D1706912

Long-Term Community Recovery
from Natural Disasters

28420

HV
553
.A68
2015

Long-Term Community Recovery
from Natural Disasters

Lucy A. Arendt and Daniel J. Alesch

INFORMATION RESOURCES CENTER
ASIS INTERNATIONAL
1625 PRINCE STREET
ALEXANDRIA, VA 22314
TEL. (703) 519-6200

CRC Press
Taylor & Francis Group
Boca Raton   London   New York

CRC Press is an imprint of the
Taylor & Francis Group, an **informa** business

CRC Press
Taylor & Francis Group
6000 Broken Sound Parkway NW, Suite 300
Boca Raton, FL 33487-2742

© 2015 by Taylor & Francis Group, LLC
CRC Press is an imprint of Taylor & Francis Group, an Informa business

No claim to original U.S. Government works

Printed on acid-free paper
Version Date: 20140926

International Standard Book Number-13: 978-1-4665-9302-2 (Hardback)

This book contains information obtained from authentic and highly regarded sources. Reasonable efforts have been made to publish reliable data and information, but the author and publisher cannot assume responsibility for the validity of all materials or the consequences of their use. The authors and publishers have attempted to trace the copyright holders of all material reproduced in this publication and apologize to copyright holders if permission to publish in this form has not been obtained. If any copyright material has not been acknowledged please write and let us know so we may rectify in any future reprint.

Except as permitted under U.S. Copyright Law, no part of this book may be reprinted, reproduced, transmitted, or utilized in any form by any electronic, mechanical, or other means, now known or hereafter invented, including photocopying, microfilming, and recording, or in any information storage or retrieval system, without written permission from the publishers.

For permission to photocopy or use material electronically from this work, please access www.copyright.com (http://www.copyright.com/) or contact the Copyright Clearance Center, Inc. (CCC), 222 Rosewood Drive, Danvers, MA 01923, 978-750-8400. CCC is a not-for-profit organization that provides licenses and registration for a variety of users. For organizations that have been granted a photocopy license by the CCC, a separate system of payment has been arranged.

Trademark Notice: Product or corporate names may be trademarks or registered trademarks, and are used only for identification and explanation without intent to infringe.

Visit the Taylor & Francis Web site at
http://www.taylorandfrancis.com

and the CRC Press Web site at
http://www.crcpress.com

We dedicate this book to the memory of the late William (Bill) Averette Anderson, a giant in his support of disaster research, a true gentleman, and a good friend. He will always be remembered and missed by those who knew him, for both his impact on public policy and for his genuine interest in making a positive difference in people's lives.

Contents

Preface

We are and have been deeply concerned with understanding and facilitating community disaster recovery. We have understood for a long time that an extreme natural hazard event is not synonymous with a disaster; a community disaster occurs when an extreme natural hazard event results in significant adverse consequences for that community. Some extreme natural hazard events result in little more than a short-term inconvenience. Others can result in catastrophic long-term and far-reaching consequences, but most lie somewhere between the extremes. The adverse consequences that extreme events trigger or exacerbate tend to continue to unfold and, often, cascade through the community long after the earth stops shaking, the wind diminishes, or the floodwaters recede. The initial losses are, almost always, just the beginning of a new normal. Restoring the built environment, while often necessary, is rarely sufficient to ensure community recovery.

We began our analysis for the book by working backward, based on our experience and that of others, about the adverse consequences that extreme natural hazard events often generate in communities. We looked into what led to those adversities—what typically triggered them and how some unfolded through the days or weeks and months following the initial event. Following the path backward from the consequences, we explored what, if anything can be done to prevent or mitigate adverse consequences and, subsequently, what actually constitutes a disaster. As we put together our analysis and conclusions, we concluded it made sense to write the book such that the reader would not have to cope with our analytical iterations. Thus, we wrote it in the reverse order of our analysis. We think that makes it more straightforward and comprehensible. We begin with a discussion of what constitutes an extreme natural hazard event and how that is different from a disaster. Then, we examine the adverse consequences that constitute the disaster, the nature of those consequences, and how they ripple through a community and, sometimes, beyond it. This analysis reinforces our belief that building a robust community—one that is disaster prepared and, should an extreme natural hazard event result in adversity, is resilient and can bounce back relatively easily—is far better than facing the daunting challenge of community recovery. Recovery, we have learned, is rarely simple and, frankly, is not in the cards for some communities. Some communities, no matter how well intended their denizens, do not recover. Finally, we outline what we believe is most often necessary for long-term community disaster recovery.

What we have written is based on decades during which we observed the myriad consequences of extreme natural hazard events and tracked, over several years, attempts at recovery in more than two dozen communities. To the extent that we could, we have incorporated specific, true examples of what happened in those communities and of efforts made to achieve recovery. To that extent, we have offered what we think are practical suggestions about building a robust, resilient community and about fostering recovery. Some of those communities recovered. Others still struggle with recovery. Although our focus is specifically and deliberately on community recovery in the aftermath of extreme natural hazard events, we strongly believe that most of what we present in the book applies to a full range of extreme events: natural, man-made, combined man-made and natural (e.g., dust bowl), terrorism, and so on. Regardless of the catalyst for a community needing to engage in recovery, most if not all of what happens next will be the same. The built environment will need attention. The natural environment will need attention. The economic environment will need attention. Most important, the sociocultural environment—the people who comprise the community—will need attention.

In addition to our own fieldwork, we have studied what others have learned, hypothesized, documented, and concluded. We are particularly grateful to those students of disaster for the insights they have shared. We, of course, have no delusions that what we have written here is the final word on mitigation and recovery. History demonstrates, time and again, that what we know today will be surpassed by improved and, sometimes, radically different sets of conclusions that come incrementally closer to a full understanding of a particular set of phenomena. Our hope is that this helps to stimulate further inquiry into reducing the adverse consequences of extreme natural hazard events and facilitating community recovery. We also hope that our thinking and writing enable decision making that reduces the adverse impacts that extreme natural hazard events can shower on individuals, families, organizations, and communities. Reducing the likelihood of preventable human and animal death, physical injury, psychological damage, economic distress, and natural and built environmental damage is at the forefront of what we do and why we do it.

Acknowledgments

Many people helped us in one way or another in our efforts to better understand what happens in communities following an extreme natural hazard event and to understand community recovery processes. We are greatly indebted to them and thank them.

We are particularly grateful to Dr. James "Jim" N. Holly. Over a piece of pie and a cup of coffee in Northridge almost 20 years ago, Dr. Holly proposed that the best way for us to learn about the consequences of extreme natural hazard events was to ask people in the disaster area, "Were you here when it happened?" If they were, we then asked, "Would you please tell us what happened to you?" In the years that followed, we, along with Dr. Holly, talked with literally hundreds of people who answered that they were there and then talked with us at great length telling us their story. Many talked with us several times over the decade following the disaster they experienced, helped us gain an understanding of the paths that attempts at recovery take, and to learn how they were working to mitigate the consequences of extreme natural hazard events. So, to the hundreds of small-business owners, residents, and public officials in California, Florida, Georgia, Louisiana, Minnesota, Mississippi, New Mexico, North Carolina, North Dakota, Oregon, South Dakota, Washington, and Wisconsin who spent so much time with us and who were so candid in telling their stories to us, we are sincerely appreciative. We are equally grateful to public officials and newspaper staff who provided us with useful statistics, maps, and documents, as well as interviews.

Over the past two decades, financial support for our research came from several sources. We acknowledge the grant from the National Science Foundation for our initial inquiry into the implications for small businesses following the Northridge Earthquake (California) in 1994 (CMMI-9416228). PERI, the Public Entity Risk Institute, provided the bulk of the financial support for us to pursue our work over the years. PERI's Claire Reiss was exceptionally supportive in that work, which resulted in a book entitled *Managing for Long-Term Community*

Recovery in the Aftermath of Disaster (PERI 2009) by Alesch, Arendt, and Holly. We extend our deep appreciation to her.

We also received support from what was then known as the Multidisciplinary Center for Earthquake Engineering Research (now MCEER) to conduct research on a public policy intended to result in enhanced seismic safety in California hospitals. That research was funded by the Earthquake Engineering Research Centers Program of the National Science Foundation under award to MCEER via EEC-9701471. The grant provided insights into organizational decision making about mitigation, and our findings are published separately in a book entitled *Natural Hazard Mitigation Policy: Implementation, Organizational Choice, and Contextual Dynamics* (Springer 2012).

MCEER also supported Professor Arendt in her reconnaissance research with Professor Daniel B. Hess to New Orleans in the wake of Hurricanes Katrina in 2005 and Gustav in 2008. That research was funded by the Earthquake Engineering Research Centers Program of the National Science Foundation under award to MCEER via EEC-9701471 and by the Small Grants for Exploratory Research program of the National Science Foundation under award to the principal investigators via SGER-0853582. The findings from this research were published by MCEER in several technical research monographs.

Finally, Professor Arendt acknowledges support provided to her and colleagues for their work on the PEOPLES resilience framework by the National Institute for Standards and Technology (NIST) under award number 60NANB9D9155_0. This research has also been published in several technical research monographs.

Many disaster research colleagues here and abroad have contributed to this book by providing ideas leading to Aha! moments, by providing a sounding board, or by reviewing all or parts of what we have written. While we were walking together maybe a decade ago on a beach in Maui on our way to a session in a conference being held there, Dennis Wenger said that what we really needed was a good theory of recovery. That comment was a stimulus to our thinking and research that has lasted for a long time. Many thanks, Dennis, for that notion and incentive. We have dedicated the book to William "Bill" Anderson, who recently and sorrowfully deceased. He graciously made it possible for us to speak at and participate in sessions sponsored by the National Academy of Sciences for which we were able to develop and test out our ideas on peers. Andre Filiatrault, professor and director of Graduate Studies at the University at Buffalo (New York), encouraged and supported the reconnaissance work in New Orleans that set the stage for Professor Arendt's immersion and interest in community recovery. Additional support for Professor Arendt from the Earthquake Engineering Research Institute (EERI) to visit New Zealand in the aftermath of its 2010

Darfield Earthquake reinforced the need to research and write about what communities can and should do to prepare themselves for extreme natural hazard events. Thanks to Marjorie Greene and Jay Berger, currently at EERI, and Susan Tubbesing, EERI's retired director, for the ongoing and always encouraging support.

In 2010, a number of colleagues met in Chapel Hill, North Carolina, for several days to discuss and share ideas about community recovery. William Siembieda and Professor Alesch met there, developed a joint paper, and subsequently shared ideas about recovery and about self-organizing systems. Professor Shigeo Tatsuki, University of Kyoto, devised the term "life recovery" and his work on that, coupled with long talks with him about it, helped us distinguish clearly between community recovery, municipal recovery, and the recovery of individuals. James Mitchel's work spurred us to look at a community's ability to perform functions as an indicator of disaster and recovery. Professor Emeritus William Petak was supportive throughout this effort and a stalwart mentor, guide, and link to everything important for the past three decades. Thanks, Bill, for everything.

Professors Jessica Jensen (Emergency Management, North Dakota State University), Jane A. Kushma (Emergency Management, Jacksonville State University, Florida), Robert Berry (Emergency and Disaster Management, Western Carolina University, North Carolina), and the ever-helpful and supportive Claire B. Rubin (president, Claire B. Rubin & Associates) were kind enough to review and comment on the manuscript. Larry Reed, retired state coordinating officer for Wisconsin Emergency Management, did the same. Their pointed commentary helped us to refine this manuscript and ensure its authenticity. Rubin was particularly instrumental in putting us in contact with Mark Listewnik at CRC Press/Taylor & Francis. Thanks so much for that and thanks to Mark Listewnik and Jennifer Abbott who have both been a joy to work with as we moved ever so gradually toward completion of the manuscript.

We acknowledge the Public Entity Risk Institute (PERI) for its permission to reuse portions of our book, *Managing for Long-Term Community Recovery in the Aftermath of Disaster* (2009), coauthored with James N. Holly. We are also grateful for the public access to FEMA's photo library, which was an outstanding resource for the non-copyrighted photos used in this work.

Finally, we gratefully acknowledge the support and forbearance of our respective spouses. Conducting the research underlying this book meant spending literally hundreds of days and nights away from home and, on those days when we were home, lots of time locked in solitude reading, writing, and rewriting. We can't thank you enough.

CHAPTER 1

The Problem

Natural hazard events resulting in community disasters occur with alarming frequency. In the first decade or so of the 21st century, hundreds of thousands have died as a result of such events. The great 2004 Indian Ocean Tsunami killed more than 200,000 people. The 2010 Haiti Earthquake killed another 200,000. The Great Tōhuko Earthquake and Tsunami in Japan in 2011 resulted in more than 15,000 deaths. The 2012 "Frankenstorm" Sandy, in addition to generating billions of dollars in damage and destruction, led to more than 100 deaths. There were 125 earthquakes worldwide greater than Richter Magnitude 6.0 in 2012, not to mention a near-Earth meteor explosion in Russia (2013) and a series of devastating tornados in Oklahoma in May 2013.

The phrase "extreme natural hazard event" and the word "disaster" are not synonymous terms. An event becomes a disaster when the event has serious adverse consequences for a society or a community. Although a natural hazard event may affect a large geographic area, it is important to remember that all disasters are local disasters. Citizens look to their local governments and those governments are responsible for preparing for, responding to, recovering from, and mitigating loss from those events. The International City Managers Association states the case succinctly, "Federal and state governments play a supporting role in the immediate aftermath and in providing guidance for long-term recovery and mitigation" (Becker 2009, p. 6). Although individuals and communities may never experience a full-blown disaster, some will experience several in their lifetime. While local government officials are seen as responsible for taking the lead in responding to and recovering from disasters, relatively few local officials will have the background and experience to know what to do and how to do it well.

Natural hazard events are often physically, psychologically, socially, and economically devastating. It does not make for light reading at bedtime, but for 400 pages Withington (2010) describes in his book *Disaster! A History of Earthquakes, Floods, Plagues, and Other Catastrophes* the human toll from volcanoes, earthquakes, tsunamis, floods, storms, plagues, wars, genocides, fire, rebellions, and terrorism from ancient times through to the present. Beyond the sheer number of injuries and deaths, events such as these result in untold damage to both the built and natural environment. The massive monetary costs of restoring and rebuilding the natural and built environments are often exceeded by the social costs to communities, organizations, families, and individuals. Opportunity costs, too, are enormous. Resources that are allocated to rebuilding infrastructure and facilities that had remaining economic life prior to the natural hazard event might otherwise have been invested in economic and social development or, in impoverished areas, to provide basic subsistence.

When the waters recede and the mud begins to dry, when the earth stops moving and the dust settles, when the wind stops and the sky becomes blue again, when the injured are cared for and the dead buried, and when the television cameras move on to another community, thoughts and concerns about recovery move to the top of the agenda. Perhaps it is better late than never, but most reasonable observers would conclude that building community resistance and resiliency to protect against inevitable events like Hurricanes Katrina in 2005 and Sandy in 2012 should begin long before the natural hazard event. If it is the goal to minimize damages and costs, the time for planning and for preemptive action is before an almost predictable natural hazard event occurs.

This book is about community recovery from disasters triggered by natural hazard events, such as those shown in Figure 1.1. The book is premised on the belief that it is essential to understand processes of community growth and change absent a disaster if we are to understand how communities recover from disaster and how to facilitate recovery. It is also premised on our conclusion that the best way to recover from a disaster is to either preclude one from occurring or to take precautions in advance of a natural hazard event that are effective in reducing its adverse consequences on the community.

Most individuals are accustomed to taking precautions against frequent events that could result in personal or financial disasters. At the very least, such precautions can reduce the severity of adverse consequences. To that end, individuals are inoculated against certain kinds of diseases, buy fire and auto insurance, have a national set of rules of the road, and add fluoride to water supplies to reduce tooth decay. At the community level, most places in the United States have building and specialty codes to protect owners and occupants from the hazards that are most likely to affect them, such as fire and wind. Where earthquakes are a common occurrence, government codes typically include provisions requiring structures be built to withstand ground motion, at least to some prespecified level. Most urban settlements in the United States have facilities to purify, distribute, and regularly test potable water and

- Earth movement
  - Earthquakes
  - Landslide
- Expansive soils
- Flooding
  - Riverine
  - Coastal and storm surge
- Excessive rain
- Fires
  - Wildfire
  - Forest fire
  - Urban fringe fire
- Volcano
  - Eruption/explosion
  - Pyroclastic flow
- Weather Events
  - Drought
  - Strong storms
  - Ice and snow
- Wind
  - Hurricanes/cyclones
  - Tornadoes
  - Straight line sheer winds
- Temperature anomalies
  - Unanticipated freezes/cold weather
  - Heat waves
- Rapid onset climactic change
- Collisions with solar system debris

FIGURE 1.1   Illustrative extreme natural hazard events.

to protect public health and the natural environment from contaminated wastewater.

We do far less to protect ourselves and our communities against what are called low-probability/high-consequence or extreme natural hazard events: events that have a low probability of occurring in any given place at a given time, but, when they do occur, are capable of generating major adverse consequences. When we do take precautions against them, those precautions are often inadequate or, sometimes, even increase the likelihood that such an event will generate even greater losses. We delude ourselves into believing that levees and dams make us secure, that some relatively minor precautions make us flood proof, earthquake proof, fireproof, or hurricane proof. We do so even though the evidence clearly indicates that is not the case.

Following disasters, we have demonstrated time and again how little we know about how to facilitate community recovery beyond rebuilding and repairing the natural and built environments. We show our concern by throwing money at the problem and sympathizing with those who suffered losses. We rarely, if ever, systematically evaluate the extent to which our efforts have been successful. We simply spend the money, build the projects, and move on to the next disaster. Frankly, we know little about what to do to help a community or a region recover from the adverse effects on that community and on other people and communities in other places. It seems that people often look at disasters as a bump in the road and that, once some critical mass of homes, businesses, and infrastructure are repaired or rebuilt, recovery will automatically occur and that all will be as it was before. This is a delusion for all but events with the most minor adverse consequences.

Reestablishing the physical aspect of the community may be a necessary but rarely sufficient step to bring about recovery as it might be understood by a preponderance of the affected population. Every significant community disaster changes individual lives and the community itself. Following a significant disaster, neither the individuals affected nor the community ever returns to what was before that event. Every disaster generates personal tragedies that will live with the survivors for the rest of their lives. People suffer serious, often debilitating injuries, lose loved ones, lose their material possessions, and, often, have their dreams dashed and never quite recover from that. Beyond personal tragedy is the economic loss and the cost of attempts at rebuilding and economic recovery that, at least in the United States, everyone bears. The failure to build resistance and resiliency into cities, towns, and villages in the United States before an extreme natural hazard event occurs is extraordinarily costly to all Americans.

A century ago, when radio was in its infancy and before television, the Internet, and electronic social networks, news of extraordinary events in distant parts of the world was sporadic and not instantly and graphically "in one's face." Today, however, places that are even a great distance from one another are increasingly interdependent and, as 24-hour worldwide news has become almost instantaneous, we see the adverse consequences of extreme natural hazard events much more frequently and much more close up than ever before. It is not only the commercial media that bring us this news. Cell phones, texting, tweeting, Skyping,

Like death and taxes, extreme natural hazard events are inevitable. For example, with an estimated 500,000 detectable earthquakes occurring per year, the Earth is never quiet. As the population continues to grow and to concentrate in places that have a high probability of experiencing extreme natural hazard events, even more frequent, deadly, and costly disasters are likely to occur.

e-mail, and other vehicles for social networking besiege us with images and information. Satellites and international television coverage ensure that we experience almost continuous, real-time exposure to the consequences of "Frankenstorms," catastrophic typhoons, deadly earthquakes, genocide, famines, pandemics, wildfires in suburban America, bush fires in Australia, and "near misses" as asteroids and other sizable space debris come close to colliding with Earth.

It is small wonder that "survivalists" are preparing for an apocalypse and are featured on what is called "reality" television programming. It is even less surprising that motion pictures and seemingly endless sequels warn us that, "There's always an Arquillian Battle Cruiser, or a Corillian Death Ray, or an intergalactic plague that is about to wipe out all life on this miserable little planet" (Solomon 1997), not to mention an imminent "zombie apocalypse." Perhaps exposure to outrageous disaster fiction as entertainment acts as a social coping mechanism against the reality of massacres in elementary schools, great storms that bring our largest, wealthiest cities to their knees, and the reality that thousands of persons who avoided genocide subsequently starved to death in Africa.

The primary focus of this book is disasters associated with natural hazard events, but the content is generally applicable to community disasters generated by or associated with disasters resulting from other kinds of events. These include willful acts of destruction, such as terrorist attacks or other acts of mass violence; unanticipated adverse consequences of intervention in natural or social systems; plagues, contagions, and pandemics; and accidents that are either large in themselves or that have significant long-term adverse consequences, including chemical spills and infrastructure failure of dams, bridges, levees, and power plants. Disasters associated with each of these are exceedingly important and certainly worthy of considerable analysis, but they are outside the scope of this book.

PURPOSE AND APPROACH

A few years ago, Levine, Esnard, and Sapat (2007), writing about population displacement and housing dilemmas stemming from community disasters, observed what a few of us have been concerned with for a decade or more. They observed that "what the Katrina experience has demonstrated is that a *poorly specified phase* occupies the period between (disaster) response and full recovery" and that "the human aspects of response and recovery do not always flow quickly or smoothly" (Levine et al. 2007, p. 4; italics added).

This book is centered on gaining greater understanding of the "poorly specified" phases between the time an extreme natural hazard event occurs and what is usually referred to as long-term community recovery. As they are traditionally understood, the four phases of the disaster life cycle include mitigation, preparedness, response, and recovery (Benjamin et al. 2011). In terms of *mitigation*, it is argued that "the best times for systematic vulnerability assessments, preventive measures, and preparedness activities" are before disaster strikes (Benjamin et al. 2011, p. 308). Mitigation might involve elevating homes in a floodplain and purchasing insurance in anticipation of a probable event. *Preparedness* includes all activities that will enable effective response to an event, including the establishment of policies and procedures to be followed by emergency responders; the testing of communication and other emergency systems; and the education and training of government officials, responders, and community residents most likely to be affected by the event.

Response includes all actions taken during or immediately after an extreme hazard event, including search and rescue efforts, provision of needed medical care, evacuation, and attempts to reduce further damage to the built and natural environments. It is the phase during which preparedness activities are expected to be executed and bear fruit. It may also be the most dramatic of the phases and therefore the most likely to garner mass media attention (Houston, Pfefferbaum, and Rosenholtz 2012). This is the phase during which we see media coverage of people being rescued from toxic floodwaters, collapsed buildings, and tornado-swept residences. *Recovery* is the last of the four phases. It necessarily reflects what has happened in the prior three phases and involves all actions intended to return the community to its preevent "state or better—and ideally to make it less vulnerable to future risk" (Center for Disaster Philanthropy 2014, para. 5). "That recovery phase, by far the longest, starts as soon as the immediate threat to human life has subsided. Due consideration must be given to when, where, and how to rebuild, mindful of not reproducing the unsafe conditions that may have existed before the disaster" (Benjamin et al. 2011, p. 313). The reader should note that both the Center for Disaster Philanthropy (2014) and Benjamin and his colleagues (2011) associate the recovery phase with actions that are intended to reduce future vulnerability to a given hazard event, without necessarily specifying what those actions might be.

Recovery efforts can be made more consistently successful, we contend, if we develop a better understanding of what constitutes a disaster, how community disasters unfold to disrupt what might be called "normal" community change, and the conditions under which communities might recover from those disruptions. Our intent is to contribute to that understanding by drawing on our field experience studying, over the years, about two dozen communities that experienced disasters and by presenting a conceptual framework that embraces (1) normal community change processes, (2) the likely consequences of an extreme natural hazard event, and (3) (sometimes) community recovery from those consequences.

We have two primary purposes. The first purpose is to explore how communities can cost-effectively enhance their resistance to the consequences of extreme natural hazard events. "Resistance" suggests that a community is able to defy the onset and defend against the potential impact of a given natural hazard event. The second purpose is to understand how community disaster recovery might be facilitated and be made more probable. We believe that "There's nothing so practical as good theory" (Lewin 1951, p. 169) and that there is a great need for good theory to guide both community recovery and efforts to make communities more disaster resistant and resilient. We are aware, too, that good theory concerning disasters and disaster recovery should result in practical means for both building disaster resistant communities and contributing to sustainable community recovery, so we have included what we believe to be ultimately practical guides.

It would be foolish to believe that we can prevent every extreme natural hazard event from leading to community disaster. It is, however, equally foolish not to attempt to gain an improved understanding of how and why extreme natural hazard events sometimes result in disaster so that we can better understand how to facilitate community recovery from such disasters. An understanding of how extreme natural hazard events result in disasters is equally critical to devising cost-effective measures to prevent some of those disasters from occurring or, failing that, to reduce the adverse impacts of extreme natural hazard events and reducing the nature and extent of community disasters. Disasters, according to Wisner et al. (2004), result from a complex interaction of natural hazard events and human action or engagement, most notably action or engagement that signifies or is the result of vulnerability. In an unpopulated area, where there is an absence of human action or engagement, a natural hazard event could engender an ecological disaster (e.g., habitat destruction), but it would not constitute a disaster in the way that we are discussing disasters.

Our efforts are premised on the belief that we can learn more about how to facilitate community recovery following a disaster. Beyond that, we believe it is possible and cost-effective to reduce the adverse consequences of many, if not most extreme natural hazard events by building communities that are disaster resistant and resilient. To understand what contributes to how extreme natural hazard events generate extreme adverse consequences in a community, what precautions are likely to reduce those consequences, and what facilitates community recovery, it is important that we learn from previous disasters.

Over the past two decades, the authors conducted a series of exploratory longitudinal and cross-sectional studies of well over a dozen communities that experienced disasters. We went to those communities almost every year for as many as 10 years following their disaster. Every year, we asked many of the same people what happened and listened closely to them. That exploratory work did not test hypotheses; what it did was to help us generate propositions about how disasters occur and how communities recover or fail to recover. This work has been augmented by research we conducted on how formal organizations make decisions about recovering from disasters and about how they make choices about what to and how much to do to protect themselves against future disasters. We combined what we have learned with the disaster research conducted by others and, importantly, on the work of still others in the fields of general systems theory and self-organizing and emergent systems. That forms the basis of both our conceptual model and our practical advice concerning building resistance and enabling community disaster recovery.

By analogy, our approach relies on the diagnostic and treatment model from the medical research field: if one wishes to increase the chances a patient will recover, one should understand the malady (and its cause) that created the need for recovery. Our approach to trying to understand disasters and disaster recovery is somewhat analogous to what medical researchers do to understand the adverse effects of a particular disease or malady on patients, how the patients became afflicted with the condition, what makes some patients more susceptible to the condition than others, and what might be done to increase the probability that patients will not develop the malady in the first place and, if they do, how to overcome its effects. That often requires autopsies. In this case, we looked at community "patients," that are, thankfully, not dead. They include, however, communities that have suffered disaster, prevented disaster, recovered from disaster, and failed to recover from disaster. In addition to taking a page from medical research, we have approached our task from the perspective of human ecology. That is, we have attempted to study community disasters in terms of the relationships between humans and their natural, social, and built environments using a perspective that cuts across disciplines and seeks new understandings.

We believe that it is critically important to examine the "life history" of disasters. We need to learn what precautions were taken and how well they served the community. Structural engineers, for example, conduct postmortems on structures following failure to learn what failed and why. They build that knowledge into their education programs and into new structural designs. We know that the initial damage from an extreme natural hazard event is not all that happens. As emergency managers, social scientists, policy makers, and disaster researchers, we collectively need to learn more about how disasters unfold and the nature and extent of cascading consequences and those characteristics of communities that make them more or less susceptible to the consequences that ripple out from the initial event. Finally, we have to learn a lot more about the dynamics of both individual and community recovery. To do that, we think it is important to better understand the dynamics of community development and decline in the absence of a major perturbation, such as a major earthquake. Only then, we think, is it possible to understand what might be done to facilitate recovery in a given community and, indeed, whether recovery in that community is likely to ever come about.

To these ends, the book is aimed at exploring, and attempting to answer, a series of questions.

- Why do relatively infrequent natural hazard events often result in community disaster?
- Given the unique characteristics of each community, how can one identify sensible precautions that, if taken, will reduce the likelihood of major adverse consequences resulting from an extreme natural hazard event?
- How do communities change through time absent a great perturbation? How might communities, in general, recover from such a great perturbation?
- What variables affect the likelihood of achieving sustainable community recovery following a disaster?

We are not so naïve as to believe our conceptual model will remain unchanged through time. In the history of science, most conceptual models are replaced as more is learned. As more communities are studied after the initial emergency period and longitudinal and cross-sectional analyses of communities having suffered or escaped disaster are conducted, we should expect improvements in our collective understanding and enhancements in our models.

Just as medical researchers sometimes encounter and then struggle to unravel what appear to be intractable problems, we too, found some questions we are unable to answer with confidence. We have faith, though, that the first step in solving a problem is to specify it in anticipation that others will contribute to finding answers. Presenting a conceptual framework requires that we explore how communities grow and change through time, how an extreme natural hazard event sometimes results in what is termed a disaster, and how communities sometimes, but not always, recover from the consequences of the event.

Pursuing the medical analogy just a bit further, we know that the best way to recover from a malady is, perhaps counterintuitively, to avoid getting it in the first place. This understanding helps to explain the widespread promotion and adoption of inoculations and vaccinations. Avoiding a potentially deadly disease can save individuals and their loved ones time, money, and their lives. Smallpox, one of history's most deadly infectious diseases, was declared eradicated in 1979 by the World Health Organization after decades of vigorous vaccination efforts (Henderson 1980). Similarly, the best way to recover from a community disaster is to prevent one from happening in the first place or, failing that, to take precautions in advance to reduce the nature and scope of the disaster by building a disaster resistant and resilient community. Thus, a significant portion of the book is devoted to practical and effective ways to recover from a disaster by preventing it from happening or, if it happens despite precautions, how to minimize the nature and scope of the disaster.

A BASIC CONSIDERATION

Natural disasters occur in places. We are interested in disasters that occur in small rural settlements, in small urban places, in large settlements comprising several local government entities, and in regions. We have spent considerable time pondering and seeking a collective, generic term that encompasses all these kinds of places. We are not comfortable with using terms such as settlement, locale, or populated place. It would sound peculiar to refer to a "populated place disaster." Nor are we comfortable using terms that have a specific, legal meaning, such as village, town, city, or municipality. Finally, we would prefer not to use a term that has a specific meaning for those in a particular discipline.

Thus, we have been perplexed; searching for a term that we can use that may be used to refer to the place in which a disaster occurs, regardless of its size or the number or types of civil divisions it crosses. Such a place could range in size from a small rural settlement to a large city and its surrounding urbanized areas, even though it encompasses a number of local government jurisdictions or even two or more states. The places might be a neighborhood, a community, a region, a nation, or even worldwide. Depending on the perspective of the analyst, the place might be described as a human settlement or some other term with special relevance and meaning to a particular scholarly discipline.

Probably because the term is used so ubiquitously and with such disregard as to precision of meaning, we choose to call the places with which we are concerned "communities." The word "community" is used by many and may refer to any of several concepts. Freilich (1963) suggests that "since a requisite of science is specificity of terminology, we must conclude ... that at this time 'community' is a non-scientific term unless separately defined in every paper which uses it" (p. 118). Hamman (1997) employed Hillery's (1955) analysis of 94 definitions of community, upon which we have based our use of the term. According to Hamman (1997), "The sociological term community should be understood here as meaning (1) a group of people (2) who share social interaction (3) and some common ties between themselves and the other members of the group (4) and who share an area for at least some of the time" (para. 4).

We are generally comfortable with this definition, mostly because it is compatible with our own sense of a community as an open system, comprising individuals and institutions with patterned relationships among themselves and with the external environment. Our focus is on communities within a generally defined geographic space, although we acknowledge the use of the word "community" to refer to groups, such as a "community of disaster scholars" that may exist without the members living or working in close physical proximity to one another but communicating through a variety of means. So, too, do we acknowledge that not every place that is called a community is actually a community, even by our generous definition. However, for our purposes, the term suffices. For us, "community" refers to a set of persons living in relatively close proximity to one another over an extended period; there is some permanence to the settlement. These individuals have generally patterned and persistent kinds of interactions with one another and with others in other places. The interactions typically include symbolic, social, economic, or political activities. The members of the "community" are likely to have a significant overlap in the way of shared values or common interests, but some of the members may share few if any of those values.

Having said that disasters occur in a place, we do not mean to imply that the natural hazard event that triggers the event must necessarily collide directly with the community that suffers the disaster. It is sufficient that the natural hazard event occur in close proximity to the community. Illustratively, a storm that destroys an ecosystem upon which the members of the community depend for spiritual or material sustenance can cause a disaster for the community just as surely as if the storm had destroyed the physical artifact of the community. If a giant oil spill were to destroy the shrimp beds on which a community depends for its livelihood, that disaster will not differ much in its consequences from an earthquake's more direct destruction. Over the years, the authors have witnessed many situations in which firms or neighborhoods suffered disaster without having been damaged directly by a natural hazard event.

SPECIFICATION

One approach to solving complex problems involves the development and consideration of theories that consider multiple causes and interdependencies. Building good theory requires an adequate specification of elements of the subject being studied. Few who have labored in the field of disaster research could be accused of having needlessly overspecified what constitutes an extreme natural hazard event, a community disaster, or community recovery. Thus, chapters following this introduction explore various aspects of disasters and recovery in an attempt to better specify what constitutes an extreme natural hazard event, a community disaster, and community recovery.

If the history of science teaches us anything, it teaches us that existing knowledge is usually proven wrong or incomplete as new understanding emerges. We certainly do not expect that we will generate anything approaching a lasting accord about these matters. We do, however, spell out what we mean by these terms so the reader can know our starting points. If our observations do contribute to some general consensus about working definitions for extreme natural hazard events, disasters, and recovery, so much the better.

To accomplish our objectives, we must also have some fundamental understanding of how communities grow, change, and develop absent a major perturbation—such as a large earthquake or hurricane—and then learn how they change following a large perturbation. Frankly, those who study urban phenomena know much more about physical urban morphology than they do about the social and economic morphology of urban settlements. Absent substantiated theory on how communities as social constructs develop and change, we get to work repairing, rebuilding, and replacing the physical artifact of a community following a disaster. We give limited or no attention in the form of money spent to the damaged social and economic aspects of the community; we hope and assume that these aspects of the community will somehow heal themselves. Unfortunately, "hope is not a strategy," as Rudy Giuliani said at the 2008 Republican Convention (National Public Radio 2008).

On a fishing trip into the Canadian wilderness, a guide told one of the coauthors that we generally fight forest fires by throwing money at them until it rains. One might argue that in the United States at least, we do essentially the same thing when addressing postdisaster community recovery. Thus, the chapter following our explorations of what constitutes extreme natural hazard events, community disaster, and community recovery will present a nascent theoretical construct concerning those matters.

TWO VIGNETTES: THE MAKINGS OF A DISASTER

Homestead and Hurricane Andrew

Driving south from Miami on essentially the only route to the Everglades and the Florida Keys, one passes through Homestead, Florida. If one knows what to look for, one can still see reminders of the impact Hurricane Andrew had on the community in 1992. To the right as one passes through, there is a sizable vacant lot with concrete pads, a reminder of the mobile homes that were there until Andrew swept them from the site.

In 1902, William Krome was surveying South Florida, looking for a route for Henry Flagler's Florida East Coast Railway, which ultimately ran from Jacksonville to Key West and through Homestead. Flagler, who helped John D. Rockefeller develop his oil empire, was a major force in promoting and developing Florida. The railroad provided a convenient means for local farmers to ship their produce to Miami and "truck" farming dominated the local economy. Some of the workers extending the railroad to Key West settled in the Homestead area, the community grew, and, in 1913, Homestead was incorporated as a town and, later, as a city.

South Florida, including Homestead, is subject to hurricanes. The "Great Hurricane of 1926" swept through the area, creating a significant pause in the South Florida development boom. In 1935, the Labor Day Hurricane destroyed the railroad in the Florida Keys, sweeping just south of Homestead. In 1942, Homestead Army Air Field was established, but 3 years later in 1945, a hurricane forced its closure. It was not until 1953 that it reopened as Homestead Air Force Base.

Florida City, Florida, is immediately adjacent to Homestead. It developed essentially in the same way and at the same time as Homestead. Florida City's population is primarily African-American. An aerial view would suggest that they are essentially one contiguous settlement split into two governmental jurisdictions; they certainly suffered similarly from the same hurricanes.

Homestead and Florida City experienced modest growth from the mid-1950s until Hurricane Andrew in 1992. One reason was the presence of Homestead Air Force Base. Not only did military personnel and their families live in and around Homestead and frequent its commercial establishments, but several thousand retired military persons lived in the Homestead area, partly because of the climate, but, perhaps, primarily because living there gave them access to the Base Exchange, the Base Commissary, and military medical facilities. The area's economy benefited, too, from a significantly large population of snowbirds: persons who escaped northern winters by spending those winters in Florida. Some also benefited by being Florida residents for 6 months and a day each year; Florida has no income tax and most northern states do. In addition to the base and the snowbirds, the economy benefited from tourists heading to the Everglades, just a few miles away, and from flourishing truck farming and landscape nursery farming, and beyond into the Florida Keys.

FIGURE 1.2   Dade County, Florida, August 24, 1992—Many houses, businesses, and personal effects suffered extensive damage from Hurricane Andrew. (Courtesy of FEMA/Bob Epstein.)

Hurricane Andrew was the third Category 5 hurricane to strike the United States in the 20th century and the second to strike southern Florida. At the time, it was the most costly hurricane in American history. The winds, which gusted to 177 miles per hour, essentially flattened Homestead, Florida City, and the surrounding unincorporated area. About 90 percent of the mobile homes in the area were destroyed, and virtually every power pole in Homestead and Florida City was snapped. Almost 14 inches of rain fell in the western part of Miami–Dade County. Reportedly, 70,000 trees in the Everglades were knocked over. Approximately 40 people were killed. More than 25,000 homes were destroyed and more than 100,000 were heavily damaged (see Figure 1.2).

To make matters worse, the Department of Defense permanently closed Homestead Air Force Base. The decision to close the base was made in 1990, long before Hurricane Andrew was born off the coast of Africa, but the approaching hurricane hastened permanent evacuation of the base, which was essentially destroyed by Hurricane Andrew. In 1993, a year after the hurricane, the base was designated as an Air Force Reserve Base. It now accommodates a few small units, including the Florida Air National Guard and U.S. Customs. It is no longer a major part of the local economy. Even without the hurricane, closure of the base would have been a major blow to the well-being of the Homestead–Florida City–South Dade economy. As a final straw, the North American

Free Trade Agreement (NAFTA) came into force on January 1, 1994. Local residents and business operators told us they believed that NAFTA had a major adverse impact on the very important truck farming business that had long supported much of the community.

Rebuilding and repairing homes, businesses, and infrastructure in Homestead, Florida City, and the surrounding unincorporated areas was a challenge. Simply replacing the power poles and restoring electricity took weeks. The destruction to the natural and built environments, however, was only one aspect of the disaster.

Perhaps the primary set of consequences that emerged from Andrew was a significant change in Homestead's demographics. The U.S. Department of Housing and Urban Development provided the local government with major funding for subsidized rental units, enabling developers to replace destroyed apartment complexes. However, the snowbirds had moved away from the community because of the hurricane, the retired military households left because the Air Force health care and Base Exchange and Commissary facilities were gone, and the military households living off base were gone. Without the pre-hurricane population, demand for the rental units was greatly diminished. Apartment owners with vacant units advertised in the Miami area that subsidized housing was available in Homestead. That attracted a large number of minority households, many of whom had recently arrived from the Caribbean and, in most cases, had significantly lower incomes and marketable skills than those who had left Homestead in the wake of Hurricane Andrew. The pre-hurricane demographic composition of Homestead was significantly different from the posthurricane demographic mix.

Municipal officials experienced problems they had never before experienced. The demand for municipal services, such as housing and electrical inspections, rose dramatically while, at the same time, local government revenues plummeted. Illustratively, Homestead operated its own electric utility, generating some electricity and buying more from other sources, and distributing it through the community. Prior to Hurricane Andrew, the electrical utility was a major source of revenue for the municipality, but the hurricane winds destroyed the distribution system by snapping off almost every power pole in the city (see Figure 1.3). The municipal electrical utility had employed far too few people to quickly replace the poles and to rewire virtually the entire city. External help was essential, but, still, the task was enormous. During repairs and during the rebuilding of the city, revenues from the utility dropped significantly at a time when the city needed them desperately. The utility could not deliver electric power for many weeks to those buildings that remained standing.

In addition to the loss of revenue from electricity sales, sales tax revenue, collected by the State of Florida and distributed proportionately

FIGURE 1.3   Dade County, Florida, August 24, 1992—Cleanup commences following Hurricane Andrew. (Courtesy of FEMA/Bob Epstein.)

to local governments on the basis of sales in the respective jurisdictions, declined to almost nothing. The State did arrange to share sales tax revenues with Homestead based on the increase in sales in other jurisdictions, but the agreement to do so was only for a 3-year period (Florida Legislature 1993, p. 11). Property tax revenues fell dramatically because the real property improvements on which the ad valorem taxes were levied no longer existed; they had been blown down or blown away. Finally, the Stafford Act, which dictates how disaster aid is to be distributed, provided for grants of only up to $5,000 to help local governments conduct normal business, unrelated to the disaster, but the city had insufficient revenue to conduct its normal activities, much less the activities made necessary by the disaster.

To make matters worse, 11 Florida property and casualty insurance companies failed following and largely because of Hurricane Andrew, further complicating the recovery. Property owners who held policies issued by those firms had to settle for as little as 10 cents on the dollar and found themselves in dire straits. The extensive damage done to many homes and buildings (see Figure 1.4) meant that many home and building owners would need to rely on other sources of funding to rebuild their properties.

Of all the cities we studied, we were particularly impressed with Homestead's bold approach to economic recovery after its disaster. Hurricane Andrew essentially flattened the city, driving out many of its residents. Closing Homestead Air Force Base drove out many more

FIGURE 1.4 Hurricane Andrew, Florida, August 24, 1992—Many houses, businesses, and personal items suffered extensive damage. (Courtesy of FEMA/Bob Epstein.)

residents. Local officials thought hard about how they could use projects funded by the Federal Economic Development Administration to launch Homestead into a new economic trajectory. The strategy seemed sound, but it did not work out as hoped, despite massive amounts of federal assistance.

The city's strategy centered on creating community facilities and amenities that they hoped would lure residents, businesses, and retirees to the community. One project was a major league spring training facility. Before Hurricane Andrew struck, the city had completed an $18 million spring training center for a major league baseball team, the Cleveland Indians. The Indians had decided to move to Florida for spring training after a half-century of conducting it in Arizona. After the hurricane essentially destroyed the facility, the city rebuilt it quickly, using federal grants. The park was opened in 1993 and refurbished in 1996, but the Cleveland Indians had already moved to Chain of Lakes Park near Orlando and were not about to move again. Homestead is now the owner of a large baseball facility that does not see very much baseball. The paint has begun to fade and peel. The sad story of Homestead's Sports Complex is available online at: http://www.digitalballparks.com/Florida/Homestead1.html.

A second major facility built by the city was the Homestead–Miami Speedway, intended to cash in on the popularity of NASCAR racing. The track is doing fairly well, hosting, as it does, a program of racing that includes NASCAR's last big race of each season. Unfortunately, a law-suit initiated by a competing city after Homestead developed the track resulted in a Florida Supreme Court decision that led to Homestead having to pay ad valorem property taxes to Miami–Dade County on the assessed value of the facility. That created an unexpected and significant drain on the city's finances just when local officials were looking forward to a significant cash infusion to the community and to the city treasury.

A third effort involved the development of a very attractive and well-developed 280-acre industrial park complete with infrastructure. The park was developed in collaboration with the Rockefeller Group Development Corporation. Local leaders had hoped to convert the former Homestead Air Force Base into a commercial airport to facilitate trade with Latin America, but that effort was unsuccessful, so the city has no large commercial airport and the industrial park remains largely vacant 20 years later.

All the effort exerted and federal grants awarded have not done for Homestead what its location near Miami finally brought about. After more than a decade of unrealized hopes for revitalization, Homestead began growing. Miami has been expanding southward and Homestead was the next available area for housing, so people from Miami turned Homestead into a bedroom community; thousands of new homes have been constructed since 2003. It reflects a fundamental change in Homestead's historic role in south Dade County as well as a new trajectory. The construction generated major increases in local tax revenue but has done relatively little to improve local employment opportunities.

New Orleans and Hurricane Katrina

New Orleans is a major port in the United States, and the largest city in Louisiana. The population was 369,250 as of the 2012 U.S. Census, a considerable decline from 455,188, its population as of July 1, 2005. Although Hurricane Katrina and the subsequent flooding of New Orleans dealt a heavy blow to New Orleans, its population had been on the decline since 1960, as shown in Table 1.1.

New Orleans is known for its distinctive architecture, music, cuisine, and its many celebrations and festivals (e.g., Mardi Gras). It is a city rich in multicultural history and traditions. New Orleans the city and Orleans Parish are coterminous, with St. Tammany Parish to the north, St. Bernard Parish to the east, Plaquemines Parish to the south, and Jefferson Parish to the south and west. Lake Pontchartrain is located at the city's north end.

TABLE 1.1   Historical Population of New Orleans

Year	Population	±%
1900	287,104	
1910	339,075	18.1%
1920	387,219	14.2%
1930	458,762	18.5%
1940	494,537	7.8%
1950	570,445	15.3%
1960	627,525	10.0%
1970	593,471	−5.4%
1980	557,515	−6.1%
1990	496,938	−10.9%
2000	483,663	−2.7%
2001	477,932	−1.2%
2002	472,744	−1.1%
2003	467,761	−1.1%
2004	461,915	−1.2%
2005	455,188	−1.5%
2006	208,548	−54.2%
2007	288,113	38.2%
2008	336,644	16.8%
2009	354,850	5.4%
2010	343,829	−3.1%
2011	360,341	4.8%
2012	369,250	2.5%

Sources: New Orleans, Louisiana Population History, http://www.biggestuscities.com/city/new-orleans-louisiana; Eggler, Bruce, 2009, "Census population estimate for New Orleans for 2008 too low, Mayor Ray Nagin says." Last modified October 2, 2009, http://www.nola.com/politics/index.ssf/2009/10/census_population_estimate_for.html.

The city was founded in 1718 by the French Mississippi Company. The French colony was ceded to the Spanish Empire in the Treaty of Paris not quite 50 years later, in 1763. The Port of New Orleans served a pivotal role during the American Revolutionary War, as it was used to smuggle needed supplies to the American revolutionaries up the Mississippi River. New Orleans was under Spanish control until 1801, when the French briefly reclaimed it. It was sold to the United States in the Louisiana Purchase in 1803.

New Orleans established itself as a multicultural city from its beginning. After the Louisiana Purchase, the city's population exploded as people willing to work the land migrated there. Americans, French, Creoles, Irish, Germans, and Africans—both enslaved and freemen—moved to New Orleans, a city made prosperous by its access to sugar and cotton plantations and the Mississippi River that transported these and other imported goods to eager customers. In addition to transporting commodities, New Orleans was instrumental in both the Atlantic and domestic slave trades. While its economy did well in part due to the tens of billions of dollars generated by the slave trade (2005 dollars, adjusted for inflation), New Orleans also boasted the largest number of free people of color in the United States at the time. Many of these individuals were well-educated members of the middle class.

French speakers represented a majority of the white population in New Orleans until about 1830, when the immigrants from Germany and Ireland began arriving. New Orleans was captured by Union forces in early 1862, thus sparing the city much of the destruction inflicted on other Southern cities during the Civil War. Louisiana was readmitted to the Union in 1868, and its Constitution of 1868 granted suffrage to both blacks and whites. Both were elected to office, and the city had an integrated public school system.

In the 1870s, the "White League," a group that supported the Democratic Party, successfully suppressed the black vote in several elections. The white Democrats, who now held the majority in office, instigated Jim Crow laws, imposed racial segregation in schools and other public venues, and disenfranchised Louisiana's freed men of color. What had been a progressive state vis-à-vis race relations, at least in terms of legal processes, became a racially segregated state that upheld Jim Crow laws. "Separate but equal" became the foundation for underfunded schools and other systems that created generations of African-Americans in New Orleans unable to defend themselves and participate in the so-called American dream.

Although the population in New Orleans continued to increase until 1960, its position as one of the largest and most consequential cities in the United States began declining in the mid 1800s. Railways and highways transformed the preferred means for transportation of goods, devaluing New Orleans' port and its access to the Mississippi River. By the mid 1900s, New Orleans was no longer a power in the American South. Those who could afford to do so began moving away from the city's central core, into its suburban neighborhoods. "White flight" took hold of New Orleans, as was also the case in many other larger and older U.S. cities in the 1950s and 1960s (Fussell 2007). In 1950, the Census Bureau reported New Orleans' population as 68 percent white and 31.9 percent black. The black population of New Orleans rose from 37 percent in

1960 to 45 percent in 1970, and became a majority of 55 percent by 1980. By 2000, blacks represented 67.25 percent of New Orleans' population. After Katrina, in 2010, the percentage of blacks in New Orleans had declined to 60.2 percent. The city, as some predicted, is "older, whiter, and more affluent" in the wake of Katrina (Fussell 2007, p. 854).

In addition to population declines after 1960, New Orleans saw its economic fortunes shift. Automation and containerization dramatically changed the availability of port-related employment. Many larger financial service organizations left New Orleans for larger cities in the South. Trade opportunities changed as interstate highways and trucking took on many of the country's transportation needs, away from the New Orleans Port and the Mississippi River. Without a substantial manufacturing sector, New Orleans was left with the less lucrative health care and tourism industries. Neither industry was sufficient to bolster New Orleans' lagging economy.

An increasingly racially segregated city in combination with a declining economy and a wealth of drugs contributed to a city with a major crime problem. Historically, much of the violent crime, including homicides, has been focused in the most impoverished of New Orleans' neighborhoods. While the rate of homicides in New Orleans had declined to 49.1 per 100,000 residents in 2010 compared to 86 per 100,000 in 1994, New Orleans still had the distinction in 2009 of being number one in homicides in cities of at least 250,000 people (McCarthy 2009).

To enable the city's expansion, New Orleans decided to drain the swamps in outlying areas such as New Orleans East. Unfortunately, these new developments were typically several feet below sea level, leaving them vulnerable to flooding. This reality was brought home to New Orleans' residents in 1965, when Hurricane Betsy killed 76 people in New Orleans, many of them living in the low-lying and poor Lower Ninth Ward. In a bit of foreshadowing for Katrina 40 years later, levees for the Mississippi River Gulf Outlet (the MR GO) and on both sides of the Industrial Canal failed. Floodwaters in the Lower Ninth Ward reached the rooflines of one-story homes; some residents drowned in their attics trying to escape the flooding. Stories of these souls influenced more than a generation of New Orleans' residents, who told of the need to carry axes with them when they went into their attics to avoid floodwaters during Katrina (*CNN Reports* 2005). After Hurricane Betsy made her way through New Orleans, it was more than 10 days before the floodwaters receded enough for people to return home.

New Orleans had a pumping system in place well before Katrina, but its weaknesses had been exposed as early as 1995, when widespread flooding resulted from rainstorms. Efforts to enhance the system's pumping capacity could not, unfortunately, keep up with the erosion of the swampland and changing topography that heightened the risk of flooding for New Orleans from storm surge, especially surge up the MR GO.

At 9:30 A.M. on August 28, 2005: Mayor Ray Nagin ordered a mandatory evacuation in advance of Katrina's landfall in Louisiana (Hauser and Lueck 2005). The evacuation order was unprecedented and reflected Nagin's concern that "The storm surge most likely will topple our levee system" (Hauser and Lueck 2005, para. 3).

On August 28, 2005 at 10:11 A.M. CDT: The National Weather Service (NWS) field office in New Orleans issued a weather message predicting catastrophic damage to New Orleans and the surrounding region (Figure 1.5).

By the time that Hurricane Katrina passed southeast of New Orleans on August 29, 2005, it was a Category 3 storm. Storm surge caused more than 50 breaches in New Orleans' drainage canal levees. Within 48 hours, 80 percent of the city—the "bowl"—was under water, with some of the worst flooding reaching 15 feet of water, well above the eaves for most one-story buildings. The French Quarter, near the city's natural ridge along the Mississippi River, was largely untouched by floodwaters. Major breeches occurred along the 17th Street Canal levee, the Industrial Canal levee, and the London Avenue Canal floodwall. The Army Corps of Engineers was called to task for having built levees that could not sustain against storm surge.

Estimates suggest that between 80 and 90 percent of the city's residents were safely evacuated before August 29. Still, many residents remained in the city, including many elderly, disabled, and otherwise vulnerable residents who did not have either personal transportation or the means to remain evacuated for several days. Some stayed because they believed they needed to protect their property. Others stayed because they believed their homes would offer sufficient protection. Some of these individuals had stayed in the city during Hurricane Betsy in 1965 and believed that Katrina would be no worse.

Eventually, many of the residents who remained behind went themselves or were rescued and delivered to either the Louisiana Superdome or the Ernest N. Morial Convention Center, "shelters of last resort" (Olsen 2005, para. 7). Neither of these facilities was equipped to shelter the thousands of residents who needed assistance. Television and other media showed the rest of the world the unsanitary and unsafe conditions that continued to deteriorate rapidly as more evacuees arrived and transportation out of the city was delayed. Some asserted that the city had not followed its own evacuation plan and had failed to use available buses to transport the city's most vulnerable citizens out of New Orleans before Katrina made landfall (Olsen 2005).

With 80 percent of the city under water, the situation was catastrophic. Stranded survivors appealed for help from their rooftops; rescue

```
URGENT - WEATHER MESSAGE
NATIONAL WEATHER SERVICE NEW ORLEANS LA
1011 AM CDT SUN AUG 28 2005


...DEVASTATING DAMAGE EXPECTED...


.HURRICANE KATRINA...A MOST POWERFUL HURRICANE WITH UNPRECEDENTED
STRENGTH...RIVALING THE INTENSITY OF HURRICANE CAMILLE OF 1969.

MOST OF THE AREA WILL BE UNINHABITABLE FOR WEEKS...PERHAPS LONGER. AT
LEAST ONE HALF OF WELL CONSTRUCTED HOMES WILL HAVE ROOF AND WALL
FAILURE. ALL GABLED ROOFS WILL FAIL...LEAVING THOSE HOMES SEVERELY
DAMAGED OR DESTROYED.

THE MAJORITY OF INDUSTRIAL BUILDINGS WILL BECOME NON FUNCTIONAL.
PARTIAL TO COMPLETE WALL AND ROOF FAILURE IS EXPECTED. ALL WOOD
FRAMED LOW RISING APARTMENT BUILDINGS WILL BE DESTROYED. CONCRETE
BLOCK LOW RISE APARTMENTS WILL SUSTAIN MAJOR DAMAGE...INCLUDING SOME
WALL AND ROOF FAILURE.

HIGH RISE OFFICE AND APARTMENT BUILDINGS WILL SWAY DANGEROUSLY...A
FEW TO THE POINT OF TOTAL COLLAPSE. ALL WINDOWS WILL BLOW OUT.

AIRBORNE DEBRIS WILL BE WIDESPREAD...AND MAY INCLUDE HEAVY ITEMS SUCH
AS HOUSEHOLD APPLIANCES AND EVEN LIGHT VEHICLES. SPORT UTILITY
VEHICLES AND LIGHT TRUCKS WILL BE MOVED. THE BLOWN DEBRIS WILL CREATE
ADDITIONAL DESTRUCTION. PERSONS...PETS...AND LIVESTOCK EXPOSED TO THE
WINDS WILL FACE CERTAIN DEATH IF STRUCK.

POWER OUTAGES WILL LAST FOR WEEKS...AS MOST POWER POLES WILL BE DOWN
AND TRANSFORMERS DESTROYED. WATER SHORTAGES WILL MAKE HUMAN SUFFERING
INCREDIBLE BY MODERN STANDARDS.

THE VAST MAJORITY OF NATIVE TREES WILL BE SNAPPED OR UPROOTED. ONLY
THE HEARTIEST WILL REMAIN STANDING...BUT BE TOTALLY DEFOLIATED. FEW
CROPS WILL REMAIN. LIVESTOCK LEFT EXPOSED TO THE WINDS WILL BE
KILLED.

AN INLAND HURRICANE WIND WARNING IS ISSUED WHEN SUSTAINED WINDS NEAR
HURRICANE FORCE...OR FREQUENT GUSTS AT OR ABOVE HURRICANE FORCE...ARE
CERTAIN WITHIN THE NEXT 12 TO 24 HOURS.

ONCE TROPICAL STORM AND HURRICANE FORCE WINDS ONSET...DO NOT VENTURE
OUTSIDE!
```

FIGURE 1.5 The National Weather Service message in advance of Hurricane Katrina on August 28, 2005.

teams took boats to retrieve survivors and take them to staging points on the accessible highways around the city. The city was without potable water and power; the pumps were unable to drain the city efficiently. Officials predicted that the flooding would continue for weeks and urged residents to stay away. Most of the city's hospitals were flooded, and generators kept in basements were unable to perform their function, leading to equipment failures and a lack of air conditioning in sweltering hospital spaces (Hess and Arendt 2006). Efforts to evacuate patients from crippled hospitals such as Charity Hospital in the Central Business District were complicated by communication systems that did not speak to each other. Most of the hospitals did not have places for helicopters to land, and with the roads made impassable, there did not seem to be any way to evacuate patients, many of whom were among the most sick (Hess and Arendt 2006). For many of the patients, the post-Katrina situation was life threatening; several died as a direct result of the storm and its aftermath. In the end, 1,464 people died in New Orleans because of Hurricane Katrina.

The infrastructure of New Orleans was severely impacted by Katrina and the flooding. Most of the major roads were damaged. Bridge supports on the I-10 Twin Span Bridge connecting New Orleans to Slidell failed, dramatically reducing available escape routes. Nearly a full year after Katrina devastated New Orleans, the U.S. Army Corps of Engineers (2006) conceded that "differences in the quality of materials used in levees, differences in the conservativeness of floodwall designs, and variations in structure protective elevations due to subsidence and construction below the design intent" all contributed to failure of the hurricane protection system (p. 10).

In the aftermath of Katrina, despite widespread reports of looting and violent crime, the city of New Orleans was in fact relatively quiet. Looting in the wake of disasters, while apparently a favorite theme of the media, is "highly unusual in U.S. disasters" (Tierney, Bevc, and Kuligowski 2006, p. 65). Specific to New Orleans in the wake of Katrina, Tierney and her colleagues (2006) write, "... no solid empirical data exist regarding how widespread (or rare) looting actually was, who took part in the episodes of looting that did occur, why they were motivated to take part, whether the goods people took could have been salvaged, or how much damage and loss looting actually caused, relative to other losses the hurricane produced" (p. 66). In other words, the media appear to have focused on looting and general unrest in New Orleans in part because of a belief that they simply must be happening, rather than because of actual evidence that they were happening. Such a belief aligns with the general mythology that people behave irrationally under the stress caused by a disaster, and by the specific perceptions that New Orleans was a place of lawlessness even in the best of times.

Once survivors were evacuated from the Superdome and Convention Center, the city was occupied by police, fire, and rescue personnel, who traversed the flooded city in search of survivors. In addition to showing individuals being rescued by emergency responders, the media also focused on the fact that up to 240 of New Orleans' 1,450 police officers could not be located during Hurricane Katrina and its aftermath

(Kushma 2007). "Role abandonment" by so many members of the New Orleans police was, in fact, an anomalous act in the midst of an extreme natural hazard event as, with the exception of Hurricane Katrina and New Orleans, "there have been no documented reports of widespread role abandonment during disasters in the United States" (Kushma 2007, p. 4). Whether warranted or not, concerns about maintaining order in New Orleans (Litke 2005) were used to justify Governor Kathleen Blanco's decision to call in the National Guard on August 31.

In response to health and safety concerns, Mayor Ray Nagin ordered a forced evacuation on September 6 of everyone in the city who was not involved in its recovery. Restoring a sense of normalcy to New Orleans would prove a daunting task. The Superdome incurred $140 million in damage from the hurricane and from those who stayed there. It reopened more than a year after Katrina on September 25, 2006. The Convention Center required repairs as well, though the damages to it were less substantial.

After the hurricane, several factors contributed to the city's precipitous decline in population, from 455,188 in July 2005 to 208,548—a 54.2 percent decline—in 2006 (see Table 1.1). As of 2012, the population had grown to 369,250, approximately 81 percent of its pre-Katrina population. The economy before Katrina had not been robust; in the aftermath, it was devastated. The only industry that saw an uptick in demand in the year after Katrina was construction. Tourism has gradually returned to New Orleans, with visitors attending the city's many festivals (e.g., Mardi Gras) and other events (sporting events, conventions).

The Port of New Orleans has returned to its position as one of the largest and busiest ports in the world. Relatively few jobs are generated by the port, however, as both mechanization and containerization have diminished the need for human resources. The region around New Orleans has also retained its role as a major contributor to oil refining and petrochemical production. Its universities have reopened, and despite several years of diminished enrollments, have begun to recover. Only one Fortune 500 company is headquartered in New Orleans: Entergy. The city lost its other Fortune 500 company, Freeport-McMoRan, in the wake of Katrina.

Since August 29, 2005, New Orleans has been in recovery mode. Urban planning experts and other well-intentioned people have converged upon the city to share their time, treasure, and talent. Plans have been made, unmade, and made anew for the city's hospitals and other employment venues. Buildings have been restored, demolished, and left to rot. A drive through New Orleans today reveals inconsistent recovery of the built environment, with some neighborhoods no longer wearing the vestiges of Katrina: the spray paint on the outside of homes indicating that they had been searched, the abandoned and ruined automobiles, the overgrown foliage, the uplifted roads, the handmade road signs, the slabs where houses used to be. Houses have been rebuilt, some elevated a few feet, and others elevated a full story. Gas stations, grocery stores, and other businesses have reopened.

In other neighborhoods, however, the built environment remains devastated. Some blocks have more slabs than homes, or empty spaces where buildings once stood. Blight well beyond that found in the city before Katrina has taken root. Basic services have not been fully restored. The roads are in dire need of repair. Overgrown lots lie between otherwise attractive homes. Many schools remain closed, with signs outside indicating that school will reopen in August 2005 (Figure 1.6). Churches are shuttered.

Beyond the built environment, the city of New Orleans continues to struggle with demographic and population changes, environmental/ecosystem issues, the provision of organized government services, its physical infrastructure, lifestyle and community competence, economic development, and social-cultural capital. These dimensions, as described by Renschler and his colleagues (2010), together contribute to a community's resilience and its ability to recover after an extreme natural hazard event. Despite infusions of financial capital and thousands of volunteer hours, the city remains a shadow of its former self.

FIGURE 1.6   New Orleans East, Louisiana, February 6, 2008—This photo, taken more than 2 years after Hurricane Katrina, tells the story of schools that never reopened. (Photograph by Lucy A. Arendt.)

One resident of New Orleans, in responding to the question, "How is the recovery from Katrina going?" says, "It's a very complicated question with a complicated set of answers" (Klein 2013, para. 2). The built environment is a constant reminder of Katrina's wrath; Federal Emergency Management Association (FEMA) markings showing whether anyone was found deceased in a given building can still be found throughout the city. Individuals and families who grew up next to each other have been torn apart. Gates lead to sidewalks that used to lead to front porches, where people gathered to exchange the news—and rumors—of the day. Simple things that make children's lives normal are only now starting to be reborn. Neighborhood schools and parks have been neglected, with charter and private schools filling the gap for most, but not all, of New Orleans' children. "Feral cats and feral chickens" roam the streets (Klein 2013, para. 17).

In the midst of all the chaos, signs of rebirth are evident more than 8 years after Katrina. Make It Right NOLA, a nonprofit organization founded by actor Brad Pitt, is building 150 new homes in the Lower Ninth Ward (http://makeitright.org/where-we-work/new-orleans/). The unique architecture of these homes seems appropriate for New Orleans, a city known for its distinctive architecture. Many of the new homes feature solar panels and other components intended to enable more sustainable living for their inhabitants (see Figure 1.7).

FIGURE 1.7 Lower Ninth Ward, New Orleans, Louisiana, March 21, 2014—New homes featuring green components, including solar panels, dot the Lower Ninth Ward landscape. (Photograph by Lucy A. Arendt.)

FIGURE 1.8 Lakeview neighborhood, New Orleans, Louisiana, October 21, 2005—One of many homes destroyed by the 17th Street Canal levee breach. (Photograph by Lucy A. Arendt.)

Not everyone has returned to New Orleans, as evidenced by the changed population statistics. So, for at least some New Orleans denizens, the answer to whether the city has recovered is a resounding no. The city's recovery is hampered by its history, which we argue has made it difficult for the city to move forward. An analogy seems appropriate to this conversation. In Lakeview, many residents whose homes were destroyed were able to restore their properties because they had resources; they had savings, they had access to credit, they had professional jobs they maintained after Katrina. In other words, they had more capacity to recover from an extreme natural hazard event than their neighbors in the Lower Ninth Ward did. Some Lakeview residents rebuilt their homes exactly as they had been (see Figures 1.8 and 1.9), figuratively "thumbing their noses" at Katrina and any future disasters.

Although many in the Lower Ninth owned their homes, that was the extent of their wealth. They did not have substantial savings, access to financial capital, or good paying jobs that continued after Katrina. Instead, they had to rely on the government, their insurance companies, and the charity of nonprofit organizations and individuals to help them rebuild. They had less capacity to recover from an extreme natural

FIGURE 1.9 Lakeview neighborhood, New Orleans, Louisiana, March 20, 2014—The rebuilt home, across the road from the repaired 17th Street Canal levee. (Photograph by Lucy A. Arendt.)

hazard event. New Orleans as a whole is akin to the Lower Ninth Ward; despite peoples' good intentions and aspirations, the city as a whole was not equipped to successfully manage an extreme natural hazard event. The community of New Orleans, with all of its rich history, may be forever altered thanks to Katrina and the failure of the city's levees.

CHAPTER 2

From Extreme Natural Hazard Event to Community Disaster

In 1793, William Smith, a British canal digger, recognized that rocks lay in different strata and that the fossils in those strata were different from one another. By 1815, he had dug trenches, mapped strata across Great Britain, and was rewriting geological understanding (Winchester 2002). As with most other things, the development of better understanding of geological forces and natural events proceeded from Smith's work in fits and spurts. One of the coauthors of this book remembers that in the late 1940s, he suggested to his fifth-grade school teacher that it looked very much as if the northeast coast of South America could fit quite comfortably into the west coast of Africa and opined that the two continents may have been joined at one time. To his chagrin, she smiled condescendingly and said that it was just a coincidence. Her response reflected conventional thinking at that time: to wit, the continents were fixed in place and always had been but that "sunken land bridges" may have once linked some of them.

Even then, however, the notion of "continental drift" had been proposed by German meteorologist Alfred Wegener in 1912 in his book *The Origin of Continents and Oceans.* His theory was met with widespread derision among contemporary scientists. Because of World War I, Wegener's book went unnoticed outside of Germany. In 1922, however, a third (revised) edition was translated into English, French, Russian, Spanish, and Swedish, pushing Wegener's theory of continental drift to the forefront of debate among Earth scientists (Miller 1983).

As *Homo sapiens* became cognizant of inexplicable phenomena many centuries ago, it was entirely reasonable for them to attribute volcanic eruptions, hurricanes, and earthquakes to supernatural forces and to seek ways to appease those forces with ritual and sacrifice. Some of the natural events were seen as useful and desirable. The annual flooding of the Nile River was generally beneficial. From time to time, however, the annual spring flood failed to materialize, leading to poor harvests and sometimes famine. Other times, the spring flooding was much greater than anticipated and caused damage, dislocation, and, again, scanty harvests and famine. Other events were far less beneficial to human settlements: massive storms, volcanic eruptions, and earthquakes certainly must have terrified people at a time when few, if any, observers understood what they were, how they came about, and had scant warning when they occurred.

Some kinds of those completely natural events came to be defined as natural hazard events because they frequently had adverse effects on people's settlements, their social and economic pursuits, and features of the natural environment important to them. Many people apparently still believe that supernatural phenomena may account for natural hazard events, but, beginning about 100 years ago, others began to subscribe to the belief that the Earth's dynamics were responsible for hurricanes, volcanic eruptions, floods, earthquakes, tornadoes, rivers overflowing their banks from time to time, and the like.

Our collective understanding of the roles of tectonic plates, solar heating of the land and water, the Earth's rotation, and the Earth's core in generating natural phenomena on and near the Earth's surface is very recent; plate tectonics did not gain a solid foothold until the 1960s. Entirely natural events have been occurring since Earth was formed. Those natural events created continents; mountain ranges; plains; canyons; and variations in climate, flora, and fauna. For hundreds of millions of years, natural processes triggered events that shaped the physical environment within which *Homo sapiens* emerged perhaps 150,000 years ago and spread across the planet.

This book is concerned with extreme natural hazard events, so we want to distinguish what constitutes extreme natural hazard events from run-of-the-mill or even medium-sized events. Everyone understands that some natural hazard events are more significant than others. One of the coauthors easily survived a completely insignificant 6-inch tsunami on Oahu in 1985. The Indian Ocean Tsunami of 2004 and Katrina's 20- to 25-foot storm surge on the Gulf Coast later in 2005 were not insignificant. The northern part of the United States routinely deals with snowstorms during the winter months. Relatively few of those are a serious danger to people, in part, because they are accustomed to such weather and they have the means to deal with it (e.g., winter attire, snow tires, snowplows, salting equipment). Still, a deep freeze that collapses power lines can lead to injury and death for those exposed to chill temperatures for too long.

What constitutes an extreme natural hazard event? Extreme natural hazard events are defined both by social interpretation of the event and by assessment of an event's "extremeness" in terms of scales devised to measure the size and frequency of those events. The scales provide a means for recording various occurrences of specific kinds and magnitudes of events, for comparing one event with another, and for estimating how often events of various "size" will occur. Both means of definition are relevant.

SOCIAL DEFINITIONS, EXPERIENTIAL CONGRUENCE, AND INITIAL CONSEQUENCES

We have come to believe that the extent to which an event is perceived by those affected as "extreme" depends, to a considerable extent, on two variables. The first of these is the social context within which it occurs. The second has to do with the nature and extent of the initial impacts of the event as measured by injuries and deaths, and damage to the built and natural environments.

Collective Experiential Congruence

One factor affecting how people who experience them differentiate an extreme natural hazard event from one that is significant but not extreme is what constitutes normal expectations for them within their context of time, place, and experience. Typically, the term "experiential congruence" is used in psychology and psychiatry with reference to an individual (Grafanaki and McLeod 2002). For us, however, collective experiential congruence has to do with the extent to which a particular event is within the range of expected events in the collective experience of people living in a given place during a given time period. Their collective experience frames their expectations of what might typically be expected to occur in that place from time to time.

Illustratively, a few successive February days with high winds, subzero temperatures, and a foot or more of new snow are typical in Wisconsin, Upper Michigan, Minnesota, and the Dakotas. That kind of weather would be likely to cause officials to call for a 2-hour delay in school openings or perhaps to close schools for a day or two. Most people living there would probably perceive the event as unusual for that time of year, but not as an extreme natural hazard event. If such a storm were to occur in the Gulf Coast or somewhere else where such weather is rarely, if ever, experienced, it would be considered an extreme natural hazard event and probably have severe consequences. Importantly, the consequences would reflect, at least in part, the degree of preparation for such an event. For example, while Wisconsin has snowplows in every municipality, it is unlikely that places along the Gulf Coast would have such equipment. Although people living in Wisconsin have attire appro-priate for walking about in subzero weather, people living in Louisiana likely do not.

An excellent example that illustrates the importance of framing and collective experiential congruence occurred on Tuesday, January 28, 2014, in Atlanta, Georgia. Despite a National Weather Service forecast on Sunday, January 26 that Atlanta would likely see up to 2 inches of snow on Tuesday of that week, government officials appeared slow to act. Meteorologists were quoted as saying that, "Snow and ice covered roads will make travel difficult or impossible beginning Tuesday after-noon into Wednesday" (Wilson and Smith 2014, para. 5). Despite a deci-sion at 3:38 A.M. to place Atlanta and its suburbs under a winter storm warning beginning at 9:00 A.M. that day, schools elected to stay open. Atlanta commuters filled the roads, buoyed by statements from their mayor, Kasim Reed, that Atlanta was "ready for the snow" (Wilson and Smith 2014, para. 12).

By 11 A.M., Delta Airlines had cancelled 840 flights scheduled to fly into or out of Atlanta that day. At noon, schools started to announce early dismissals. By 1:35 P.M., Atlanta's roads were gridlocked. The cars made the work of clearing the icy roads a near impossible task. The Georgia National Guard went to work rescuing children trapped in buses and stranded motorists. Citizens were told to stay home if pos-sible, something that most would have gladly done—if they could have gotten home (Wilson and Smith 2014). Some motorists elected to stay with their trapped vehicles; others walked up to 5 miles in 20 degrees Fahrenheit before reaching their homes. Governor Nathan Deal declared Georgia closed on Wednesday, January 29, as state police and the National Guard continued working to clear the roads of vehicles.

In the aftermath of the storm, there was plenty of finger-pointing (Payne 2014). Although it might be convenient to blame this or that political figure, in truth it was everyone who found themselves on the roads who bore some responsibility for the disastrous outcomes of what would have been a fairly innocuous winter storm in any Northern state. Because Atlanta and its citizens were unprepared for a couple inches of snow and ice, the storm may as well have been a blizzard. The kind of weather faced on that day in January was outside the collective experien-tial congruence of Georgians. Oh, they had experienced winter weather before. An ice storm in 2011 had prompted calls for better preparation and response. Then, as now, the wintry mix of snow and ice was seen as an anomaly, not something that people needed to add to their rep-ertoire of "normal" happenings for which they would develop coping mechanisms. Local government had not substantially added to the snow and ice clearing equipment and contracts needed to ensure fast action to prepare roads in advance and make them passable during and after the storm.

Over time and generations, people learn which kinds of natural hazard events occur frequently enough where they live that residents are very likely to encounter them more than a few times during their lifetimes. Absent precautions, those events are life threatening. Through their personal experience as well as through social and intergenerational learning, people generally know the kinds of precautions they can take to protect themselves against those events to preclude or reduce major adverse consequences from them. The extent to which they take precautions against the more or less normal range of natural hazard events depends on their understanding of those events and the likely consequences that may ensue and their experience with those kinds of events.

To the extent they have sufficient resources, people usually, but not always, take the precautions that are necessary to protect their lives, property, and patterns of interaction among themselves and with the outside world. In climates with severe winters, such as in Wisconsin, those who can do so have adequate insulation in their buildings, have two-stage entries to buildings to reduce the amount of cold air entering the building when people enter or leave; have warm clothing; and have vehicles that are very likely to operate during intense cold, snowy, and icy conditions. They also keep an eye on weather forecasts. Unless those same people also have experience with earthquakes, they are likely to build with attention to extreme cold and the forces of wind and gravity, but they are unlikely to build with attention to forces generated by horizontal ground motion. It simply is not a part of their collective experience and is incongruent with their expectations for where they live.

Collective experiential congruence is relevant for events other than natural hazard events. Certainly, the slaying of 26 children in a Newtown, Connecticut, elementary school by a crazed gunman in January 2013 and the bombs detonated in April 2013 at the Boston Marathon were well beyond and completely incongruent with the collective experience of residents there and in most other places in the United States. Yet, there are many places in the world today where similar events would not be nearly so out of the ordinary. Iraq and Syria, for example, have experienced numerous terrorist bombings and many fatalities over the past decade (Global Terrorism Database 2013).

Along with experiential congruence and social expectations, context has temporal and spatial dimensions. What is rare and extreme in one place during one period in time might not be in another. *Hans Brinker* or *The Silver Skates* was first published in 1865 by Mary Mapes Dodge. Our literary hero, Hans, won the silver skates in an ice skating race over frozen canals in the Netherlands. Of course, Hans did so during the tail end of the Little Ice Age, which dominated European weather for 400 years, roughly from the 16th to the 19th century. Because of global warming, if Hans were to try to skate on a canal in the dead of winter in Haarlem today, he would likely drown because the canals rarely freeze since the Little Ice Age. Today, a winter in the Netherlands like those that were common 150 years ago would no doubt be construed by its residents as an extreme natural hazard event.

Initial Adverse Impacts

Sometimes, an event is perceived, defined, and described as an extreme natural hazard event, not because it was unusually large or rare, but because it resulted in major adverse consequences. Absent adequate precautions, even relatively common and comparatively modest earth-quakes, storms, and floods can result in major damage to a community. For most of history, some natural hazard events have been defined as extreme both because of their incongruence with "normality" and because of the nature and extent of their initial, visible consequences: damage or destruction in the built environment, land deformation, injuries, death, and destruction of natural environmental features.

Hurricane Katrina will be remembered not so much because it was an unusually powerful hurricane: Katrina had been a Category 5 event but made landfall in Florida as a Category 1 hurricane and on the Gulf Coast as a Category 3. It is the double whammy of hurricane winds and flooding brought on by levee breaches, along with the fact that so many people died because of the double disaster, that make the storm so memorable. First, much of New Orleans and parishes to the seaward side of it (e.g., St. Bernard Parish) were flooded by the storm surge as levees and floodwalls failed. Antiquated municipal sump pumps failed, exacerbating the flooding caused by breached levees, and leaving up to 80 percent of the city to sit for weeks in water up to the rafters of one-story buildings. Next, although "the evacuation of New Orleans had some unprecedented successes ... (it also had) glaring failures" (Wolshon 2006, p. 27). In particular, "low-mobility individuals" (Wolshon 2006, p. 32), such as many of New Orleans' disabled, elderly, and poor, did not have access to the personal vehicles that many used to exit the city. Others elected to stay because they did not have the means to afford a long-term evacuation (e.g., credit cards to pay for hotel bills). Still others chose to stay because they believed that their residence would stand up to the hurricane's forces; they could not know that the levees would be overtopped and breached, and that the streets would become canals. Television coverage of the government's response to the flooding showed thousands of people stranded in wholly unsustainable circumstances

(Wolshon 2006, p. 32) and told of human bodies floating in floodwaters. An article in *The Washington Post* by Coates and Eggen (2005) described New Orleans as "a city of despair and lawlessness" (para. 1).

It was the combination of a moderately strong hurricane, a city that was mostly at or below sea level, inadequate precautions exercised by municipal government officials, and massive infrastructure damage that defined Katrina as a catastrophic and extreme natural hazard event.

The length of time that the city was under water also affected people's perceptions of the event's extremeness. Some people were not allowed back into their neighborhood to view the damage to their homes until more than a month had passed. By then, any hopes of salvaging their homes and the contents were dashed. Many of the Lower Ninth Ward residents indicated that they would not likely return; the neighborhood that had boasted relatively high homeownership no longer resembled itself. This last point is an important one. A major reason for the collective perception that Hurricane Katrina was an extreme natural hazard event was the highly visible nature of the destruction and the high contrast between the "life" in the community before and after Katrina. Whereas before people sat on their front porches and chatted up their neighbors, in the aftermath of Katrina, there were not enough people living in enough houses to chat up. Blocks looked like jack-o-lanterns when power was finally restored; there were a few lights on here and there, but the neighborhood was mostly cloaked in darkness. The neighborhood had taken on an eerie and forbidding appearance; it no longer felt like home.

Population statistics compiled by the Greater New Orleans Community Data Center (2013) tell the tale of a community in transition. Census data from 2000 indicated a total of 14,008 people, 4,820 households, and 3,467 families living in the Lower Ninth Ward. By 2010, there were 2,842 people, 1,061 households, and 683 families living in the neighborhood. Eighty percent fewer people in a formerly densely occupied zone tends to be rather obvious. A conversation that one of the coauthors had with a resident of the Lower Ninth Ward in March 2014 confirmed the observation that the neighborhood had been irrevocably altered by Katrina and the flooding that followed. "There used to be neighbors all around me," said the older gentleman. "When I came back, my house wasn't here. It was blocks away. I rebuilt on the same spot, but almost no one else has come back. It isn't the same." A look around the gentleman's block confirmed his statement that relatively few homes stood where once the neighborhood had been densely populated (see Figure 2.1).

Although the City of New Orleans tends to dominate conversations about Hurricane Katrina and its aftermath, St. Bernard Parish experienced similar, if not more dramatic, changes to its population

FIGURE 2.1   Lower Ninth Ward, New Orleans, Louisiana, March 21, 2014—The Lower Ninth continues its recovery nearly 9 years after Katrina. On a stretch of land where once there would have been dozens of homes, now there are fewer than a dozen. (Photograph by Lucy A. Arendt.)

and housing stock in the wake of Katrina. Located southeast of New Orleans, St. Bernard Parish was a residential community with 67,229 residents and 26,790 housing units, according to the 2000 U.S. Census. Katrina swept the eastern part of St. Bernard Parish, propelling a 25-foot storm surge into the Mississippi River Gulf Outlet, and destroying the parish's levees. "Most of the parish was flooded directly from the surge, in the early dawn of August 29, 2005, but the section that was spared was subsequently flooded in midmorning, along with NOLA's (New Orleans) Ninth Ward, when the Industrial Canal levee walls failed" (Kieper 2006). Of all the residential buildings in St. Bernard Parish, only a handful was considered habitable in the aftermath. The water that drowned St. Bernard was "contaminated by a large oil spill—millions of gallons—from a storage tank in the industrial portion of the parish" (Kieper 2006). The 2010 U.S. Census reveals the extent of the damage to St. Bernard's built environment: The population decreased 47 percent to 35,897 and the housing units decreased 38 percent to 16,553. More than 10,000 housing units were destroyed directly by Katrina or demolished in the years following. What remains in many neighborhoods are extensive swaths of open green where before there had been tightly clustered homes (see Figures 2.2 and 2.3).

A Richter Magnitude 3.5 earthquake in Los Angeles is not a particularly rare event. It would be noticed by most of the residents, but then

FIGURE 2.2 St. Bernard Parish, Louisiana, March 21, 2014—Few neighborhoods in St. Bernard Parish have maintained their pre-Katrina character, as significantly fewer homes fill each block. (Photograph by Lucy A. Arendt.)

FIGURE 2.3 St. Bernard Parish, Louisiana, March 21, 2014—Where homes used to be, in 2014 all that remain are addresses painted in white on the curbs. (Photograph by Lucy A. Arendt.)

soon forgotten as they refocused their attention on daily activities. If a similar earthquake were to happen in a city that has not experienced an earthquake in its recorded history or one in which the residents have not built structures to resist the ground motions generated by such an earthquake, many structures would be likely to sustain significant damage or even fail. People would likely die. One need only review the effects of modest to moderate earthquakes in parts of the Middle East, where traditional building practices make structures particularly vulnerable to the Earth's movement to know that. When an earthquake does occur in such places, it usually results in many failed structures and many injuries and deaths. The reasons for the differential impacts are clear. Since the early 1930s, California has enacted and enforced increasingly stringent building codes that resulted in an inventory of structures resistant to moderate earthquake forces. Structures in cities in other places in the United States where even a Richter Magnitude 3.5 event is extraordinarily rare tend to be vulnerable to even modest ground motion or deformation.

The media frequently contributes to an event being socially defined as an extreme natural hazard event because the event results in significant initial damage, even when observers that are more objective might disagree about whether either the magnitude of the event or the losses experienced were exceptional. The media might also characterize an event as extreme based on its rareness or novelty. For example, the 2011 Virginia earthquake occurred on August 23, 2011, at 1:51 P.M. EDT in the Piedmont region of Virginia. The epicenter, in Louisa County, was 38 miles northwest of Richmond and 5 miles south-southwest of the town of Mineral. It was an intraplate earthquake with a Magnitude of 5.8.

Although the quake was felt by people across more than a dozen U.S. states and in several Canadian provinces, no deaths and only minor injuries were reported. Minor damage to buildings was widespread. For the most part, this earthquake was a nonstory in terms of its initial impacts. The damage to the built and natural environments, while not inconsequential for the owners of affected buildings, was relatively minor and not terribly visible. With no deaths and only minor injuries, there was not much of a human interest story to relate. That said, the media did emphasize the relative rareness of the earthquake and used that to discuss the East Coast's relative lack of preparation for an earthquake of any great magnitude. Experts spoke to the differences between earthquakes on the West Coast and the one that so many people had experienced in 2011. As one expert blogger wrote:

> Overall, seismic waves are transmitted more efficiently through compact, elastic materials. East coast rocks are relatively old and cold, and thus more dense and more capable of transmitting seismic energy. California and the west, in contrast, has a higher rate of heat flow

through the crust and so those rocks are more "poofed out" by being warm—they take up more volume, and so it's harder for seismic energy to swiftly pass through them. Furthermore, in comparing the great distance that these waves traveled to a similar magnitude event in California, it's worth keeping in mind that many of the fractures which would retard the transmission of seismic energy in the east have been sealed shut by mineral veins, while a lot of the west coast's fractures are still relatively fresh. It's hard for seismic energy to cross empty space. Those two factors—temperature and fracturing—may have something to do with explaining why this event was felt so widely up and down the eastern seaboard.

Bentley 2011, para. 18

In looking for evidence that the Virginia earthquake was worth writing about, the media focused on damage to the Washington Monument. The estimate to repair the damage to the monument is $15 million. Though not insubstantial, the cost of repairing this building alone pales in comparison to the damages wrought by other extreme hazard events. For example, Hurricane Sandy (also known as Superstorm Sandy) made landfall along the eastern seaboard in October 2012. It affected 24 states, including the entire seaboard from Florida to Maine and west across the Appalachian Mountains to Michigan and Wisconsin, with particularly severe damage in New Jersey and New York. Damage was estimated to be $65 billion in the United States alone. Clearly, there was a substantial difference between the "extremeness" of the 2011 Virginia earthquake and Hurricane Sandy.

METRICS AND EXTREME NATURAL HAZARD EVENTS

The magnitude of most kinds of extreme natural hazard events has been measured through history in terms of observable on-the-ground effects. More recently, metrics and means have been devised to measure various aspects of individual kinds of events. The new tools do not depend on the recollections of those who experienced the event; they are more objective and generally replicable.

The new tools and metrics provide the means for logging the frequency with which events with certain characteristics occur and a means for comparing events. Importantly, they are able to measure both the kinds of forces and the magnitude of those forces to which the built environment will be subjected when such events occur. This information provides invaluable insights for those charged with incorporating resistance and resiliency against hazardous events into the built environment.

Over the decades, scientists have devised metrics and associated scales for specifying the magnitude and frequency of a wide range of natural hazard events with greater accuracy and reliability. For earth-quakes, we have the Richter scale (Spence et al. 1989). The Enhanced Fujita Scale (Texas Tech University 2006) measures tornadoes, the Saffir-Simpson Scale (Iacovelli 1999) measures hurricanes, and the Beaufort wind force scale (Huler 2004) measures wind velocity. The Torino Impact Hazard Scale (Morrison et al. 2004) is for assessing the likelihood that a particular asteroid or comet will strike the Earth and result in a particular level of destruction. We even have the Szilagyi Waterspout Index (Sioutas et al. 2013).

The scales and metrics for the different kinds of natural hazard events typically evolve through time, going through a number of iterations and refinements. Earthquake scales serve as a good example. A 10-point scale for assessing earthquake magnitude was developed in Italy by Rossi and Forel in the late 19th century (Stover 1989). It was based on on-the-ground observations of the immediate consequences of an earthquake. Closer to the turn of the century, Giuseppe Mercalli modified Rossi and Forel's work, resulting in the Mercalli Intensity Scale (Stover 1989). Shortly thereafter, another Italian, Adolfo Cancani, expanded Mercalli's 10-degree scale to 12 degrees. That scale was subsequently refined several times. It emerged in English in 1931 as the Modified Mercalli Intensity Scale (MMI) but was still based on on-the-ground observations of the immediate consequences of the earthquake (Stover 1989). The U.S. Geological Survey (USGS) interprets the scale this way. According to the USGS description of the MMI, "The lower numbers of the intensity scale generally deal with the manner in which the earthquake is felt by people. The higher numbers of the scale are based on observed structural damage. Structural engineers usually contribute information for assigning intensity values of VIII or above" (USGS 2013a, para. 3).

In 1935, Charles Richter at the California Institute of Technology devised a scale based not on the immediate effects of an earthquake, but on the amplitude of waves generated by the event as measured on a seismograph (Spence et al. 1989). The Richter scale was the first earthquake magnitude scale not based on on-the-ground observations at the time of the quake. The scale is logarithmic, so an increase of one whole number on the scale represents 10 times the amplitude of the size of waves generated by the quake. However, in terms of energy released, each one whole number increase in the scale represents about 31 times more energy released than that released by an event measuring one whole number less on the scale.

Earthquakes occur frequently. The USGS estimates that several million occur in the world each year (USGS 2013b). Most of us who have experienced a number of earthquakes know that some are small, others

TABLE 2.1   Frequency of Occurrence of Earthquakes
Greater Than Richter Magnitude 2 by Average
Annual Occurrence

Magnitude	Average Annual Occurrence
8 and higher	1[a]
7–7.9	15[a]
6–6.9	134[b]
5–5.9	1,319[b]
4–4.9	13,000 (estimated)
3–3.9	130,000 (estimated)
2–2.9	1,300,000 (estimated)

Source: U.S. Geological Survey, "Earthquake Facts and
Statistics." Last modified November 29, 2012.
http://earthquake.usgs.gov/earthquakes/eqarchives/
year/eqstats.php.

[a] Based on observations since 1900. The numbers were
updated based on data from the Centennial Catalog
(from 1900 to 1999 and the Preliminary Determination
of Epicenters [PDE] Bulletin since 2000).

[b] Based on observations since 1990.

are moderate, and some are strong. A few very rare earthquakes approach
what is known as a maximum credible event for any given place.

The USGS maintains earthquake records and published data on the
average annual frequency of earthquakes on the globe by magnitude.
Since 1900, an average of 16 earthquakes of Richter Magnitude 7 or
more have occurred on average somewhere on Earth. That is, on average over the past century, only about 1 in 100,000 (0.001 percent) of
the earthquakes that occur annually and that are greater than Richter
Magnitude 2 measure more than 7 on the Richter scale (see Table 2.1).
These, indeed, are both rare and extreme natural hazard events. About 1
in 10,000 earthquakes (0.010 percent) that occur each year are measured
between Richter Magnitude 6 and 6.9. Although sometimes referred to
as moderate or moderately strong, even Magnitude 5 to 5.9 earthquakes
are relatively common, but they still account for less than one-tenth of
1 percent of all earthquakes that occur each year over Magnitude 2.

The relationship between the magnitude of an event and the likelihood that it will become an extreme natural hazard event in terms
of a community is anything but linear. Context is critically important.
So, too, are preventive measures taken by and within the community.
Because of contextual variability, even the Richter's scale, which has
proven to be both useful and durable, does not provide all the information engineers and scientists find useful in measuring the characteristics

of specific earthquakes. It is important for structural engineers and geo-scientists to know the nature of the ground motion generated by earth-quakes, including vertical and horizontal displacement and horizontal ground acceleration. Mitigating the effects of an earthquake at a specific location requires knowledge of the microgeology of the site, knowledge of wave propagation through different kinds of soils with different levels of moisture content, and other contextual variables.

Extremely rare events that release massive amounts of energy are more likely than smaller events to result in extreme consequences for a community, other things being equal. If we are trying to determine the likelihood that a natural hazard event will be one that is extreme for a community, the magnitude of the event is clearly one variable that must be taken into account. However, as will be subsequently seen, magnitude is only one of several critical variables when determining whether the natural hazard event is an extreme natural hazard event for a community.

WHAT, THEN, IS AN EXTREME NATURAL HAZARD EVENT?

It makes sense to identify extreme natural hazard events in terms of the energy release associated with it, their magnitude, intensity, dura-tion, and probability of occurrence. It also makes sense to define them socially in terms of context based on time, place, and collective expe-riential congruence. It makes less sense to measure them in terms of the initial and the subsequent damage they inflict upon a community. The problem with attempting to specify whether a natural hazard event is extreme in terms of damage inflicted is that the nature and extent of damage inflicted on the community often depends on the extent to which the community has taken precautions against the event and the effectiveness of those precautions. In other words, "damage inflicted" as a postevent measure is confounded by actions taken or not taken prior to the event.

If a community is sufficiently resistant and robust against an event, then an ensuing disaster is unlikely and the event, while it may have been powerful, will have both fewer immediate and cascading consequences. If the community fails to adapt proactively to an event with the same characteristics and is demolished, then, we suppose, the event would be labeled extreme, even though it is the consequences that are extreme and not the event. This poses the somewhat discomforting question of whether, absent metrics such as the Richter scale, events are viewed as extreme only if we are not successfully prepared for them.

From Extreme Natural Hazard Event to Community Disaster

As L. J. Carr (1932) wrote, "Not every windstorm, earth-tremor, or rush of water is a catastrophe" (p. 211). Historical ideas about disasters have gone through three basic changes, according to Quarantelli, a pioneer in the sociology of disaster (2001). First, they were characterized as Acts of God. As scientific understanding developed, they were thought of as Acts of Nature. Today, they are generally thought of as resulting from the Acts of Men and Women (Quarantelli 2001). Furedi (2007) observes that "throughout history people's explanations of what caused a disaster, what would be its likely impact on their lives and what meaning they should attach to it have gone through important modifications" (p. 483). In our time, we have come to understand that disasters are defined socially and not by the triggering event itself. As Carr (1932) states, "Social change in disaster is catastrophe, plus cultural collapse, plus peril and perhaps death, plus disorganization, plus reorganization—it is no one of these alone, but all of them together. In other words, it is not a single event or even a single kind of event: it is a series of events, linked one with another" (p. 215).

Rodriguez and Dynes (2006), examining the Hurricane Katrina experience, discuss how Katrina was "framed" by observers. They identify five themes that, for all practical purposes, defined Katrina. They are finding damage, finding death, finding help, finding authority (who's in charge and who's responsible for doing what), and finding the "bad guys." They illustrated the "finding death" theme by pondering whether the early high estimates of those that died in the event were either useful or accurate. The "finding help" theme in their article focuses on the perceived and reported difficulties of those exposed to the event finding help in the immediate aftermath. We could perhaps abbreviate their framing themes to five themes we would call damage, death, help, authority, and human failings. Regardless of the frame used, what matters is that people tend to use them to help them understand what is happening when an extreme natural hazard event collides with a community.

The primary point of the historical development and discussions about social definitions of disaster is that today, more than ever, informed observers agree that extreme natural hazard events are not the retribution of supernatural beings but the consequence of phenomena that are intrinsic to the natural processes changing the face of the Earth. Individuals often disagree about a particular phenomenon because, figuratively, the phenomenon is buried deep within a cloudy crystal and the observers view it through different facets of that crystal. The view through one facet is never quite the same as the view through another.

The facets through which individuals choose to peer reflect their predilections, dominant values, or disciplinary interests. Sociologists, for example, might examine disasters by looking for patterns that shape both smaller interpersonal interactions as well as institutional behaviors. Public policy scholars might focus on how policy influences behavior of both individuals and agencies. Environmentalists might be most interested in the interaction between humans and ecosystems, and the effect of human decision making on ecosystem resilience. Occasionally, the view through a particular facet changes with new insights. Students of disasters agree there are some commonalities among their various perceptions of disasters, but there appears to be no consensus about what constitutes a "community disaster."

Even within a discipline, it is often difficult to gain consensus for a definition of disaster. Perry and Quarantelli (2005) report that sociologists have been defining and redefining what constitutes a disaster for at least 60 years. In *What Is a Disaster?* Perry and Quarantelli (2005) asked what is a disaster and then explored the question with the help of a dozen prominent sociologists long involved in disaster research. In his introductory chapter to the work, David Alexander (2005) described "disaster" as "a definitional minefield" and it certainly appears to be just that (p. 26). The absence of a consensus definition of what constitutes a disaster has not appeared, however, to limit inquiry into disasters, at least within several interested disciplines. Actually, it may be useful to have different foci of interests and definitional differences among anthropologists, sociologists, economists, political scientists, engineers, organizational behaviorists, and others. As a complex topic, disaster research demands a multidisciplinary effort (Dynes 1989). But, without a common language or set of concepts, it seems less likely that the potential intellectual synergies that can emerge from truly interdisciplinary research will be realized.

More than two decades ago, Kroll-Smith and Couch (1991) attempted to resolve the definitional debate among sociologists. They examined two approaches to defining a disaster and suggested a third approach. One of the approaches they examined focuses on the social consequences of the event. The other approach includes the physical dimension of the event. Kroll-Smith and Couch call their approach an ecological-symbolic approach. For them, "the real issue is not the quality of the disaster agent per se, but whether or not it significantly alters the relationship between a community, its built, modified or biophysical environments, and how people interpret and experience the changes in those environments" (p. 361). This observation is congruent with the view that disasters are socially defined and linked with the extent of the consequences that are caused by or triggered by the extreme natural hazard event (Carr 1932).

Disasters as Complex, Disruptive Social Events

Community disasters are typically associated with an event or a combination of events. Although people may believe that the natural hazard event itself constitutes the disaster, we do not think this is a useful construction. For decades, sociologists, including Carr (1932), have viewed an extreme natural hazard event as a catalyst to the disaster and not the disaster itself. We concur: the disaster comprises the adversities and the dysfunctions that develop following the natural event, primarily as a consequence of the event. Other events or historical patterns in the community may contribute to the disaster, but the natural hazard event is only a trigger for what follows. Injuries and death are consequences of natural hazard events. So, too, are homelessness, unemployment, anomie, and a host of other social phenomena.

Oliver-Smith and Hoffman (1999) spell out that view: "The conjunction of a human population and a potentially destructive agent does not … inevitably produce a disaster. The society's pattern of vulnerability—or in other words, its adaptive failure—is an essential element of a disaster" (p. 29). Oliver-Smith and Hoffman see disaster as an array of socially derived effects. Dynes' (1989) view is similar but not the same. He sees a disaster as largely a behavioral phenomenon associated primarily with the behavioral response of humans and groups in the context of disruption or damage.

This notion of vulnerability is supported by the work of Cutter, Boruff, and Shirley (2003). They write, "There are three main tenets in vulnerability research: the identification of conditions that make people or places vulnerable to extreme natural events, an *exposure* model; the assumption that vulnerability is a social condition, a measure of societal resistance or *resilience* to hazards; and the integration of potential exposures and societal resilience with a specific focus on particular *places* or regions" (pp. 242–243; italics added). As a result of their empirical research, they concluded that "those factors that contribute to the overall (vulnerability) score often are different for each county, underscoring the interactive nature of social vulnerability—some components increase vulnerability; others moderate the effects" (Cutter et al. 2003, p. 242). This reinforces our view that natural hazard events have the potential to trigger disasters, and that what happens in the aftermath of a disaster is a complex "stew" that will vary by community.

Sometimes, it may seem unreasonable to view a disaster as a failure of a community to adapt. The massively destructive flooding in Colorado in September 2013 occurred because an extraordinary amount of rain fell in a very short period—up to 21 inches in parts of Boulder, nearly double the area's annual rainfall. Meteorologists estimate that such an event has a probability of one in a thousand of happening in any given year.

Reuters reports that the flooding ultimately encompassed 17 Colorado counties across an area roughly the size of Delaware (Coffman 2013). It may, in fact, be unreasonable to expect a community, or dozens of communities as in this case, to be fully resistant to an event with 0.1 percent probability of occurrence in any given year.

Nonetheless, the scale of the consequences was likely to have been abated by human activity or lack thereof. Dams failed in the face of the flooding (Olinger and Finley 2013), and some have suggested that because funding for dam maintenance has been inadequate, the failure of the dams was partly the fault of human inaction. This argument parallels the one in which the U.S. Army Corps of Engineers was considered responsible by many for the failure of New Orleans' levees after Katrina. Most people can be expected to acknowledge that New Orleans is located in such as way as to virtually ensure flooding; after all, most of the city is well below sea level. Still, most people are also aware that the flooding that drowned New Orleans for weeks could have been reduced significantly if the levees had held.

It is virtually impossible for humans to protect themselves completely against the very rare natural hazard events with the extraordinary potential for generating widespread, intensive destruction. Competing priorities butt up against scarce resources, and trade-offs must be made. Still, our failure to mitigate the potential consequences of such events is just that: a failure to adapt. And, sometimes, not adapting to an extremely rare hazard event that would require most or all of our resources makes sense.

As anthropologists, Oliver-Smith and Hoffman (1999) see disasters as being within a major focus of anthropology: that being human use and adaptation of the natural environment. This perspective contributes to understanding a disaster as encompassing the adverse consequences triggered by a natural hazard event. After all, depending on how humans have adapted to the physical environment and how they have modified the physical environment to their purposes, natural hazard events of the same magnitude and characteristics may have serious adverse consequences for humans in different places at different times. Taking precautions to reduce adverse consequences from anticipated natural hazard events can mitigate the consequences of those events.

On the other hand, using the physical environment heedless of what kinds of natural hazard events are likely to occur in that location often results in disaster. Failure to recognize the types of natural hazard events in a given location may reflect a lack of knowledge about possible natural hazard events or perhaps hubris that nature has been subjugated to the desires of humans. Regarding the latter possibility, Carr (1932) spoke scathingly, "despite our boasted conquest of nature it is estimated that more than a million people died in disasters somewhere in the world in 1931. Even in the United States, where nature is supposed to be most completely subdued, there were 938 disasters in the forty-eight years from 1881 to 1928, each large enough to induce the American Red Cross to give aid" (p. 209). In New Orleans, for example, the city filled in what had been swamp and marshland in order to expand the city's boundaries. Presumably, this was done in part to expand the property tax base and to increase the possibility that people would choose to live in the city and parish of New Orleans rather than in an adjoining parish. Thus, decisions about land use are often politically motivated and thoughts of natural hazard events pushed to the background.

Oliver-Smith and Hoffman (1999) elaborate the point, suggesting that there is nothing particularly easy about understanding disasters in the context of "the complex internal differentiation that is particularly characteristic of contemporary human societies" requires an approach that "can encompass the interaction of environmental features, processes, and resources with the nature, forms, and effects of the patterns of production, allocation, and internal social differentiation of society" (p. 29).

Perry (2005) references half a dozen sociologists who see disasters as possessing common themes. Among these is the "definition of disasters as social events in social time" (p. 313). This implies that disasters constitute a major disruption to social intercourse and should be seen in the "context of social change" (Perry 2005, p. 313). This is an important commonality among sociological and anthropological perceptions of disasters: they represent significant disruptions in the normal course of activity and interaction because of a failure of the community to successfully cope with an event or combination of events.

When Communities Cannot Perform One or More Critical Functions

Sociologists and anthropologists make a convincing case for viewing community disasters as situations in which some catalyst, such as a major flood, are a significant disruption in the normal course of activity by the members of the community and by the community as a whole. Presumably, then, the activities that comprise the "normal" activities of the community have to do with the ability of the community to perform critical functions sufficiently well so as to meet community needs or expectations. Thus, it makes sense to look at the nature of communities (cities, villages, human settlements) in terms of the functions they are expected to perform and, then, to look at how a natural hazard event might compromise the ability to perform them (Alesch and Siembieda 2012).

Functionalism, a long-time social science approach to understanding social and political phenomena, is a useful tool for beginning to understand the normal course of activities for human settlements. Lewis

Mumford, in his 1938 classic, *The Culture of Cities*, described the contemporary city as having developed from the earliest roots of "the need for a common fortified spot for shelter against predatory attack (which) draws the inhabitants of the indigenous village into a hillside fortification" (p. 5). Mumford (1938) concluded, "Cities arise out of man's social needs and their methods of expression. In the city remote forces and influences intermingle with the local: their conflicts are no less significant than their harmonies. And here, through the concentration of the means of intercourse in the market and the meeting place, alternative modes of living present themselves" (p. 4). Mumford described the development of the city through history in terms of its symbolic and practical functions and how those functions are expressed in its physical characteristics (c.f. Mumford 1961).

James K. Mitchell (2004) elaborated on the functions that communities perform. Mitchell identifies the following functions of communities: material and economic, metabolic, learning, performance, creative expression, and regulatory. "Material and economic functions of communities," he writes, "involve the accumulation of resources and their conversion into products and services that sustain both the physical fabric of the built environments and the livelihoods of associated human populations" (p. 16). Metabolic functions are described as those that "involve natural and human-modified life-support systems including, among others, those that generate, nurture, circulate and absorb air, water, biota, and wastes" (Mitchell 2004, 16).

Mitchell (2004) says that each function he defines is linked with "a characteristic kind of analytic model or metaphor" (p. 16). This approach replicates and extends the use of metaphor by Gareth Morgan (1986) to explain the different functions of organizations (e.g., organizations as machines, organisms, brains, cultures, political systems, psychic prisons, flux and transformation, and instruments of domination). Mitchell (2004) identifies his city-based metaphors as cities as machines, cities as organisms, cities as information exchange networks, cities as performances, cities as muses, and cities as power structures and regulated places. Cities, he says, are a complex form of human settlement, but like all open systems, they are not self-sufficient. They draw upon external resources to function, interacting with the external environment because they need those linkages to adapt and to survive.

Verhoef and Nijkamp (2004) also listed what they perceived to be the primary roles that communities perform. These roles (or functions) are shelter, religious, cultural, political, economic, engineering, and network roles. The city, they suggest, "brings together a triple-C potential: communication, competence, and creativity" (p. 90).

Renschler and his colleagues (2010) discuss a community's functions in terms of their contribution to the community's resilience. They identify seven interdependent dimensions of community resilience, as follows: population and demographics, environmental/ecosystem, organized governmental services, physical infrastructure, lifestyle and community competence, economic development, and social-cultural capital (i.e., the PEOPLES framework). They suggest that population and demographics may be measured using a "social index that describes the socioeconomic status, the composition of the population (elderly and children), development density, rural agriculture, race, gender, ethnicity, infrastructure employment, and county debt/revenue" (Renschler et al. 2010, p. 4). The environmental/ecosystem dimension "is typically measured by the amount of disturbance an ecosystem can absorb without drastically altering its functions, processes and structures, or by the ability of an ecosystem to cope with disturbance" (Renschler et al. 2010, p. 5).

Organized government services include legal and security services (e.g., police, emergency and fire departments), along with the services provided by public health and hygiene departments as well as cultural heritage departments (Renschler et al. 2010). The physical infrastructure dimension includes housing, commercial facilities, cultural facilities, and lifelines (e.g., food supply, health care, utilities, transportation, and communication networks). Lifestyle and community competence deals with community action, critical reflection and problem-solving skills, flexibility and creativity, collective efficacy, empowerment, and political partnerships (Norris et al. 2008). This dimension "captures both the raw abilities of the community (e.g., ability to develop multifaceted solutions to complex problems, ability to engage in meaningful political networks) and the community's perceptions of its ability to effect positive change. Communities that collectively believe that they can rebuild, restructure, and revive themselves are more likely to be persistent in the face of environmental, governmental, and other obstacles" (Renschler et al. 2010, pp. 6–7).

As described by Renschler and his colleagues (2010), economic development includes "both the static assessment of a community's current economy (economic activity) and the dynamic assessment of a community's ability to sustain economic growth (economic development)" (p. 7). As described by the Research Institute on Christianity in South Africa Poverty Project (2010), economic activity takes into account the supply of labor for the production of economic goods and services, which includes "all production and processing of primary products whether for market, for barter or for own consumption, the production of all other goods for the market and, in the case of households which produce such goods and services for the market, the corresponding production for own consumption" (para. 10). Economic development addresses the future and growth of the community.

Finally, social/cultural capital incorporates categories such as education services, child and elderly services, cultural and heritage services, and community participation. Aldrich (2012) describes social capital as "the ties that bind people together" (p. viii). He uses the example of the neighborhood of Mary Queen of Vietnam within Village d L'Est in the northeast corner of New Orleans to illustrate the importance of social capital (social networks and their resources) to a community's recovery. "The absence of social capital can stall a community's recovery" (Aldrich 2012, p. 2), in part because of the relationship between social capital and community competence. Social/cultural capital is a prerequisite to community competence (Norris et al. 2008). Proponents of social capital as "the core engine of recovery" believe that it is more essential to recovery than "socioeconomic conditions, population density, amount of damage or aid" (Aldrich 2012, p. 15).

While agreeing that social capital is critical to community functioning and recovery, we do not see the need to prioritize or elevate it above other community functions, knowing that all elements in the system are interdependent and essential to the community. Recognizing that community health requires more than good jobs and infrastructure, the function of social/cultural capital incorporates the array of formal and informal services that the community has chosen to provide itself. It also includes several intangible "goods," such as social support, sense of community, place attachment, and citizen participation (Norris et al. 2008). For many, social/cultural capital is the "extra" or "icing" that makes a community's quality of life something worth promoting.

From the perspective of someone viewing the community in terms of the functions it performs, a disaster is a disruption—a significant disruption—in the ability of the community to perform one or more of its functions at a satisfactory level. The functions may be construed as the material and economic function, the metabolic function, any of the others, or a combination of several functions. The functions may also be understood as the dimensions that comprise the PEOPLES framework (Renschler et al. 2010). This view of disasters is congruous with a view of disasters as social events associated with the inability of the community to cope with a disruptive event. The inability to perform critical functions at a level consistent with contemporary expectations is very likely a consequence of a great disturbance and an inability of the community to cope with that.

This view of communities and coping with disasters is consistent with social psychologists' thinking about experienced stress at the individual level. McGrath (1976) describes a model of stress in which individuals experience stress as a function of three factors, all of which are measured as perceptions rather than as "objective" data: consequences of meeting a demand, a demand, and ability or coping to meet the demand.

When there is an imbalance between perceived demand and ability, and perceived consequences are high, individuals experience high levels of stress. By analogy, then, one might assert that communities experience high levels of collective stress when there is an imbalance between perceived demand (the natural hazard event) and ability (specifically, the community's arsenal of tools to cope with the natural hazard event, or the efficacy of its functions/dimensions), and perceived consequences of dealing with the event are high.

Disasters and Damage to Complex, Self-Organizing, Open Systems

An extreme natural hazard event is not a disaster in and of itself: the disaster is triggered when the event has serious adverse consequences for a society or a community. We concur with those who see extreme natural hazard events as a catalyst that may result in a disaster, depending on the extent to which the community has effectively precluded exceptional adverse consequences from the event. As suggested by the analogy of individuals experiencing stress, a disaster occurs when a community's coping mechanisms are insufficient to preclude or reduce the extent of the initial consequences of the event and the seriously adverse consequences that may follow primarily because of that event. Consequences matter. The disaster occurs when the community is unable to perform its essential functions because of the disturbances generated by the event.

A major contribution to the understanding of disasters from sociology is the perspective of the disaster as a social event centering on the failure of the community to adapt effectively to its natural environment. Mitchell's (2004) central contribution is his focus on disaster as the inability of the community to perform its central functions. Together, these views add significantly to our understanding of what a disaster is. They do not, however, help us very much with the dynamics of disaster: how the natural hazard event actually triggers the disaster and how the disaster unfolds. Nor do they contribute much to our understanding of how recovery from disasters might come about. A new layer of complexity is necessary for that.

We have come to believe that viewing a community as a complex, self-organizing social system enables one to add a dynamic that contributes to greater understanding of how community disasters occur and unfold. As described by Ludwig von Bertalanffy in his classic work, *General System Theory: Foundations, Development, Applications* (1968), a system comprises a set of component parts, each of which is linked to other components within the system in generally persistent patterns. Performance of the system as a whole depends on performance of the various component parts. A disturbance of one component part of the system has consequences for the other components. When one or more of the component parts is compromised and unable to perform its role with regard to other parts, then the system itself is in danger of being compromised in terms of performing its aggregate functions. Individual components of the community system experience a major interruption when sufficient other components are unable to perform their functions.

Disasters have their own dynamics. What begins as a disaster for an individual component (element of the system) becomes a system disaster when a sufficient number of individual elements fail to prevent disruption to the overall system or are unable to cope with the disruption sufficiently soon and effectively enough to preclude individual element failures from generating consequences that ripple through the system, crippling, at least temporarily, its ability to perform the functions described by Mitchell (2004) and to maintain the dimensions articulated by Renschler and his colleagues (2010). Because open systems are necessarily interdependent, performance failure of one part of the community system contributes to performance failures in the larger system (Bertalanffy 1968). And, failure of the larger system to perform one or more of its functions adequately contributes to subsequent and consequent failures in other parts. If the community is not disaster resistant or sufficiently robust to attenuate the cascading consequences, then the disaster spreads and deepens.

Not all natural hazard events are sufficiently damaging to result in a major failure of the community to perform its essential functions such that systemic failures spread unabated in every disaster. Every extreme natural hazard event is unique, as is every community. We do not want to understate the importance of disasters for individuals, families, and organizations because of our focus on community disasters. In our interviews over the years with those who experienced their own disaster within the community disaster, we found some individuals were still suffering long after observers claimed "recovery" for the community. Disasters and disaster recovery for individuals, their households, and individual organizations are critically important subjects for study, but are, unfortunately, largely beyond the scope of this book.

CHAPTER 3

Communities as Complex, Open, and Self-Organizing Social Systems

If we hope to understand the anatomy of disaster and recovery, it is essential to consider the dynamics of community change absent a great disturbance. Then, we must consider how that disturbance results in the reduced capacity of a community to perform its functions. Finally, we must consider how the community may be able to restore its capacity to perform its essential functions and, thus, recover. Considerable progress has been made to define and understand complex, adaptive, self-organizing social systems. The concept appears particularly promising in terms of contributing to improved understanding of how communities develop through time, how a catalyst, such as an extreme natural hazard event, can result in a community disaster, and how communities might recover from a disaster. This chapter presents a framework based on work done on complex, adaptive, self-organizing social systems for viewing those phenomena.

We concur with those who think of community disasters as a consequence of a great interruption in the "normal" activities of a community and reducing the ability of the community to perform those functions critical to that community through the aggregate behavior of its inhabitants. We believe that in order to understand how the "great interruption" results in a disaster and how communities might recover from the disruption, it makes sense to explore and to understand how communities change absent a significant perturbation. We believe that such understanding will shed considerable light on how communities recover and why some communities fail to recover.

Over the past few decades, many physical and social scientists have found that it is less useful to think of linear models than it is to think of nonlinear models. Kiel (1995) says that a "new paradigm of social and human dynamics is emerging" (p. 186). Phenomena that were not understood or explained in terms of linear cause-and-effect models have been subjected to, with increasing frequency, examining them as nonlinear systems. People have begun to use terms like emergence, chaos, near chaos, complexity, fractals, cellular automata, agent-based models, and self-organization. These concepts, while still evolving, provide useful insights in processes of growth, change, system discontinuities, and a host of related, dynamic processes.

In 1987, F. Eugene Yates edited a volume comprising articles by 36 life scientists in which they examined the development of biological entities through the perspectives of differentiation, self-organization, and related concepts. In his preface, Yates (1987) states, "Complexity and self-organization can be found on technical agendas of fields as diverse as cosmology, geology, linguistics, artificial intelligence, communication networks, fluid mechanics, sociology, economics, embryology, paleontology, atmospheric science, and evolutionary biology" (p. xii). To that list, scholars have added community processes and the morphology of urban places.

Models of urban form and spatial development have been around for well over a century, but the dynamics of change processes took a leap forward in the late 1950s and early 1960s with the development of the field of regional science, with the emergence of computer-driven urban transportation planning models and particularly with the publication of Forrester's *Urban Dynamics* (1969). Still, those approaches focused primarily on the spatial characteristics of cities and of urban growth. Batty's (2007) *Cities and Complexity: Understanding Cities with Cellular Automata, Agent-Based Models, and Fractals*, while still examining spatial development, focuses on change processes in a compelling volume exploring the emergence, change, and complexity of cities. His discussion of cells and agents in shaping urban systems stimulated our consideration of communities as self-organizing social systems. Batty's (2007) work informed, to a considerable extent, our consideration of how the spatial dimensions of communities change through time. He did not, however, examine social and economic changes over time from the perspective of self-organizing systems. Nor had he, at the time he published his book, contemplated the consequences and implications of a great perturbation, such as an extreme natural hazard event, to a community system and to its subsequent response.

MEANING OF "COMPLEX," "OPEN," AND "SELF-ORGANIZING"

In this book, we have attempted to expand Batty's (2007) work by examining changes in the social and economic dimensions of community life through essentially the same processes that Batty uses to examine changes in the physical artifact of the community. That is, we view communities as complex, open, self-organizing, and adaptive social systems. What follows is an extension of our writing in Alesch, Arendt, and Holly (2009).

As mentioned previously, cities, villages, small towns, and rural communities comprise social, economic, and political patterns and relationships, typically within a place associated with a built environment. The built environment facilitates the functioning of the community, but in and of itself, it obviously does not constitute the system. Together, the component parts of the community comprise a system (or a set of related systems and subsystems) that is complex, open, adaptive, and self-organizing (Bertalanffy 1968).

A social system is an artificial system; it is devised, whether intentionally or inadvertently, by humans. This contrasts with biological or natural physical systems. Again, and as mentioned previously, open systems are comprised of a set of elements that are interrelated with one another in complex networks, such that a perturbation or disturbance of one element has consequences for other elements in the network and in the system (Buldyrev et al. 2010; Kast and Rosenzweig 1972). Systems are often defined as a set of elements interrelated in such a way that the whole is more than the sum of the parts. In community systems, each individual or organization is an element within that system. A disturbance to one or more elements will have implications for other elements that make up the system.

An open system is one that has mutual interactions with its external environment (Bertalanffy 1968). They import inputs such as information, energy, and resources from the outside world, and export outputs such as information, waste, and "things" to it (Kast and Rosenzweig 1972). In a community, at least some individuals and organizations will have extensive relationships with the world outside the community—with its environment. Individuals migrate from one community to another, local firms buy and sell in other communities, material resources needed in the community come from other places, information flows between them, and the community provides needed goods and services to other communities.

The description of the system's elements as existing within a set implies the existence of a boundary that encompasses the elements. Boundaries of open systems are permeable, with some being more permeable than others (Kast and Rosenzweig 1972). Individuals and entities in contact with their counterparts in other systems are known as boundary spanners (Tushman 1977); the boundary spanning function is essential to a system's existence. Open systems interact with other systems and with elements within those systems, importing from them and exporting to them, depending on the extent of their permeability.

The relationships among elements of a system are generally persistent in nature, but the elements themselves and relationships among them may not be in equilibrium (Kast and Rosenzweig 1972). Elements may adapt when they or other elements in the system are disturbed and adapt their behavior to accommodate or to cope with the perturbation. The disturbances may come from either within or outside the system. The adaptations may be mutual or not.

The interrelationships between and among elements comprising the system are generally patterned and persistent, producing an apparent stability that helps define the community. At the same time, both the elements and the generally persistent patterns among them are continually adapting to changing circumstances. Elements come and go, just as the population changes because of births, deaths, and migration. The relationships among the elements change, too, as community members, organizations, and institutions either innovate at their own volition or adapt to changes from both within the community and outside it.

Communities maintain their stability by means of the continuing and collective adaptations by the constituent parts, while, with each new adaptation, the community as a whole changes, usually marginally. Comparing and contrasting snapshots of a community from year to year helps to demonstrate such change, not just in terms of buildings, streets, and parks, but also in terms of who lives where, what they do, how they do it, where they do it, and when they do it. Because the changes are largely evolutionary rather than revolutionary, they may not seem obvious to those who are fully immersed in the community but are readily apparent to those familiar with the community who leave and then return months or years later. Thus, change in communities might be understood using a "punctuated equilibrium" model, in which the community seems to "exist in essentially static form (equilibrium) over most" of its history, with occasional "revolutionary 'punctuations' of rapid change" (Gersick 1991, p. 11).

Communities are systems that adapt to change and increase in complexity through time without being guided or managed by either an "invisible hand" or some agent, such as Robert Moses, the "master builder" of mid-20th century New York City, Long Island, Rockland County, and Westchester County, New York (Gratz 2010). Individual and organizational behaviors can and do change over time. Those changes can take any of several directions. The aggregation of those changes can maintain the existing developmental trajectory of a community, or it can result in any of several new community trajectories. A community system may survive an extreme natural hazard event, but it will necessarily change as its component parts adapt to new realities. It might, for example, become smaller than the preevent community was or have significantly different demographic characteristics. Alternatively, the community system that emerges in place of the old one may actually be bigger and better as so often promised by elected officials in the aftermath of an extreme natural hazard event. For example, C. Ray Nagin, the Mayor of New Orleans during Hurricane Katrina, promised in the aftermath, "It's time for us to rebuild New Orleans—the one that should be a chocolate New Orleans. This city will be a majority-African American city. It's the way God wants it to be. You can't have New Orleans no other way. It wouldn't be New Orleans" (Martel 2006, para. 5). Change, however, is not always for the better. The new community may be inferior to the old one in any number of ways. The economy may not be as strong, a historical district might be destroyed, or the postdisaster population may have fewer marketable skills than the preevent population.

Many of the terms that might be used to characterize the physical, social, economic, and political changes in communities through time are already in use for other purposes. We would like to use the term "urban morphology" to describe the process, but, unfortunately, it has been appropriated by those concerned primarily with changes in the physical characteristics of urban settlements. According to Bentley and Butina (1990), urban morphology "is an approach to studying and designing urban form which considers both the physical and spatial components of the urban structure of plots, blocks, streets, buildings and open spaces, all of which are considered as part of the history/evolutionary process of development of the particular part of the city under consideration" (p. 67).

"Urban ecology" might be a useful term for examining dynamics of community change, but it seems to be the domain of those interested primarily in the interrelationships among humans and their built and natural environments. This leaves us to rely on a number of terms mostly from general systems theory, each of which refers to some aspect of change through time, but none of which is inclusive of the process. Moreover, some of the terms, such as "negentropy" are particularly pedantic and actually painful to use in polite conversation (Kast and Rosenzweig 1972). It probably, then, makes sense for us to use the term "community morphology."

Community Systems Change through Time

Mumford's (1938, 1961) view is that communities, as human settlements, emerged when humans began to develop agriculture. Those engaged in agriculture were able to live in a place for an extended time in contrast to hunter-gatherers who were generally obliged to move from place to place, at least seasonally. Mumford suggests that humans began to move closer to one another for social purposes, not the least of which was defense. Medieval European communities retained many of the characteristics of those ancient communities. Within defensive walls, the church and the castle dominated the skyline and were surrounded by housing and shops. Farmlands were outside the protective walls of the community and farmers walked to their fields to tend their crops.

Obviously, communities have changed through time and they continue to change. Some change or morph more quickly than others. Community morphology is largely the result of adaptations made by individuals and organizations that constitute the community. Individual elements (i.e., agents, individuals, organizations) of the community, more or less, respond to cues from other elements and from changes in their environment. Since each element is interconnected with other elements, a significant change in behavior of one or more of those other elements is likely to trigger a change in behavior of other elements. Either element may change what it does, how it does it, where it does it, and when it does it. For example, as the number of women with children entering the workforce has increased over the past several decades in the United States, so too has the prevalence of day cares. This has created the need for education credentialing for individuals employed by day cares, which has affected the array of educational training programs offered by local and regional community and technical colleges. Whereas it may be the case that some adaptations are proactive, others are reactive.

Adaptive behavior is a coping mechanism employed by humans as well as other animals. Songbirds, for example, move away from a copse of trees when a pair of sharp-shinned hawks sets up housekeeping near them, at least until the hawks move on. In the case of individual elements (agents) in a community, changes in what, how, and where may be made by mutual accord (cooperation) or to gain a competitive advantage in relationships with other elements. For our purposes, it does not really matter what the motivation is; the important feature of the adaptation is that it is a change in the community system. As adaptations accumulate, the change in the community becomes more easily observable and identifiable.

Ashby's (1958) "law of requisite variety" is critical to understanding the importance of adaptation to changing circumstances to both the aggregate community and to the individual members that constitute the community. Ashby's law, greatly simplified, states that a system, or element within it, can survive only insofar as it has an array of coping mechanisms at least equal to the array of environmental challenges it encounters (Ashby 1958). By environment, Ashby is referring to elements outside the system's boundaries. Thus, survival of the community, much less its growth and development, is dependent on the community's aggregate ability to be sufficiently adaptive or proactive to continue to perform its functions when faced with significant challenges.

Adaptive behavior is essential for systems if they are to survive. *Homo sapiens* have flourished, often despite themselves, not because they are bigger, stronger, or less subject to disease than other animals, but because they are capable of generating an amazing array of coping mechanisms and sharing them with one another. This ability to cope with change begins, presumably, with having opposable thumbs, but it is mainly because of the development of the human brain. The human brain is an amazing general-purpose symbol manipulator, enabling humans to solve complex practical and theoretical problems. Dogs and cats may be lovable, eat foods, and drink water that would send us to the emergency room, but they cannot build bridges, solve differential equations, or think up a better way to adapt to a changing market.

Ashby (1958) speaks of adaptive behavior within a system as being sparked by a change in some feature, characteristic, or behavior of another element either within the system or in its environment. We concur, but we prefer to look at the forces that drive adaptive behavior as changes that are perceived as being incongruent with the individual, household, or organization's current behaviors and that, unless that individual element is somehow able to adapt successfully to those changes, it is unlikely to be able to perform either effectively or at all. The environmental change might involve a change in technology, such as from arrows to guns, from horses to automobiles, or from analog to digital communication. The changes might be economic: manual labor being replaced by machines, a shift in technology where production of automobiles is more efficient, automation replacing telephone operators, a shift from shipping by boat to shipping by rail or auto. Until Great Lakes shipping by sailboat and steamers was replaced by shipping by rail and truck, Green Bay, Wisconsin, was actually larger than Chicago, Illinois, simply because of its excellent harbor and its favorable location for trade on the Great Lakes.

In general systems theory, development and growth are differentiated from one another (Kast and Rosenzweig 1972). Development implies an increase in complexity associated with increased division of labor. Thus, in a community, the general store is replaced by specialty retailers (butchers, bakers, and candlestick makers). They are subsequently replaced by big-box stores owned by giant national and international retailers (e.g., Walmart) and are located conveniently along major thoroughfares near where people live. Those stores are threatened by online commerce (e.g., Amazon). Specialization and differentiation increase along with the density of networks and complexity of relationships. Illustratively, warehouses are replaced by just-in-time contractual relationships between suppliers and processors, thus reducing the amount of slack in the production process—slack that affords a cushion for operations and adaptation—and, simultaneously, increasing the complexity and the time-interdependency involved in process and supply chain management.

Growth, on the other hand, can occur when a system (or community) simply increases in size without associated increases in complexity or differentiation among its parts. (Imagine, if you will, a 250-pound amoeba, still a one-celled entity but frighteningly large.) The larger community with little differentiation may be generally less susceptible to crippling damage from an extreme natural hazard event, simply because it has fewer social, economic, and political linkages and dependencies among its parts, but, at the same time, it is likely to have fewer coping mechanisms than a more complex community. Without differentiation and interdependency among the parts, each part of the system is less vulnerable to a large disturbance in some other part. Extremely complex, highly differentiated and interdependent systems are more frequently vulnerable (Bashan et al. 2013; Buldyrev et al. 2010) when disruptions affect one or more individual elements within the system.

Katz and Kahn (1978), in their classic work *The Social Psychology of Organizations*, employ general systems theory constructs to examine change in inorganic systems, primarily formal organizations, which, like communities, are artificial constructs. Thus, their analyses are applicable to communities as well as formal organizations. Absent a major perturbation, they say, employing a biological system analogy, "The catabolic and anabolic processes of tissue breakdown and restoration within the body preserve a steady state so that the organism from time to time is not the identical organism, but a highly similar organism." Minor changes take place constantly in the system, whether natural or contrived, as it adapts to minor changes (disturbances) from either within or outside the system. To paraphrase an Army saying, "Soldiers come and soldiers go, but the unit remains and goes on" (pp. 26–27).

The term "dynamic homeostasis" was coined in the 1920s to describe a condition in which the system adapts continually to cues from and changes in its environment simply to remain, figuratively, even in the same place. Katz and Kahn (1978) suggest that "the initial adjustment to such disturbances is typically approximate rather than precise. If it is insufficient, further adjustment in the same direction will follow. If it is excessive, it will be followed by a counter adjustment. The iterative process will then continue to the point of equilibrium or until the process is broken by some further disruptive event" (p. 27).

Katz and Kahn (1978) further suggest that adaptations to disturbances are made as part of the effort to maintain the system's dynamic homeostasis. They posit that "The basic principle is the preservation of the character of the system" (p. 27). We know that communities are not thinking, decision-making entities. Their status at any given time is the result of a myriad of events, including historical accident, geographic constraints, and the largely independent actions of the many actors comprising the community at any given time. This is consistent with the notion that the basic principle of adaptation to disruption is the preservation of the basic character of the system. The key is that the system changes, mostly at the margin, as the self-organizing actors and elements within the system take actions to retain their viability within the overall system. The community system itself does not make choices intended to achieve dynamic homeostasis: it is, after all, an inanimate social construct. Corporate systems, for most practical purposes, have unitary decision makers (an owner, a board of directors, etc.) that make decisions concerning adaptation and systemic change to preserve the essential characteristics of the firm. Nonetheless, the cumulative actions of (most) members of the community system do reflect or constitute efforts to maintain stability of the overall community system, including adaptation, leading ultimately, to a system with many changed characteristics.

Self-Organization and Individual Choices: What, Where, and When

One of the authors, at the time a young university student from a small town, stood on the sidewalk looking up and around at midday in midtown Manhattan for the first time and wondered, "How does this thing work?" Certainly, notwithstanding Robert Moses (Gratz 2010), there was no man behind the curtain orchestrating the movement of all the parts of the city so that they worked together at least somewhat harmoniously. City hall did not orchestrate the behaviors of all the actors. How, then, did and does the community system work?

The answer is that the community is self-organizing. Each of its member parts makes choices about what to do, where to do it, when to do it, and how to do it. Some of the members of the system behave dysfunctionally; their individual actions generate friction in the community. What is good for one element of the system is not necessarily good for other elements or for the system as a whole. Most members, however, perform activities intended to maintain themselves at an acceptable level of well-being over time: they engage in activities that help ensure their continued individual and collective viability. Taken together, the aggregation of activities conducted by the various elements (agents) that comprise the system result in the aggregate community performing its critical functions at some level of mutually acceptable competency (Alesch et al. 2009).

Contrary to Adam Smith's beliefs, when each of the individual elements pursues its individual interests in the quest for viability, it does not necessarily result in the most efficient, most effective, or best community. Attempting to optimize subsystems will generally lead to suboptimization of the overall system (Katz and Kahn 1978), in part because competition between subsystems can yield a premature and unanticipated exhaustion of shared resources. Even self-organizing systems require some regulation to ensure that most behaviors are consistent or at least congruent with mainstream community values and expectations: self-organizing systems left alone do not always result in optimal outcomes. The purposes and goals of the aggregate community system are not necessarily the same as those of the individual members of the system. Presumably, however, there is some significant overlap between community purposes and those of most of the individual members of the community; else, one would expect members in disagreement with the purposes and values to vote with their feet and find a new community. Still, it is likely that, under some conditions, the extent of commonality among interests of community inhabitants may diminish and various individuals will pursue paths that in their best interests do not contribute to the stability of the community.

Communities develop and grow continually as individuals and organizations make choices in response to what they see as opportunities, obligations, competition, constraints, and other cues: to repeat, they make choices about what, where, when, and how to do it. Communities that are developing or growing have one or more *raison d'être* sufficient to create an effective magnet that attracts other elements from outside the community system. The magnet may be economic, social, religious, political, recreational, or related to one or more of the critical functions a community performs. Communities form around mining sites, ports, colleges, government centers, religious centers, the arts, entertainment, recreational opportunities, retirement locations, medical complexes, and military bases, or some combination of those things, among others.

We have, however, seen large human settlements that are growing and, perhaps, developing, not so much because they have a powerful magnet, but because those who move to those cities have few if any other options. Jakarta, Indonesia, for example, a city of about 11 million, continues to grow, in large part because of migration from the countryside and small villages. The migrants see few or no opportunities for themselves in the countryside and hope for opportunity in the larger community. The result is large numbers of people living off the formal economy in squalor in pockets of the city and its periphery. The same story is true for Mexico City, with a population of 20.1 million and growing. As the economic, political, and cultural hub of Mexico, Mexico City is a natural draw for rural people looking to better their economic futures.

Although individuals and organizations come and go in the life of a community system, the community itself tends to persist and through decades may retain many of its distinguishing characteristics. Few, if any people who were living in Philadelphia a century ago are still living there now. Yet, the Philadelphia community continues to exist as a system and to morph as adaptations are made by some and not by others. Firms that prospered at one time are now defunct, replaced by other firms in the same or different industries. The dynamic of the community is one of continual change fueled by adaptation by individual elements as they are challenged by new opportunities or threats. Those that adapt successfully survive.

All communities change continuously, some more quickly than others do, as some individuals and governments adapt to new circumstances more quickly than others and still others do not adapt at all, thus putting themselves at risk. Although there is continual marginal change, some of the more significant changes in communities may occur episodically—the "punctuations" described by Gersick (1991). Significant episodic change may occur with the introduction of a new technology or exploitation of a resource that is suddenly in demand. Illustratively, mining oil through fracking, a rapid onset new technology, generated rapid change and adaption in many communities in North Dakota during the second decade of the 21st century. Another source of episodic change may be an extreme natural hazard event.

Just as individuals survive or fail to survive based on how effectively they adapt to a continuing set of challenges, so too do communities as a whole. Sociologist Kathleen Tierney (2005) told us that her sociologist colleagues refer to communities that have lost their reason for being and are caught in a downward spiral as "dead cities walking." Communities sometimes find a replacement for a disappearing *raison d'être* with another one that promises new viability. Watertown, New York, located near the St. Lawrence River in northwestern New York State, was once a thriving mill town, largely because of the available water power from the Black River and an available workforce from neighboring farms. The mills eventually disappeared, leaving large, generally attractive gray stone buildings that once housed the mills. Most of the buildings are empty, along with remnants of dams and other concrete structures that once drew power from the river. Pine Camp, a small military base just outside Watertown, was active in WWII as a training site and prisoner of war facility. In 1974, it became Fort Drum and, in 1984, it became the home of the 10th Mountain Light Infantry Division. Between 1984 and 1992, the Department of Defense spent $1.3 billion developing Fort Drum, thus providing a new economic engine and relative prosperity for Watertown. Today, Fort Drum is home to thousands of troops and thousands more of their dependents, providing nearby Watertown with an economic reason for existing.

Only a few communities that have lost their reason for being are as fortunate as Watertown. Detroit, Michigan, which boasted a population of approximately 1,670,144 and was the fifth largest U.S. city in 1960, had a population of 701,475 and was ranked 18 in 2012. On July 18, 2013, the city filed for bankruptcy protection under Chapter 9 of the bankruptcy code in federal court in Detroit, saying the city was insolvent and could not meet its financial obligations. In filing its bankruptcy petition, Detroit became the largest city in U.S. history to do so. Since then, Detroit emergency manager Kevyn Orr has been working to create a plan that would allow Detroit to exit bankruptcy by September 2014. This aggressive timetable may be difficult to achieve, since "the city will need to get a majority of its creditors to approve the plan of adjustment—and the city's labor creditors have vigorously contested (emergency manager) Orr's plan to reduce pension payments" (Free Press Staff 2014, para. 15).

The Rust Belt is filled with communities in which the number of jobs has declined along with the population. In addition, small communities across the country that depended on serving agriculture are withering away as improved access to larger centers made them dispensable. The declining communities reflect the same self-organizing behaviors as vibrant communities: individual actors respond to cues from their environment. When the small town grocer finds his convenient location is not enough to enable him to compete with the supermarket or big box store that is now very accessible because of better roads and faster cars, he closes his store and retires or moves on, thus contributing to the spiral of decline in that community. As each of the components of the community system makes choices that take them away from the declining small town, eventually the feed mill closes, the U.S. Postal Service closes its post office, and the local church merges with one in another community. If a few extended families remain living there while working in a nearby city or while retired, the community hangs on as a small, largely undifferentiated settlement until it is eventually swallowed by a larger community or becomes a ghost town.

No one is really in charge of a community, although some organizations wield more influence on individual choices than others do. Municipal governments that place controls on land use patterns, make choices about where streets and highways go, and decide what areas will have water and sewer utility service provide both cues and constraints for the individual members of the community. Major employers, often owned by out-of-state or foreign companies, make choices about when and where they will invest their resources: where facilities will open and where they will close. A decision made thousands of miles away from a community may spell its ultimate demise or immediate prosperity. The actions of individual agents in the community are influenced, whether consciously or not, by geographic, political, and organizational constraints and opportunities (Alesch et al. 2009).

Batty (2007) notes that the growth paths of cities have "sensitive dependence on initial conditions" (p. 28). Historical accident plays a role in establishing an initial trajectory. The site of New Orleans, for example, had been inhabited by native peoples for perhaps a thousand years prior to the arrival of French fur traders in the last years of the 17th century. They built a small community on the banks of the Mississippi River because it was adjacent to their native fur trading partners and provided a convenient transport route for shipping furs to Europe. The rag-tag settlement was destroyed by a hurricane in 1722, presaging the city's future. Batty (2007) notes, too, that some aspects of community trajectories are affected by "whim," "often of course in association with some other more obvious reasoning" (p. 21). Other forces shaping the trajectory of communities include physical constraints in the area within which the community is developing as well as natural and comparative advantages affecting decisions about where various kinds of development would take place. Illustratively, the well-to-do typically built homes in close proximity to one another and almost invariably in the choicest locations—usually sites offering pleasant views, away from mosquito-filled swampy areas, and away from areas with frequent floods.

We suspect it is common for people to view communities as existing in some kind of equilibrium prior to being disrupted by some extreme natural hazard event. Batty (2007) and Kiel (1995), however, believe that communities that are developing are characterized by disequilibrium, "as our focus is on dynamics, we consider disequilibrium to be a more characteristic state of urban systems" (Batty 2007, p. 31). This view is wholly consistent with the notion that community change occurs as individual agents within the community adapt to changing circumstance. The ideal circumstance is to have some disequilibrium in the system, enough to propel innovation, but not so much as to yield chaos. Batty (2007) describes the typical kind of changes in a community in a way fully congruent with our perceptions: the changes "reflect a system far from equilibrium, in disequilibrium whose elements are changing at different rates and whose impact is diverse across different spatial scales and time frames" (p. 31).

Without disequilibrium and adaptation (what Ashby calls "directive correlations"), the community would stagnate and, unable to maintain its dynamic equilibrium, eventually cease to be a community. Even standing still in one place requires adaptation as the treadmill beneath one continues moving.

AND THEN, A GREAT DISTURBANCE

As seen in the previous chapter, community systems continually experience disturbances. These disturbances create what we might call "quiet disequilibrium" in the community system. The quiet disequilibrium triggers adaptation and community change and, one hopes, further development along a positive, generally desirable trajectory. What happens, however, when the disturbance to the community system is beyond the bounds of an ordinary, normal "quiet disturbance?" Under what conditions does the unusual disturbance result in a community disaster?

Initial and Cascading Consequences of Extreme Natural Hazard Events

As we have mentioned, disasters consist of the consequences of an extreme natural hazard event. We are all familiar with what we choose to call initial consequences: they are the most immediate results of the collision between the extreme natural hazard event and a human settlement, the built environment, or the natural environment. The disaster is exacerbated as secondary and tertiary consequences, triggered by the initial event and the initial consequences, cascade through the community and beyond (Alesch et al. 2009).

Initial consequences often include injuries and deaths, as well as damage to physical infrastructure, buildings and their contents, vehicles, trees, landforms, and bodies of water. Immediate consequences are usually highly visible: the January 1994 Northridge Earthquake resulted in the collapse of buildings and damage to natural gas and water pipes. Many apartment buildings were badly damaged. One that collapsed resulted in a score of deaths. Some hospitals had to evacuate patients. Whole villages were swept away by the 2004 tsunami in the Indian Ocean (Iwan 2006); upward of 230,000 people were killed. Bridges and buildings—some buildings six blocks or more from the shore in Gulfport and Biloxi, Mississippi—were smashed by Hurricane Katrina's storm surge in 2005. An EF5 tornado struck Joplin, Missouri, on May 22, 2011, killing 158 people and causing approximately $2.91 billion in damage (see Figure 3.1). Similarly, an EF5 tornado tore through Moore, Oklahoma, on May 20, 2013, killing 24 people and injuring 377 others. Damages were estimated to be $2 billion. Photographs taken by professional media and amateurs attest to the widespread and catastrophic initial consequences of these extreme natural hazard events.

Homes in California are consumed annually by wildfires and almost every year a heavy snow load from an unusually severe storm collapses a roof on a commercial or industrial building somewhere in the United

FIGURE 3.1   Joplin, Missouri, June 4, 2011—Volunteers and debris fill the streets of Joplin after an EF5 tornado touched down on May 22, 2011. (Courtesy of FEMA/Steven Zumwalt.)

States. In September 2013, more than 4,000 homes and buildings in Colorado were destroyed by flash floods. These are all initial consequences. So, too, are people killed or injured by the force of a blast, the ravages of tornado winds, a rioting mob, or any other extreme natural hazard event. People are killed or injured when falling from buildings or through windows during an earthquake; others have lost control of their vehicles during the shaking and have crashed and died. Again, these are all initial consequences.

We are not purists; for example, we choose to treat tsunamis as events in and of themselves and not as secondary consequences of the initial earth movement. We are satisfied to treat the initial consequences of the tsunami, for example, without investigating the initial events that triggered it—at least for our current purposes. Our reasoning is that one could almost endlessly go behind every earthquake or landslide to find some prior chain of events that either triggered or contributed to the earthquake. We do not want to get involved in a lengthy discussion of either cause and effect or emergence and probability for us to deal with how the earthquake came to be. We have neither the desire nor the patience to trace a hurricane that makes landfall back to the individual butterfly whose wing flap triggered the movement of some air molecules that eventually may or may not have triggered the birth of a tropical depression off the west coast of Africa which, in turn, may or may not have become the hurricane under question. Sometimes, it is enough to start with the latest extreme natural hazard event in what is no doubt a series of events. We will assume their occurrence and look at their direct and cascading consequences.

What Determines the Nature and Extent of Initial Consequences?

The nature and extent of the initial consequences to the community system are a function of the characteristics of the event itself, the exposure of the areas damaged, and the vulnerability of the areas exposed to the event (Alesch et al. 2009).

The Event Itself

Three primary characteristics of an extreme natural hazard event describe its potential for generating initial damage to communities and their natural environments: how big, how close, and how long.

In terms of "how big," what we are generally describing is the amount of energy released. Obviously, an earthquake with a Magnitude of 3.0 on the Richter scale releases much less energy than one measuring 7.0 on the same scale. A tornado classified as an EF5 (Enhanced Fujita scale) is much more likely to create major initial damage to a community or a forest than an EF1. A tsunami generating a chain of waves in excess of 3 meters in height is much more likely to generate extensive initial damage than one generating waves of only a few centimeters in height. The good news is that the most frequent earthquakes, tornadoes, and tsunami waves are small. The bad news is that some few rare natural hazard events are massive and release almost unimaginable amounts of energy within a very short time in a relatively concentrated place. Size matters.

In terms of "how close," we mean the proximity of the event. It almost goes without saying that the closer an extreme natural hazard event is to a given place, the more likely it is to generate substantial initial damage. Sometimes, even a small difference in proximity is extremely important. When the flood reaches 14 feet above flood stage, being 15 feet above flood stage makes a big difference. Being a hundred meters outside the path of an EF5 tornado usually can mean the difference between total destruction and minor damage.

On the other hand, earthquake epicenters can be quite distant from a community and still cause major damage. The epicenter for the 1985 earthquake that damaged Mexico City so badly was about 220 kilometers from the city, offshore in the Pacific Ocean. Geological peculiarities overcame the distance. The seismic waves were transmitted through rock to Mexico City. The city is built on a dry lakebed that resonated with the earthquake wave, apparently amplified them, and transmitted them to buildings built on it. The geological anomaly was heightened because

FIGURE 3.2 Northridge Earthquake, California, January 17, 1994—
Buildings, cars, and personal property were all destroyed when the
earthquake struck. Approximately 114,000 residential and commercial
structures were damaged and 72 deaths were attributed to the earthquake. Damage costs were estimated at $25 billion. (Courtesy of FEMA
News Photo.)

the earthquake was measured at 8.1 on the Richter scale: a massive and
exceptionally rare event.

The Northridge Earthquake of 1994 and the Nisqually Earthquake
in the Seattle area in 2001 measured about the same (6.8) on the
Richter scale. The Northridge Earthquake generated major initial damage (see Figure 3.2), but the Nisqually Earthquake did not. The difference in the consequences was a matter of proximity. The Northridge
Earthquake occurred on a thrust fault and ruptured the surface of the
Earth in the heart of Northridge. The Nisqually event, on the other
hand, occurred 52 kilometers below the surface of the Earth. Similarly,
the February 2011 Christchurch, New Zealand, earthquake was
centered 2 kilometers (1.2 miles) west of the port town of Lyttelton,
and 10 kilometers (6 miles) southeast of the center of Christchurch.
The Christchurch Earthquake killed 185 people. The epicenter of the
September 2010 Canterbury, New Zealand, earthquake was 40 kilometers (25 miles) west of Christchurch, near the town of Darfield. While
the February 2011 earthquake had a 6.3 Magnitude compared to the 7.1
Magnitude of the September 2010 earthquake, no one was killed due to
the September 2010 event. Proximity matters.

Finally, "how long" refers to the duration of the event. Other things being equal, earthquakes during which the shaking lasts for only a few seconds are usually not as damaging as those in which the shaking lasts for a minute or more. Floods that inundate an area for as little as an hour are usually far less damaging than those that persist for days and weeks. New Orleans was submerged for weeks; buildings, cars, and other physical artifacts in the flooded bowl were thoroughly saturated. Generally speaking, the longer an area is exposed to an extreme natural hazard event, the more likely it is to experience damage from that event. Duration, exposure, and vulnerability (discussed next) have much to do with the extent of initial damage to landforms, buildings, and communities. Shaking, pounding from waves, and high winds that last for a long time are likely to result in successive or cascading failure of natural or constructed artifacts. This can happen because of gradual erosion of the landform or the failure of one or two critical elements in the structure, elements that might have withstood one or two blows, but which could not withstand repeated blows. Time matters.

Exposure

Exposure is the second variable associated with initial damage. If a building is outside the flood channel or floodplain, it is unlikely to be damaged from flooding. If a business is not on the beach, it is unlikely to be demolished by storm surge. If a building is not on a steep, unstable landform in Santa Monica or the Palos Verde peninsula in southern California, it is unlikely to slide down the cliff and end up destroyed on the Pacific Coast Highway or in the Pacific Ocean.

People continually take risks by building in very dangerous places: on top of or next to known earthquake faults, in canyons known to have experienced violent flash floods, on the shore of places with frequent hurricanes, in areas that experience brush or forest fires, and so forth. They also tend to buy for the view or for access to transportation routes and desired locations (e.g., a place with a view, work), without necessarily considering carefully the possible hazards to which their property may be vulnerable. Typically, they both underestimate the risks associated with their decisions and place their reliance on others to cover their losses when the inevitable occurs. With respect to the former, they misunderstand the meaning of probabilities. For example, many people will interpret a 100-year floodplain to mean that floods only happen in the area once every 100 years. From there, they conclude that since the last major flood was in 1990 (or some other year), that they have 76 years before another flood will decimate the area—long after they will have moved on to a new location.

Sometimes, people believe they are safe from disastrous events because structures have been built to hold back the water that would otherwise inundate them. The protection afforded by floodwalls, levees, and dams against flooding is largely mythical. How many communities have been badly damaged or destroyed because a floodwall, levee, or dam that failed because of unusual rains, spring snow melts, or misjudgments in design or construction? We have come to believe that there are only two kinds of levees: those that have failed and those that are going to fail. Sometimes, they are deliberately made to fail, perhaps to save a larger settlement further down the river. This was the case when about 30 tons of dynamite were set off on the levee at Caernarvon, Louisiana, in 1927 to spare New Orleans from further flooding (Barry 1998). Unfortunately for the people of St. Bernard and Plaquemines Parishes, the destruction of the Caernarvon levee proved unnecessary as other levees upstream naturally breached, saving the city of New Orleans without human intervention.

The lesson is simple. The best way to avoid a natural hazard event from destroying one's home, business, or community is to build it in a place not subject to the most frequent and predictable extreme natural hazard events. There are no guarantees, of course, but some bets are better than others.

Vulnerability

If a man is a bald person of Scandinavian descent who loves to fish, he may expose his scalp to harmful rays of the sun and they are very likely to cause skin cancer on his scalp. Since he chooses to be out in the sun, the wise course of action is for him to reduce his vulnerability by wearing a hat and using sunscreen. The same may be said of any beachcomber or person who enjoys the sunny outdoors. Similarly, if one's business has to be along the shoreline, it makes sense to reduce one's vulnerability to loss by storing most of the inventory in a place that is safe and by building a structure that can withstand at least minor flooding. The State of California works diligently to ensure that structures built in areas prone to earthquakes are built to standards that will protect them against small and moderate earthquakes and reduce the likely extent of collapse from strong earthquakes. Design and construction codes for critical facilities such as hospitals contain high standards in an attempt to ensure the usefulness of such structures following earthquakes and to minimize deaths during them. Enacting and enforcing stringent standards to protect the public is often difficult and requires careful policy and program design (c.f. Alesch, Arendt, and Petak 2012).

No one can build a structure that is completely safe from all fires, earthquakes, tornadoes, blasts, or meteors falling from the sky at 20,000 miles per hour. What can be done is to build structures that are resistant to commonly occurring events that can damage or destroy them. This is why there are building, electrical, and plumbing codes almost everywhere in the United States. This is also why many of us buy insurance against fires, wind damage, flooding, and so forth. Insurance is a backstop for instances in which our other attempts to reduce vulnerability fail.

Nature of Cascading Consequences

The extreme natural hazard event is the initial trigger, the catalyst. But the initial consequences of the event trigger subsequent consequences that extend through the community and beyond (Alesch et al. 2009). Engineers use terms like cascading failure, progressive collapse, and sequential collapse to describe phenomena associated with various kinds of failures in buildings, bridges, or complex structures and machines. In some cases, failure of one structural element leads to the subsequent failure of other elements. Sometimes, the linked, sequential failures end only when the structure fails completely, like a bridge collapsing into the Mississippi River in Minneapolis in 2007. Other times, the sequence of failures is attenuated for some reason, such as when the structure includes "fuses" that limit sequential failure. In those cases, some of the structure remains intact or at least minimally functional when the dust settles. Essentially the same thing happens in communities, except that communities are much more complex systems than are bridges, buildings, or machines. Bridges and buildings may be dynamic in terms of response to wind and ground motion within limited ranges, but they are not self-organizing and they are not adaptive to a changing environment. Nonetheless, the notion of cascading consequences is useful in illustrating what happens in communities following an extreme natural hazard event.

Sometimes it seems as though the adverse consequences following an extreme natural hazard event in a community radiate out almost seamlessly, like the ripples in a pond when a stone is dropped into it. In such cases, it may be difficult to distinguish the sequential consequences of an event from the immediate effects of the event itself. Was the collapse of the twin towers of the World Trade Center in September 2001 an immediate consequence of the impacts and explosions of the airplanes flown into them, or was it the outcome of a complex chain of events, starting with the towers' design and construction? For most of us, it does not matter, because the sequence of the most salient events occurred within a short time period and we can think of it as a single, continuous event.

Still other times, the consequences are not as readily apparent as ripples in the pond. Thousands of small businesses went out of business in the immediate area of the World Trade Center following the collapse of the twin towers; the businesses' customer base collapsed along with the towers. This is a consequence, though not as visually dramatic as the collapse of the towers. In addition, some of those who were exposed to the dust and smoke of the explosions, fire, and collapse, and who removed the debris, suffered and will continue to suffer chronic illnesses long after their exposure to it (Lite 2008).

Over the years, we studied diverse community experiences following extreme natural hazard events (Alesch et al. 2009). Two points were hammered home time and again. The first is the importance of the consequences that cascade out from the initial event on cascading consequents and on the outcomes of recovery efforts. The second is that it is difficult for anyone to anticipate the outcomes from the event because of the large array of possible outcomes from chance events and the complexity of cause and effect relationships. Some might say that what happens in the aftermath is a simple matter of cause and effect, and, as such, should be predictable, but we are not convinced of that. That kind of thinking presumes a linear causality of discrete events, something that does not align with the nonlinear nature of extreme natural hazard events (Kiel 1995). Our observations suggest that multiple causes generate multiple effects, along varying timelines. Consequently, postdisaster consequences are less like a chain of events than they are a cascade of interrelated events, the outcomes of which are largely a function of chance influenced by some degree of environmental chaos.

Disasters typically unfold episodically in fits and spurts as initial events trigger subsequent adverse consequences that, in turn, trigger other adverse consequences and as seemingly random events occur (Alesch et al. 2009). Kiel (1995) observes that we often make linear estimates of what will follow initial losses because we tend to think of disasters as linear processes. He notes, "But when we look at real disasters do we see such prediction, such simplicity, or such linearity? The potential for nonlinearity and erratic behavior to occur in complex human environments emphasizes the overly simplistic assumptions we often make about system behavior and real outcomes" (p. 187). At any given point in time during the emergency period immediately following the event and in the weeks and months following the event, it is often extremely difficult to predict what might happen next. Consequences interact with one another, unanticipated relationships appear, individuals make choices that may or may not be surprising or rational, that have surprising outcomes, and that mean some phenomena may proceed, apparently, randomly. We believe that it is virtually impossible before an event to reliably predict all the major consequences of that event. One can anticipate some of the most likely consequences and prepare accordingly. Nonetheless, no matter how well prepared a community may be, some consequences will arise that no one will have anticipated.

Some observers have suggested that extreme natural hazard events simply accelerate existing trends in a community (Haas et al. 1977). We agree that extreme natural hazard events do tend to accelerate preexisting trends in affected communities, but we are inclined to believe that they can also result in discontinuities and altered trends that might be represented as an interrupted time series. Although it is generally possible to sketch out the broad picture of what is likely to happen in or to a community following an extreme natural hazard event, it is difficult to predict its outcomes reliably. Too much prediction is actually hindsight bias (Roese and Vohs 2012) in action. Saying something like, "I knew that would happen," does not suggest that one is a good predictor so much as it suggests that one is able to piece together events after the fact. The conclusion that extreme natural hazard events simply accelerate existing trends is likely the outcome of too small a sample of disasters.

Increasing Complexity and Cascading Consequences

Perrow (1999) writes that accidents and failures are much more likely to occur in very complex systems. This is simply because an increase in the number and nature of interfaces among the component parts increases the number of places where failure may occur. Extraordinarily complex systems with high degrees of differentiation among the parts rely on predictable functioning of not only each element but of the interfaces between each of those elements (Bashan et al. 2013; Buldyrev et al. 2010; Perrow 1999). Complex mechanical networks require high maintenance and extraordinary management to ensure continued viability. Communities are extraordinarily complex systems in which the individual parts are interdependent on generally predictable functioning of the other parts. When one part, such as the built structures that constitute the artifacts within which the community function, is damaged or broken, one must expect dysfunctional consequences for the other parts of the community.

The initial impacts of a natural hazard event usually generate damage to the built or natural environment, but that is not always the case. Sometimes, the physical artifact of the community remains largely intact and initial impacts are on some other aspect of the community that results in the community's inability to perform its critical functions. Illustratively, the Anasazi people inhabited Mesa Verde from about 600 to 1300 CE. They left their home in Southwestern Colorado more than 700 years ago, leaving behind more than 600 cliff dwellings that were essentially undamaged. Despite vandals and treasure hunters, many remain undamaged today. Many archaeologists believe the Anasazi suffered an extended drought and left in search of a place where they could grow food. The initial impacts of the natural hazard event, if that is the case, were a number of successive years yielding very scanty harvests.

The example is not as remote as it might first appear. As more and more materials and biota with the potential to do great harm are introduced into the environment, one must be concerned with the potential for various kinds of toxicity that might be released in an extreme natural hazard event. A flash flood might do little more than destroy a train trestle, but might cause a train carrying toxic gasses to crash and a tank car to break open, releasing the gas into the air, forming a cloud that goes wherever the wind takes it. Perhaps more common, industrial fires triggered by a natural hazard event can release toxins into the air or water. A Midwestern flood released Asian carp from a farm in Arkansas, and those "leaping carp" with no natural enemies are reproducing rapidly. They have destroyed existing ecosystems in many rivers and now threaten the ecology of the Great Lakes. It was not a natural hazard event, but it might as well have been one. Similarly, ships from Eastern Europe, emptying their ballast tanks in the Great Lakes, introduced zebra mussels and round gobies into the Great Lakes with extensive consequences for the native ecosystem.

Actions beget reactions and subsequent events. These events can cripple a community even more than the initial damage from the extreme natural hazard event itself. We have come to understand that the extent to which a natural hazard event results in a disaster depends largely on its initial impacts, most often, on the community's built environment and, then, on the extent to which there are cascading consequences for the individuals and organizations that comprise the community and, often, individuals and organizations outside the community (Alesch et al. 2009). We have come to understand that if the event results in damage to the physical artifacts of the community alone, recovery is relatively easy. It is when the initial damage results in consequences that ripple through the community with major adverse social, economic, political, and symbolic effects that recovery becomes extraordinarily difficult.

The extent of the disturbance generated by an extreme natural hazard event depends on the extent to which components of the community system are resistant to those challenges and the extent to which, if needed, they are able to adapt quickly to them. If the disturbance to the status quo of one or more of the community's component parts exceeds their resistance to the event and, as consequences ripple through the community, the entire community may be unable to perform its requisite functions satisfactorily. The ability of the community as a whole to continue to perform its key functions depends on the ability of a critical mass of its component elements to perform their functions adequately. When the community is unable to perform those functions, we call it a community disaster. The extent to which a disturbance disrupts a community's ability to continue to perform its critical functions defines both the nature and extent of the disaster. Not all disasters, of course, are equal in terms of their consequences. Some are truly cataclysmic, while others are extremely limited in scope and consequence.

CATEGORIZING CONSEQUENCES

Alesch, Arendt, and Holly (2009) devised a relatively simple classification scheme to clarify the differences in consequences (see Figure 3.3 and Table 3.1). In the schema shown in Figure 3.3, an extreme natural hazard event triggers both initial and immediately following consequences for the community and, subsequently, additional, cascading consequences. The initial effects of the event result in consequent events. In an earthquake, the ground moves, a building shakes, parts of it fall off, and the building may collapse. People below are pelted with falling bricks and rubble. Many are injured and some die. These we class as initial and immediately following consequences. Similarly, building contents become water soaked if the earthquake triggers water sprinklers that were put in place to protect against fire. A bridge fails and cars that are on it plunge into the river or gorge and people die. Or, as in the 1906 San Francisco Earthquake, fire ravages the city because the earthquake has broken the water pipes and firefighters are unable to fight the flames.

In our schema, the initial consequences frequently generate systemic consequences for the community. Systemic community consequences occur when initial and immediately following consequences trigger or

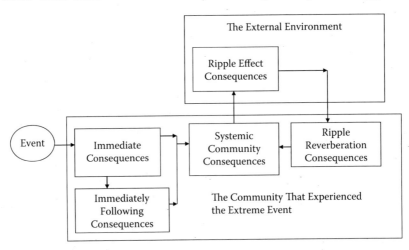

FIGURE 3.3   Relationships among the consequences of extreme natural hazard events.

TABLE 3.1 Classification of Consequences Following from Extreme
Natural Hazard Events

Type of Effect	Definition	Example
Initial consequences	The immediate consequences of an extreme natural hazard event for life and the built or natural environment.	Structural damage, damage to the natural environment, consequent death and injury or illness.
Immediately following consequences	Consequences tightly coupled to and causally related to immediate consequences, usually resulting in consequences to the built or natural environment.	Fire follows an earthquake because flammable gasses or liquids are released by structural damage, or because water is unavailable.
Systemic community consequences	Social, political, and economic consequences that emerge in a geographically, socially, politically, or economically defined area following an extreme natural hazard event that are triggered, exacerbated, or ameliorated by immediate and immediately following consequences of the event.	An employer permanently closes a factory because qualified workers are not available. They are not available because of inadequate supply of affordable housing. Workers with options leave the area. The loss of the employer contributes to extended unemployment and an economic downturn in the area.
Ripple effects beyond the community	Consequences that ripple out from the area that suffered the event and that affect other places.	A port is unable to receive shipments for more than a year following an earthquake, so other ports are able to compete successfully for an increased market share. A community becomes the location of choice for thousands of refugees from a community that experienced the disaster.
Ripple reverberations returning to the initial community	Consequences for the community that suffered the initial disaster because ripple effects lead to changes in other communities and those changes subsequently ripple back to adversely affect the place that experienced the initial event.	A port loses a significant share of the market and, even after restoring its port facilities, cannot regain its previous market share. The developmental trajectory of a community is changed forever by subsequent development of a nearby community deemed to be safer and more convenient.

cause part of the community to no longer adequately perform its critical functions. Illustratively, an industrial firm may need to cease operations if a flood were to damage its buildings, machines, raw materials, and inventory of in-progress and finished goods. The closure may be temporary, lasting only as long as it takes to repair or replace damage. Or it may close permanently for any of several reasons. Perhaps the firm's customers found a new supplier during the time the damaged firm was out of operation and cannot be lured back.

Perhaps the multinational that owned the firm decided that it could use the resources that would be necessary to bring the facility back into operation would be better invested somewhere else. Perhaps the company that owned the firm had inadequate insurance to rebuild and decided to cut its losses. One cannot assume that the rest of the world simply takes a timeout while organizations that suffered initial losses get everything back in place. It simply does not happen that way. In any event, the loss of the firm results in unemployment and lost income, at least temporarily. The households affected by the loss of employment make choices that affect others and a chain of subsequent events are set in motion. The events do not occur all at once; they unfold through time.

When jobs evaporate and the housing stock is reduced, at least temporarily, people relocate, either temporarily or permanently and either within the community or elsewhere. Preevent relationships among parts of the community are damaged or destroyed and the community cannot function as it did before the event. If the firm chosen for our example closes for an extended period, those who worked there become unemployed. The unemployed make choices about what to do, when to do it, where to do it, and how to do it. This is central to both the notions of cascading consequences and self-organizing communities. One may choose to leave the community to live some place not subject to earthquakes or hurricanes. We have seen that happen time and again. In the wake of Hurricane Katrina, for example, many people evacuated New Orleans, never to return (Kammerbauer 2008). By the time they had the green light to return, many had rented new housing in a new community, found themselves a new job, enrolled their children in a new school, and so on. Others stay in the community and try to find work in a different business. Regardless of whether they stay or leave, there are impacts on what is spent in the community on rentals, home sales, grocery stores, and so forth.

It was in Northridge, following the 1994 earthquake, that we first realized the existence of cascading events. We interviewed dozens of retailers whose businesses suffered either no damage at all or minimal damage, and who went out of business 6 months to 2 years following the earthquake. Their former customers stopped shopping in those shops because their priorities for spending the money available to them changed: they were busy repairing the damage to their homes and replacing what they had lost. Many moved away and did not come back. Business owners that did not or could not adapt effectively went out of business, usually after they had run out of savings, credit, and hope. Some owners we interviewed adapted by moving to another neighborhood or by changing what they did and how they did it. They prospered, at least sometimes.

Some economists have suggested that insurance payments and government benefits offset the losses to local business, but that is not always the case. When Northridge, California, was being rebuilt following the 1994 earthquake, local carpet suppliers, most of whom were out of business for a few weeks or months, found that they lost out to large dealers from other states that made deals with contractors to sell them boxcar shipments of carpet at prices the locals could not meet, even if they still had a store from which to sell and carpet with which to stock. The loss to local merchants showed up as revenue in other states. In addition, many of the contractors who rebuilt apartments and homes damaged by the earthquake came from other parts of California or from out of state; wages and profits followed them home and did not end up in Northridge. Nothing is as simple as it might seem.

We do not mean to imply that every community that experiences a natural hazard event experiences extensive, cascading adverse systemic consequences, but in the case of an extreme natural hazard event in a community that is not disaster resistant, they usually do. Adverse systemic consequences for the community occur when a part of the community system suffers initial consequences that preclude it from functioning "normally" and is, therefore, unable to perform its role in maintaining the community's "normal" functioning (Alesch et al. 2009). Moving from the abstract to the concrete, significant damage to Kobe, Japan's, harbor in the 1995 earthquake resulted in major problems for the community because the port was central to Kobe's economy. In the wake of Hurricane Katrina, damage to beaches, hotels and motels, workers' housing, and recreational facilities along the Gulf Coast generated cascading adverse consequences for businesses, employees, municipal revenues, and the ability of local governments to provide essential services (see Figure 3.4). Should a community experience a natural hazard event that does not generate sufficient damage to preclude community subsystems from performing their functions at an acceptable level, then there is little potential for the community system to unravel because of the event.

Ripple Effects: Consequences for Other Communities

The economic and social connections among communities within a nation, such as the United States, are closely linked. Businesses are tightly coupled with one another; that is, businesses rely on one another

FIGURE 3.4 Gulf Coast, Mississippi, March 15, 2007—More than 18 months later, little remains of a motel destroyed by Hurricane Katrina's storm surge. (Photograph by Lucy A. Arendt.)

with little room for slippage, delays, and discontinuities between them. Often, the tight coupling of activities depends on precise timing between firms and facilities in widely separated places. These days, there is little "slack" in the relationship between businesses, thanks in part to three phenomena: globalization, the Internet, and supply chain efficiencies. Tight coupling and the consequent lack of systemic slack is a defining characteristic of our time. An influenza strain that originates in a small community in Asia yesterday is a major concern in New York tomorrow, thanks to intercontinental transportation and travel. A joke that enters cyberspace this morning will be on everyone's e-mail, Facebook, or Twitter this afternoon. The advent and widespread adoption of "just-in-time" inventory systems and other efficiencies in the supply chain means that piston rings built today somewhere in Michigan's Upper Peninsula or Malaysia may be needed "just in time" for assembling lawn mower engines in Milwaukee or Georgia tomorrow.

Tight coupling and widespread interconnectedness mean that a major disruption in one community can easily trigger a crisis or an opportunity in another in a matter of hours or days. In our hypothetical lawn mower example, a fire in the piston ring factory can mean that purchasing orders from a firm specializing in lawn mower assembly will be unmet for weeks or months, unless a competing piston ring supplier steps in to meet the demand. Such a fire could lead to unemployment in the hypothetical little community in Upper Michigan and enhanced prosperity in a different community, if the firm specializing in lawn mower assembly decides to permanently source its piston rings from a new supplier in another community.

Charity Hospital in New Orleans closed following Hurricane Katrina. The hospital was the city's primary facility for caring for uninsured and poor households. Following closure, people who needed hospital care and who would have gone to Charity Hospital, went instead to other hospitals, most of which were in communities outside of New Orleans. This placed a major burden on those facilities. The State of Louisiana was slow to shift financial support from the defunct Charity Hospital to the facilities now bearing the expense of caring for the poor and uninsured, leading to significant financial problems for those hospitals.

Another ripple effect example from the Hurricane Katrina experience has to do with Baton Rouge, about 40 miles and 50 minutes from New Orleans. It became an overnight boomtown in the wake of Katrina. About 200,000 persons and 2,000 businesses rushed within a few days from the devastated areas to make Baton Rouge their temporary home (Steinberg et al. 2011). No one knew how long the refugees would stay. In the meantime, Baton Rouge local government was hard-pressed to deal with the increase in traffic, the need for housing, school facilities, increased crime, and all the other problems associated with a mass influx of storm survivors. By the end of the sixth week, more than 1,000 hospital beds and 5,000 medical personnel were added to the Baton Rouge inventory to help meet the vastly increased local need. While aid was being rushed to New Orleans, Baton Rouge got few headlines and not much help.

Still another example of external ripple effects centers on Kobe, Japan. Before the 1995 earthquake that destroyed Kobe's harbor, the seaport handled the most tonnage of any seaport on the Asian Pacific shore. Following the earthquake, harbors in other cities on Asia's Pacific shore captured most of the shipping that had gone to Kobe. This was a major economic problem for Kobe that contributed significantly to its post-earthquake problems. Still another example comes from Katrina. A small town on the Gulf Coast suffered badly in 2005 from Hurricane Katrina. About 16 months later, in January 2007, Oreck decided to move its production facilities to Cookeville, Tennessee, citing the high costs of doing business in hurricane country and costing Long Beach, Mississippi, 450 jobs (WLOX-TV 2008). Local officials seemed to think that the looming end of local government tax breaks to the company had something to do with the relocation.

When there are systemic consequences of a natural hazard event in a community, the consequences rarely stop at the boundaries of the community. They ripple out to other communities that may be proximate to the community suffering the immediate and systemic losses or to communities far from the damaged community (Alesch et al. 2009). These extra-system consequences occur because communities are open systems. The elements within them interact with, support, or compete with individuals and organizations in other, external communities. If we want to understand the consequences of extreme natural hazard events, it is unacceptable to ignore the consequences that extend beyond the borders of the community receiving the initial damage from the initial event.

Ripple Reverberations

Ripple reverberations are often the outcome of ripple effects. They are consequences for the community suffering the initial losses because the impact on outside communities have come back to contribute to a second or third round of adverse effects for the initial community (Alesch et al. 2009). In our experience, ripple reverberation consequences appear to occur most in the economic and employment sectors. Adverse ripple reverberations seem to result when firms or industries in outside communities either benefited or suffered economically because of things that happened in the community experiencing the natural hazard event and then adapt to those consequences in ways that generate further adverse consequences for the community that was initially damaged. Illustratively, when Katrina shut down New Orleans' French Quarter, Las Vegas benefited by being able to attract tourists, gamblers, and conventions that might otherwise have gone to New Orleans. New Orleans then had to struggle to regain its previous share of that market. An even better example of ripple reverberations is that Kobe has yet to recover its pre-earthquake share of the Asian Pacific coast seaport activity. It went from first or second in the Pacific Rim to about 15th and does not look as though it will regain its preeminence any time soon.

Sometimes the ripple effects that benefit external communities change the developmental trajectory of the damaged community. Ripple reverberation consequences do not occur following every disaster. Sometimes, for some reason or other, they are attenuated or dampened.

REAL PROBLEMS FOR REAL PEOPLE IN REAL PLACES

Unless a community is sufficiently resistant to the effects of an extreme natural hazard event, the consequences of that event generate problems for individuals, families, businesses, not-for-profit organizations, and local government itself. The following few chapters describe some of the problems that have arisen in communities across the country.

CHAPTER 4

Postdisruption
Real Problems for Real People in Real Places

A very large portion of this book is focused on trying to understand community disaster and recovery in the abstract, with the objective of learning how to facilitate recovery and to find ways to make communities more resistant to extreme natural hazard events. Disasters, however, do not occur in the abstract: they create real pain and real problems for real people in real places. Sometimes, the physical and emotional pain last for a lifetime. Here, we underline the importance of the task of learning how to reduce the impacts of extreme natural hazard events and to help communities quickly recover from disaster.

THE LOCAL ECONOMY MAY UNRAVEL

It was a 360-degree disaster: home, job, business, every aspect of life.

**Banker in Homestead, Florida,
looking back at Hurricane Andrew**

I think we'll be OK. I got a job cleaning restrooms.

**Flood victim in the Midwest
who lost his small business**

In a complex modern community, a thriving economy is the driving force for community survival and development. Frequently, however, a significant natural hazard event creates havoc even in thriving economies or significant portions of it. When there is a major disruption in economic activity for key employers, the potential for serious adverse cascading consequences is very real and predicting the long-term effects for the community is difficult (Alesch, Arendt, and Holly 2009).

Krugman (1996), referencing physicist Phillip Anderson, speaks of complexity as stemming from the science of "emergence," "how large interacting ensembles ... exhibit collective behavior that is very different from anything you might have expected from simply scaling up the behavior of individual units." He goes on to discuss how urban sprawl, as in Los Angeles, for example, is not simply "a homogeneous, undifferentiated mass" (pp. 3–4). On the contrary, he says, it is a "patchwork of areas of very distinct character," and that it is the result of a self-organizing system, not only in terms of its geographical characteristics, but, as he discusses later in *The Self-Organizing Economy*, in its economic structure.

Like the rest of the community, the local economy is largely self-organizing. Depending on decisions by those who own or control the firms that operate locally, the behaviors of individual firms in the community may take actions following the natural hazard event that result in a vibrant local economy. The reorganization might also result in a significantly different pattern or extent of economic activity. Self-organization, of course, implies the possibility that parts or all of that economy will "self-disorganize" or in systems terms, become entropic (Kast and Rosenzweig 1972). Ghost towns exist and some cities in the Rust Belt have experienced the falling apart of their respective local economies. For example, Gary, Indiana, which boasted a population of 178,320 in 1960, had a population of 80,294 in 2010. Median family income, according to Bogert (2013) is $32,000, about half the national average. Where U.S. Steel "once employed 25,000 people in its Gary operations; now only 5,000 locals work for that company" (Bogert 2013, para. 12). Following a major disturbance, local economies do, sometimes, begin to unravel and may even collapse.

Business Activity and Cascading Consequences

Just as a community depends on its economy for survival, businesses often depend on the community within which they exist for their viability. One of our very first big surprises about disasters when we began examining the consequences of extreme natural hazard events for small businesses two decades ago was when we found numerous businesses in Northridge that failed because of the Northridge Earthquake without having experienced any physical damage from the event. One can visualize business interruption or termination for an organization when the earthquake or storm surge destroys its facilities. Business facilities, however, are only one of the prerequisites for doing business. When the World Trade Center was destroyed, for example, many of the larger businesses that had occupied space there and that had facilities in other locations survived. They found new locations or moved activities to other existing facilities they operated. The same was not true for many of the small businesses in lower Manhattan whose customer base consisted almost entirely of those working within the World Trade Center. Many of them failed without having suffered immediate damage from the terrorist attack. In Northridge, the exodus of residents from the area because of reductions in employment in the defense industry and because their homes were damaged or destroyed meant that small businesses lost some of their customer base even before the earthquake. In addition, households that received damage from the earthquake had their purchasing priorities changed. Only about 10 percent had earthquake insurance and the homes had to be repaired. Some, while they were repairing that damage, decided they might as well add that extra bedroom they had been contemplating or make other improvements. Purchases for goods and services that could be deferred often were and the purveyors of those goods and services suffered financially.

The local economy starts to unravel when firms operating in the community suffer losses to their production, sales, or distribution capacity—particularly when they are unable to restore that capacity relatively quickly (Alesch et al. 2009). Unraveling also results when there is damage to a resource on which the community's economy largely depends, such as attractive white, sandy beaches and warm tropical waters on the Gulf Coast. Over the past few decades, hurricanes in the Gulf of Mexico erased homes, hotels, and rental accommodations from barrier islands and oceanfront property, depositing the debris on the sandy beaches and in the adjacent water. When the beaches are not usable, tourists stop coming. Then, too, customer capacity is limited when hotels, motels, and restaurants are damaged or, quite literally, ripped from their foundations and dragged out to sea. Undamaged businesses may be affected as well if they cannot ship products; if power, water, and sewerage are not available; and if suppliers or customers are unable or unwilling to do business with them.

Workers often disappear, at least for a while, as the storm approaches and even as it recedes. For the first few days or weeks, they are busy taking care of their families and their immediate needs. However, if a substantial amount of housing is damaged or destroyed, many of them leave, at least until the Federal Emergency Management Agency (FEMA) helps arrange for temporary housing days or weeks later. Workers also leave if they cannot find work that matches their skills or expectations. This can end up in an ugly spiral: workers are not there because there is no work, and employers do not reopen because there are not enough workers.

If a company's suppliers are damaged or cannot get the supplies to the company, and if there is no convenient substitute for those supplies, then the firm cannot produce its goods or services. Unless it has large inventories, the firm may have to close—at least temporarily. The same holds true when the firm loses its customers because they have either moved away or changed their spending priorities.

Following disaster, businesses that are parts of chains or franchises frequently have adequate insurance and access to capital from the corporate headquarters. After a hurricane or storm surge, those are usually among the very first retail outlets, restaurants, and motel/hotels repaired or rebuilt. Locally owned small businesses may have skimped on or failed to buy insurance and often do not have a large financial flywheel to help them through difficult times. We have seen many fail as long as 5 years after the flood or hurricane when they ran out of cash, credit, and hope. Many times, small-business owners told us that they had maxed out not only the company's credit cards, but their personal credit cards and lines as well. They were hoping for customers who did not return to them because they were gone, were themselves in financial trouble, or had found a new supplier.

In some smaller communities we studied, a locally owned bank extended credit to small businesses that were in trouble, often at very favorable rates. The banks and the businesses had a symbiotic relationship: they depended on one other. Many communities, often led by a local chamber of commerce or business association, worked with banks to provide small loans to small businesses. This sometimes worked out well, but, too often, the loans included provisions that made it difficult for the business to become flexible enough to survive and, too often, both the lenders and the business owners did not pay attention to the fact that one or more of the critical pillars supporting business was no longer capable of providing its essential support.

We have heard a few professors of economics, more committed to theory than to empirical research, tell audiences of people in the disaster field that a small disaster is actually good for business because all of the federal disaster aid and the insurance payments flowing to the community will stimulate the local economy. In reality, it rarely works out that way. Although some local businesses may profit from "day after the disaster" sales of various materials, all too often a large share of the money flowing into the community flows right back out, leaving the local economy with little or no gain. The stimulus is too little and for too brief a time to yield long-term, sustainable gains for the community's economy.

Businesses That Drive the Local Economy

Every community requires an economic reason for its existence. The reasons may be manufacturing, mining or other extractive industries, regional distribution, transportation, financial and insurance services, regional health care, education, or tourism. Larger communities typically have several economic bases and organizations whose activities drive the local economy and create significant linkages with the outside world. The larger and more diverse the economic base of a community, the more resistant the community itself is to events that may significantly reduce employment in any one of those economic drivers.

The same is not true of many smaller and midsized American communities. Often, their economy is based on employment in one or a few organizations or a single primary economic activity. In such communities, the dominant firms were often owned by people who came from the community, started the business, grew it, and passed it on to family or trusted colleagues. The individual owners typically had a real stake in the community. They were attached to it for reasons that went beyond short-term profit-and-loss statements. They contributed to the economic integrity of the community in myriad ways: through employment; through the attraction and then support of complementary industries; and through basic support of community members, both as individuals (e.g., with scholarships) and in the aggregate (e.g., with financial support of community events and facilities). The names associated with these businesses and individuals were found throughout the community on buildings, parks, streets, and so forth. For many reasons, this model of doing business in one's local community is no longer dominant.

The story of one community with which we are particularly familiar mirrors a national pattern. A very successful company producing frozen ice cream treats was created and owned by a local family. It is now owned by a huge international conglomerate. It did not take long for the conglomerate to move 400 premium jobs from the original home of the business halfway across the continent "to achieve greater efficiency." Most of the shareholders of a huge papermaking firm once lived in the community, but the firm went through a leveraged buyout, and was subsequently sold and resold to a series of multinationals. Its future is not certain. A meat packing plant across the river was created and owned by a local family, but was bought and operated by a large national firm and is now owned by a large foreign firm. If any of the production facilities in those dominant firms is damaged or destroyed, the decision as to whether to repair or rebuild the plant will be made far away by people who may never have been to the plant, who do not know the employees, and who may not even know where the community is. Their decision will be based not on what is best for the community but on what is best for the shareholders and managers of the conglomerate. If it makes financial sense to the firm's decision makers to rebuild in the damaged community, the business will be rebuilt; otherwise, it will not.

The decision about whether to rebuild operations in the community depends on many things: replacement costs, shipping costs, market shifts, and production costs. It depends, too, on the availability of an adequate labor force at affordable costs. If the workers have left the community and cannot return because there is not enough housing or because it is too expensive for them, that will factor negatively into the equation. However, if the firm has limited relocation options, has the prospect of being able to operate profitably in its predisaster location, or is tied to the community by virtue of its mission, it may provide temporary housing for workers. Faced with a housing shortage in New Orleans after Katrina, several hospitals committed to the area chose to house their employees rather than lose them to other cities.

Communities that are home to a large and presumably permanent institution—a public university, military base, a Veterans Affairs hospital, or the like—benefit substantially from the continual flow of money from the state or federal government to support that institution. The resulting jobs and income help sustain them after extreme natural hazard events. And, unlike the case with a large investor-owned firm, the local community may be able to exert pressure on its state legislature or Congress to stall or preclude any closure (e.g., of the military base) that might be considered. Unfortunately for Homestead, Florida, the decision to close Homestead Air Force Base had been made long before Hurricane Andrew destroyed so much of the community. When the air base was closed a few days before the hurricane, the loss of customers and members of the community confounded the seriously difficult recovery challenge in that city and the area south of Miami.

Smaller Businesses and Not-for-Profit Organizations That Serve the Local Community

As noted earlier, there is only a weak relationship between the amount of damage to its building or inventory that a business sustains following an extreme natural hazard event and that business's subsequent recovery. If a business cannot provide what its customers want when they want it, it is in jeopardy. Customer loyalty does not extend very far when a need is urgent and one's regular supplier cannot provide what is needed. The customer usually goes somewhere else, especially if it is convenient to do so. In Northridge, California, a local carpet dealer lost most of his inventory because the earthquake set off the sprinkler system in his warehouse, and then heavy rains poured more water into the building through the broken roof and missing back wall. While he was trying to get the landlord to repair the building that the business occupied, large manufacturers from Georgia and distributors from elsewhere in California cut deals with the big contractors, offering truckload prices and immediate delivery. Like other small retailers, the beleaguered merchant finally acquired suitable space and an inventory just in time to learn that there was no longer a need for his product or services. Virtually all the immediate demands for carpeting had already been met, and when most of the buildings in the market area get new carpeting all at once, there is little demand for it for several years thereafter. With the replacement carpet business essentially gone for years, this businessman had to rely on growth in the area, which proved insufficient to keep his business afloat and his business folded 2 years later.

If a business loses a critical mass of its customers for an extended period and cannot replace them, it is in serious trouble. Businesses lose customers for several reasons. First, some customers move away after the disaster and may not come back. Second, customers' priorities change: the new priorities have to do with repairing damage and rebuilding, perhaps to replacing automobile and home furnishings. At least for a while, discretionary money dries up, and people do not buy expensive new fishing gear or expensive jewelry, or eat in expensive restaurants, and they may postpone their annual or semiannual eye exams as well as nonessential work on their cars.

Businesses that provide goods or services that are purchased with discretionary income usually make a mistake if they rush to reopen. Their insurance companies will urge them to reopen, citing wholly unfounded statistics about how many businesses fail if they do not reopen immediately following a disaster. However, if the business has business interruption insurance, the insurance payments will stop the day the firm reopens, regardless of whether that business ever has another customer or makes another dime.

In nearly every community we studied, small-business owners struggled to reopen only to learn that they no longer had customers. A long-flourishing upscale fishing-tackle shop found that no one was interested in buying high-end fishing gear in the wake of the disaster. Hobby shops, jewelry stores, specialty restaurants, and other small firms experienced the same thing. Some closed shortly after they reopened. Others, tied to a lease or an unrealistic dream that things would return to the preevent normality, continued to pour their savings into a dead business until they were out of savings, credit, and energy. Some years after a flood, we interviewed an elderly woman who had been in business for many years with her husband. They had nothing left but the building in which the dying business was located. She asked, "Do you know how to find someone who will start a fire?" We hoped she was speaking in jest, but we were not sure.

Instead of reopening right away, it makes sense for the owner to assess whether there are still customers for the business and whether his or her business plan still makes sense in the postevent milieu. If not, it makes sense either to move to a new location where customers did not suffer as much loss or to shift to another business that is in demand. An optometrist in Northridge chose the first option: after cleverly sending out a "please return if not delivered" letter to all his patients and receiving 40 percent of the letters back, he decided to move to an undamaged area and rebuild his practice. Others chose the second option. We learned of a woman in a Gulf Coast city who was in the catering business; since there was no one to whom to cater following the hurricane, she mothballed the business and went into the temporary storage business. A couple with a cooking school saw no one come through the door for some time, so they opened a small restaurant to meet the growing needs of recovery workers. The last we heard, both entrepreneurs were doing just fine and meeting important needs in the community as it struggled toward recovery. Following the earthquake, a young man who owned a brake and transmission repair shop had no customers for several weeks. He kept busy by repairing his own racecar and then by starting to repair racecars for friends. It did not take long for him to decide to change his business into a repair shop for sports and racing cars. A year later, when we interviewed him again, he said that the earthquake had "made my dream come true."

Prerequisites for Doing Business and for Postevent Recovery

Whether an individual business can operate successfully or whether it can recover in the aftermath of a disaster depends on the extent to which the prerequisites for success exist for it. We have identified seven prerequisites for an organization to engage successfully in business activities: customers, suppliers and support services, means of producing its products, goods or services for sale, supporting infrastructure, labor, and operating capital. If any of these pillars is missing, then business operations are hindered or stopped (see Figure 4.1).

Customers are the first prerequisite for business success. Firms that depend on local customers for most of their business (grocery stores, retail shops, optometrists, and the like) find themselves in serious trouble when those customers change their shopping priorities and habits and if they move away. They change their shopping priorities and habits if they suffer losses from the event or if a shopping magnet on which small retailers count for drive-by shoppers is destroyed. Extensive damage to the Northridge Fashion Center led shoppers who had shopped there to go to other shopping centers and, when the center was rebuilt, many did not come back.

Second, a firm may experience adverse ripple effects if its suppliers are unable to provide it with products or raw materials for it to continue operations. If the supplier is damaged in the natural hazard event, then

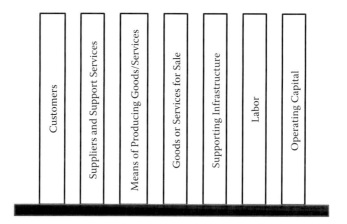

FIGURE 4.1   The requisite columns supporting business operations.

the adverse effects may show up in another community as well. The firm in that other community will search for a new supplier if it appears that delays in shipments from the original supplier may extend for weeks or months. If the customer is happy with the new supplier, the original supplier may have permanently lost a customer.

Suppliers also include those organizations that provide services for our illustrative firm. Support services include those others that provide transportation and delivery services, provide or maintain or repair equipment, and others that provide a wide array of support services.

A third prerequisite consists of facilities for creating the firm's goods or services. We have seen a business whose workers were assembling computer products in the company parking lot after the earthquake had damaged its building to the point at which occupancy was unsafe. It is not always necessary to have a fully functioning factory, laboratory, or other facility to continue business operations, but often it is. Sophisticated processes requiring sophisticated machines or other equipment require specialized space in which to function. Some retailers can sell their wares on a street corner, but others require space that enables them to store and to demonstrate sophisticated products. One retailer we interviewed on several occasions sold sophisticated medical and health equipment. When his retail space was flooded, it took 6 months to find appropriate space in his community. By then, his competitors had taken over his market share and he was not able to recover the lost business.

This leads directly to the fourth pillar: the organization, whether investor owned or not for profit, must have sufficient quantity and quality of products or services to provide to customers. Without goods or services to sell, the business becomes defunct. When inventory is destroyed, firms sometimes fail, particularly when it is difficult to replace that inventory and other providers have inventory to sell.

Fifth, the organization needs supporting infrastructure: electricity, telephone, computer networks, roads, water and sewage services, shipping services, and the like. Fred, who sold fish and seafood products from his shop, lost power for a day following the earthquake and found himself with refrigerators filled with rotting product. Hospitals relied on emergency power as long as they could when earthquakes, hurricanes, and storm surges disrupted the primary power sources, but when the emergency power sources were exhausted the hospitals were faced with problems of major proportions. San Francisco burned in 1906 when the water system failed because of the earthquake.

The sixth pillar and prerequisite for business operations is labor. Just ask restaurateurs and shop owners in New Orleans what it is like to try to open and operate when former and prospective employees simply are not available. Even if all the other pillars remain standing, if labor is gone, then the organization faces serious problems. In New Orleans, we observed small-business owners working extraordinary hours and calling in family members to help staff their operations, while regular employees searched for housing.

The final requisite pillar is operating capital. When revenue slows or stops, money is still required to cover fixed costs, payment to employees, repairs, and replenishment of supplies and inventory. Adequate cash flow is essential to continuing operations. Without it, firms cannot pay the utilities or other bills on time; lateness may be tolerated for a short while, but eventually employees and other creditors want and need their money. The business with limited reserves, inadequate insurance, and limited credit faces serious problems when disaster strikes and the normal course of affairs is disrupted.

The availability of financial resources is critical to firms that lose assets in the extreme natural hazard event. This usually means having the right kind of insurance in the right amounts from a reliable, viable insurer. Most of the small businesses we studied had inadequate coverage, no coverage, or the wrong kind of coverage. The proportion covered by flood insurance in other communities was not much higher. All too often we were told, "I didn't think I needed flood insurance. I'm in the 500-year floodplain." Apparently, the insurance agents for these businesspeople failed to tell them that a large proportion of the annual losses due to floods in the United States are in the 500-year floodplain, not just the 100-year floodplain.

Among those who were covered by flood insurance, most had inadequate coverage. Many of those who were insured in areas struck by hurricanes became embroiled in conflict with their insurer over whether damage was caused by wind or water. Water damage was typically not covered by anything other than flood insurance. And, in Florida following Hurricane Andrew, 11 Florida property and casualty insurance firms failed, leaving policyholders in the lurch.

Finally, small-business owners in particular must be able to adapt quickly and appropriately to new realities in the postevent environment. Suppliers with whom the business enjoyed long-standing relationships may have gone out of business or left the area, or may have stayed but now need to renegotiate pricing to remain viable. New suppliers may need to be found; and their expectations for contract negotiations and inventory management may be radically different from those of the former suppliers. Employees may have left the area (perhaps because their homes were destroyed, or their children's schools destroyed, or their partner's employer went out of business) or may have stayed but now demand higher compensation because of increased opportunities. As was the case with new suppliers, new employees' expectations for compensation, working hours, job requirements, and so on may differ from those of former employees. Longtime customers may have moved away, and new customers may demand better, faster, cheaper, and easier products or services; their needs and expectations having little or nothing in common with those of former customers.

Trying to do the same old thing usually does not work. Often, the owners need help in understanding this. The new normal is one fraught with uncertainty and ambiguity; adaptation is required to survive and thrive under the new conditions. For some business owners and their firms, doing something other than what they had been doing prior to the natural hazard event is unthinkable. Others understand that the ultimate goal is to stay vital and in business. The business people who understand this have a better chance of recovering.

Conditions under Which Economic Unraveling Is More Likely

Although an economy will not necessarily unravel following a disaster, in most of the smaller communities we studied, it did. The fundamental lesson seems clear: it is not enough to rebuild the infrastructure and the buildings. In fact, rebuilding the buildings as they were may be especially unwise in terms of the community's recovery; consider again the case of the rebuilt baseball stadium in Homestead, Florida, that never became home to a team.

We have identified the following factors that from our research appear to be correlated with a greater likelihood of economic calamity after an extreme natural hazard event.

Massive damage and massive systemic effects. When there is massive damage to the critical parts of a community's physical artifacts, and where the social and political systems become dysfunctional, we believe that economic recovery will be difficult and time-consuming.

A weak preevent economy. When the preevent economy in the community and the surrounding area is in trouble and has been for some time, the economy is more likely to unravel. By "in trouble," we do not mean that unemployment is up because of a nationwide recession. Rather, we mean that the community's economy has serious, long-term structural weaknesses. For example, some communities that began as service centers for an agricultural area are no longer needed for that purpose; larger centers and good highways have made them superfluous. Cities in the Rust Belt, such as Gary, Indiana, that depended on manufacturing steel and heavy machinery no longer do that as the industry moved away.

Nonlocal owners. From the communities we have studied, it appears that the local economy has a better chance of rebounding when the larger employers are locally owned. Owners with local ties seem more likely to reinvest in the community than owners who are unfamiliar with the community except as a line on a spreadsheet they review quarterly.

Inadequate quality or quantity of workers. In one struggling community we visited several times over the years, a local told us that the community had serious labor problems: "Chances are, if they can read, they can't pass the drug test." An untrained, numerically inadequate labor force will not support economic recovery. Firms that were in the community before the extreme natural hazard event occurred will be seeking another location with an adequate workforce, even if wages are lower in the disaster-stricken community, other things being equal.

Inadequate infrastructure. If the local infrastructure was marginal before the disaster and indications are that it will not improve, we would expect business owners and managers to seek an alternative location. It may be as close as the suburbs or a nearby community near a major highway, but it could be in another place altogether.

Increased costs of doing business. Sometimes the consequences of a disaster increase the costs of doing business. If housing becomes scarce and prices rise, workers may become scarce and wages may rise. Delays in construction may increase the cost of doing business for only a few years, but that may be enough to induce the firm to seek a better location.

Heavy "penalties" for rebuilding. Johnstown, Pennsylvania, has been badly damaged by floods on more than one occasion. During one particularly destructive flood, steel manufacturing facilities were severely damaged. One condition of rebuilding the facilities was that they would have to meet contemporary environmental safety standards. The steel firms balked at what they perceived to be extraordinarily high costs. They did not rebuild the steel mills and Johnstown's economy precipitously declined.

A deteriorated location relative to other places. Relative changes often have as much impact as absolute changes. An area can become less desirable simply because another area has been created that is far more desirable. Heavy public investment in interstate highways, recreational areas, universities, research parks, airports, or other important facilities can influence relative spatial desirability. And a community that has benefited from public and private investment in infrastructure and amenities is likely to realize economic recovery faster and more completely than one that has not benefited from such investment.

HOUSING AND REBUILDING ISSUES

Not going home is already like death.

—E. Catherine Tobler, *Vanishing Act*

Along the Mississippi coastline, steps and slabs were all that remained after the storm surge from Hurricane Katrina cleared a path extending several blocks back from the beach. The photograph in Figure 4.2 was taken in March 2007 near Pass Christian, Mississippi. This was one of several larger homes swept away by the surge. Some have called Katrina the worst historic preservation disaster in U.S. history (Huffman 2005). Along the 90-mile stretch of Mississippi coastline, hundreds of historic homes and structures were damaged significantly or washed completely off their slabs (Huffman 2005).

Housing accounts for the majority of building stock in any community (Comerio 1998). While housing represents a significant portion of a community's financial infrastructure, it also represents a significant portion of a community's social infrastructure (Comerio 1998). In the case of New Orleans, for example, we know that the history of its various neighborhoods is closely tied to the distinctive styles and designs of the homes found within. New Orleans is known for its Creole cottages, its American and Creole townhouses, its shotgun houses, its double-gallery houses, its bungalows, and more. Each of New Orleans' neighborhoods

FIGURE 4.2   Pass Christian, Mississippi, March 17, 2007—More than 18 months after Hurricane Katrina, only the slabs remain of the many homes that once dotted the Mississippi coastline. (Photograph by Lucy A. Arendt.)

(e.g., Treme, the Lower Ninth Ward, St. Charles) has its own style, its own history, and its own subculture. Maintaining and extending these neighborhood housing styles has an important role in the recovery of the community, for both financial and social reasons.

What Happens?

The nature and extent of housing problems following extreme natural hazard events vary considerably among communities, depending on the *event* itself, the *exposure* of the areas damaged, and the *vulnerability* of the areas exposed to the event. With respect to the event itself, the *size* of the extreme hazard event is critical. For example, an EF5 tornado that cuts a swath through a town in Oklahoma is likely to damage a greater proportion of the town's housing than an EF1 tornado. The *proximity* of the event will also affect the event's impact on housing. Does the EF5 tornado travel the path of the community's Main Street, or does it touch down on the outskirts? Finally, the duration of the extreme natural hazard event is likely to impact housing damage. Does the EF5 tornado briefly touch down in the community, or does it take its time weaving its destructive path?

Exposure is the second variable associated with initial damage to housing. If an apartment building is outside the flood channel or flood-plain, it is unlikely to be damaged from flooding. If a condominium is not on the beach, it is unlikely to be demolished by storm surge. People build homes in dangerous places, and the result is that their homes may be destroyed by extreme natural hazards. Those who love the forest may choose to build their dream home in an area prone to wildfires. Sometimes, municipalities make it easy for homes to be exposed to haz-ardous events. For example, cities like New Orleans look to expand their property tax base, so they fill marshes and swamplands, hoping that floods will not reclaim the land that new housing rests upon. In the end, one of the steps that a community can take to minimize exposure of its housing stock is to make it impractical or even illegal to build housing in areas where exposure to extreme natural hazards is moderate to high.

Finally, communities can take steps to reduce the vulnerability of their housing units. Design and construction codes can be implemented to minimize loss from fire, earthquake, flooding, tornadoes, and more. Homeowners living in tornado alley can be incentivized to build tornado safe rooms, consistent with FEMA P-320. Owners of large apartment units in earthquake country can be encouraged to explore base isolation and other contemporary options for minimizing both structural and nonstructural damage after earthquakes. Beyond structural and design considerations, homeowners can buy homeowners' insurance and other types of insurance specific to their location (e.g., flood insurance, earth-quake insurance). Tenants can buy renters' insurance. All of these mea-sures can reduce the vulnerability of a community's housing.

Beyond thinking about the event itself, exposure, and vulnerability, other aspects of the community also affect the impact of an extreme natural hazard event on the community's housing and the ability to rebound after the event. For example, the size of the community mat-ters. The housing in a small, sparsely populated town in Nebraska is likely to be impacted differently by an extreme natural hazard event than the housing in a major, heavily populated city in California. Older housing may be affected differently than newer housing. Housing owned by middle-class homeowners may be affected differently than housing owned by a community's upper class. The availability of vacant housing can influence what happens in a community after an extreme natural hazard event. More available housing likely means a reduced depen-dence on temporary housing (e.g., FEMA trailers). Housing that is well maintained may be impacted differently than housing that is blighted by poverty, disuse, and neglect.

In line with this thinking, Comerio (1997) describes housing losses and recovery problems in a number of U.S. and international cities. She argues that the "common denominator in urban disasters is housing and that recovery issues are quite different in cities than in rural areas, precisely because the losses are concentrated in densely populated areas and the housing loss not only represents a significant financial investment, but also a unique component of the urban infrastructure" (p. 166).

The 1994 Northridge Earthquake seriously damaged approximately 60,000 housing units, most of which were apartment buildings (Comerio 1998). Having observed severe housing problems after the 1989 Loma Prieta Earthquake, the city of Los Angeles acted quickly to "expedite temporary housing assistance for tenants of damaged buildings and to enhance standard housing recovery programmes" (Comerio 1997, p. 167). Most of the displaced tenants found alternate housing within 2 months of the event, in part thanks to the swift action on the part of city officials, and because there were relatively high vacancy rates in the rental housing market when the earthquake struck.

Comerio (1997) suggests that owners of multifamily apartment buildings were in some ways worse off than their tenants were after the earthquake. Fewer than half of the seriously damaged multifamily units were eligible for either Small Business Association (SBA) loans or special Department of Housing and Urban Development (HUD) allocations to the city of Los Angeles. The result was that owners who wanted to repair their buildings had to use their own funding to do so. Owners of more affordable housing were often able to repair their no-frill units with a combination of federal low interest loans and personal funds. Owners of larger apartment buildings with more amenities typically faced a combination of more expensive repairs and reduced cash flow from higher vacancy rates. Many of these owners had to take loans from the city, as they were often not eligible for SBA loans. Within 3 years of the earthquake, "three out of four vacated units had been repaired" (Smith 1997, cited in Comerio 1997).

The impact of the 1994 Northridge Earthquake on single-family homeowners was significant. Whereas the city's initial estimates of housing damage were $1.5 billion and insurers' initial estimates were $2.5 billion, total expenditures were 10 times more (Comerio 1997, 1998). What accounted for the difference? "An analysis of insurance claims and government assistance programmes suggest(ed) that there was much more damage than originally estimated and that the damage was distributed over a much wider area" (Comerio 1997, p. 169). Whereas 64,000 homes were evaluated during the initial postdisaster inspections, "as many as 500,000 homeowners received compensation to repair damage, and these were distributed in areas as far as 50 km from the fault rupture" (Comerio, Landis, Firpo, and Monzon 1996, cited in Comerio 1997, p. 169). This supports our contention that more of the built environment tends to be affected than the initially identified houses and other buildings thought to have been affected by a given extreme natural hazard event. Especially in the case of earthquakes and floods, housing and other buildings can sustain structural and nonstructural damage that may not be apparent even to skilled and knowledgeable inspectors in the immediate aftermath of an event.

According to Comerio (1997), what struck insurance companies and disaster researchers looking at the costs associated with the 1994 Northridge Earthquake was the extensive "financial cost to repair what was largely minor damage" (p. 170). Although initial estimates of damages tended to focus on multifamily apartment units, in the end at least half of the damage was associated with single-family homes (Comerio 1998).

Comerio's (1997) comparison of her Northridge findings to other urban disasters revealed several interesting observations. First, housing units most likely to sustain damage were those that were poorly constructed without much attention to proactive regulation or enforcement of existing building code standards. Second, existing vacancy rates affected the need for alternative forms of temporary housing. This factor greatly influences the need for long-term temporary housing solutions. Third, the proportion of low-rent units affected by an extreme event affects the ability of a community to rehouse their occupants. Whereas single-family homes may be quickly repaired, reconstruction of multiple-family units, especially those catering to lower-income individuals and families, can take considerable time as owners look to affordable housing development programs for assistance. Another factor that apparently influences the reconstruction of multiple-family units is the availability of employment for people living there. Without jobs, people will move away from a community, reducing the demand for multiple-family units.

Comerio (1997, p. 177) summarized eight lessons from her research on urban disasters and housing:

1. Damage to residential stock constitutes the majority of the damage;
2. The major structural damage commands media attention and often frames government response, but it is the minor damage that costs the most to repair;
3. Just as we have learned that there is a surprising amount of redundancy in the transportation infrastructure, so too is there redundancy in the housing stock;
4. ... there has been little preparation for the much bigger task of coordinating and paying for post-disaster rebuilding;
5. Private insurance is, and will continue to be, the primary fund source for private rebuilding;

6. ... governments need to improve loss estimation and rate setting models ...;
7. Government re-building programs need to be more efficient and targeted to complement rather than substitute for insurance coverage; and
8. Mitigation policies and programmes must be viewed as part of the funding for recovery and not simply as disaster preparedness.

Housing Costs and Land Values

What happens to housing costs and land values depends, of course, on the interplay of supply and demand. That interaction has played out a little differently in every community we have studied and appears to be affected by several factors. In some Gulf Coast areas with severe damage at the shoreline, land values appeared to have escalated almost immediately after Hurricanes Katrina and Rita. Almost everywhere at the water's edge, smaller homes that were damaged or swept away were being replaced by much larger homes, and small buildings with rental units are being replaced by larger hotels and condominiums or by commercial buildings catering to shoreline business. In other local jurisdictions, housing prices appear to have increased in direct proportion to the amount of housing that was damaged or destroyed. However, land prices do not seem to have increased as they have along the Gulf Coast shoreline. Other variables include the availability of housing in a nearby surrounding area, the number of residents who left the community in the wake of the event, and the extent of activity by speculators bent on acquiring special land, such as beachfront property.

Housing Availability

In every community we studied, temporary housing was needed for people who lost their housing and did not evacuate to undamaged areas. Emergency response and relief teams, including hospital staff, public safety officers, local government officials, and utility crews, also need temporary shelter (see Figure 4.3). Some of these workers will have homes that have been damaged or destroyed, while others will have come from elsewhere. Cleanup crews that arrive from outside the community sometimes bring their housing with them in the form of trailers, campers, and recreational vehicles, but they still need water and sanitary hookups or facilities. After the cleanup crews come the construction crews—usually single people or people traveling alone who are from out of town; because they plan to be there only temporarily, they look for simple, inexpensive

FIGURE 4.3   Dade County, Florida, August 24, 1992—Emergency shelters being set up by the Army. (Courtesy of FEMA/Bob Epstein.)

housing, such as motels and hotels. Housing is also needed for those who provide services to all these workers: the restaurant workers, hotel staff, and gas station operators. And at some point, temporary housing is needed for returning workers and their families.

Providing the needed housing seems to always have raised a series of issues as emergency shelters were replaced with temporary shelters, which eventually gave way to more or less permanent housing. The horror stories from New Orleans about emergency shelter in the Super Dome and the convention center are atypical experiences in the United States, at least judging from the communities we studied. Our communities did not rely much on tents for emergency shelter; more often, local schools and YMCAs became temporary shelters for a few days or, at most, a few weeks. People who were unable to return to their homes often found places to stay with friends and relatives or in vacant, available rental apartments or houses. Some families left town to find housing, especially if the primary breadwinner had become temporarily unemployed. Before too much time had passed, FEMA mobile homes, often called trailers, began to arrive (see Figure 4.4).

Residents interested in receiving a FEMA mobile home complete an application. The time between applying for a mobile home, or trailer, and receiving one can be a few weeks or even months. Trailer installation is a complicated process that involves the efforts of numerous contractors; the area suppliers of energy, water, and sewer; and finally, a FEMA inspector. While many homeowners may seek to have FEMA

FIGURE 4.4   FEMA trailers passing through Slidell, Louisiana, on their way to New Orleans. (Photograph by James C. Alesch.)

trailers installed on their private lots, other individuals and families, for example those who had been living in a rental property prior to the natural hazard event, find themselves living in FEMA trailer parks. These parks usually begin to take shape within a month or so after the dust has settled or the water has receded. As necessary as they are, however, they are not without issues. Some local officials reported to us that they believe FEMA has a tendency to locate the parks on the outskirts of the community where there are no grocery stores, no gas stations, no parks, no public transit, and no access to school for children. From FEMA's perspective, those sites probably make sense because it is often difficult to find a site in the center of the community that is sufficiently flat enough, large enough, and vacant enough to put a trailer park. The urgent need to get the facility up and available should presumably be traded off against the need for convenience, but there often seems to be some friction between local and federal officials concerning the location of the trailer parks.

We also heard from local officials about conflicts over which organization had primary responsibility for policing the trailer parks. As described earlier, residents already suffering stress from the storm or earthquake often find themselves in cramped quarters living next to people who are very different from them. Clashes arise and, over time, can become frequent and intense. If the trailer parks are located outside the city, police services may be thought to be the responsibility of the county or parish sheriff. Sometimes, however, FEMA officials on site have maintained that they are responsible for policing the park. To the best of our knowledge, the issue remains unresolved, worked out from state to state and disaster to disaster.

Although FEMA trailers are intended to provide temporary housing, typically for a period not to exceed 18 months, recent disasters such as Hurricane Katrina have led to FEMA trailers being used for more than 4 years. Clearly, the extent of an extreme natural hazard event's impact on a community's built environment will affect the amount of time needed for temporary housing. In New Orleans, for example, and neighboring St. Bernard Parish, where so much of the built environment was damaged, residents had little recourse but to stay in the temporary housing provided by FEMA. The same has been true in communities along Mississippi's Gulf Coast, all of which also sustained severe damage to their built environments in the wake of Katrina's storm surge. With so many residences so badly damaged and destroyed, the rate of repair and reconstruction was necessarily slowed, and the need for temporary housing made greater.

POSTEVENT DEMOGRAPHIC CHANGES

I've developed a new philosophy ... I only dread one day at a time.

—Charles Schulz's *Charlie Brown*

Often, but not always, extreme natural hazard events lead to population changes in both the stricken community and those communities to which people have fled for safety or because their homes were damaged or destroyed or their jobs disappeared. In the days and weeks following the extreme natural hazard event, as the disaster is unfolding, some people leave while others arrive. Some leave temporarily; many of them, at least initially, plan to return. New people move in shortly after the event to help clean up, restore services, and rebuild, and then they usually leave. Others come to live and work in the community as it rebuilds. Following an extreme natural hazard event there are typically disjoints between the number of people and the availability of housing, labor, and services. Displacement usually involves personal and family disruption. As suggested by Aldrich (2012), "Whereas popular press accounts hope to see results within weeks or months, ... population levels may never reach pre-disaster points" (p. 6).

Wright and his colleagues (1979) examined the long-term effects of natural hazard events. They concluded, "For the period 1960 to 1970, there are no discernible effects of the natural disaster events occurring in that period which materially altered population and housing growth trend for counties or for census tracts" (p. 27). They were, of course, talking about the long term: everyone understands there are often major changes in population numbers in the near aftermath of such events. We found, in our research, significant demographic long-term changes in a variety of demographic characteristics, if not in total population.

Estimating Postevent Population Changes: Important But Difficult

It is important for public and private policy makers to have reliable estimates of how the community population has changed as a consequence of a disaster. Such estimates provide a basis for establishing priorities and allocating resources during and after the postevent emergency period. They are valuable in understanding the nature and scale of the recovery challenge. The value of reliable demographic information in the days, weeks, and months after the extreme natural hazard event does not, however, make the task of obtaining that information any easier.

Relatively few analyses have been conducted identifying demographic changes in communities that have experienced significant disasters. One reason is that the work is methodologically challenging. Another is that very few analysts conduct longitudinal studies of communities to learn how communities change as time passes after the disaster. Consequently, there is little basis for generalizing about those changes and for predicting what is likely to happen in any specific disaster.

Work by the University of Florida's Bureau of Economic and Business Research (Smith 1994) points out the difficulties associated with making reliable estimates, in the near term following disasters, of both initial population displacement and community repopulation. Smith notes the "impact of the hurricane (Andrew) on the housing stock, occupancy rates, active residential electric customers" and so forth, as well of use of temporary shelter by residents, made it impossible to use traditional means of estimation (1994, pp. 462–463).

McCarthy and his colleagues (2006) employed measures of housing habitability and the rate of reconstruction or repair, along with "a conceptual framework based on the costs and benefits of migration and on the role of social networks and physical constraints" (p. xi) to make their estimates. They made estimates of the population for the very short term following Katrina as well as for up to 3 years following the flooding.

Sometimes a household's move away from the community is intended to be temporary. When damage is widespread, everyday life becomes burdensome and sometimes unaffordable. "I took the kids and moved in with my sister in [insert name of town] until the power was back on and the supermarket reopened. My husband stayed there to [help clean up, to work, because he was a fireman]." "My apartment was destroyed and I couldn't find an affordable place to live so I moved to [insert name of town] where I got a job [waiting tables, at a hotel, driving cab]. I'll come back [when I can find a place I can afford to live, when I can get my old job back, in a few months]." A woman in Minnesota moved away after the tornado destroyed her home: "I moved to a house trailer in [a city about 15 miles away], but I continue to work in the family business. It's been almost 10 years and I still can't find housing in [her hometown]. I don't know when I'll be able to move back."

Other times the move is intended to be more or less permanent. Thousands of middle-class homeowners left Northridge after the 1994 earthquake with no plans to return. Many were at or near retirement age. The area's defense industry had seen cutbacks, so some of these people had been laid off or offered early retirement packages. But taxes were high for retirees, and the value of homes had softened or actually declined. For many, the earthquake was the last straw. In Homestead, Florida, of the many people who left just before or just after the hurricane struck in 1992, a large number were Air Force personnel, their dependents, and retired career military people (who lived near the base to avail themselves of medical services, Base Exchange, and Commissary privileges). Others were retired snowbirds who left because almost everything was destroyed and other places beckoned.

Long-term projections of population change in communities that have experienced disasters or that are disaster prone present different problems from estimating short-term displacements. Based on the longitudinal analyses we have conducted, we believe that the major regional and sectorial economic forces and mobility patterns dominate the population trajectories of communities, even those that experience a disaster. That having been said, disasters with systemic consequences for the community usually create significant, although perhaps temporary, variations in both the characteristics and the long-term trajectory of population numbers.

Each community and each disaster is unique. This contributes to the problems of projecting the likely trajectory of each community. In addition to long-term shifts in economic activities and mobility trends, significant long-term demographic changes in a community seem to depend on several variables, including community economics; the availability of housing, health care, schools, and employment; and the mobility of the existing population. The most important appears to be the economy of the community, both pre- and postevent. If the economic magnet has not been weakened, people are likely to stay or return as they are able, depending on available housing, jobs, and so on; if it has been weakened, people are likely to drift away permanently. Before generalizations can comfortably be made about what is likely to happen under various conditions, much more research needs to be done on the demographic consequences of disaster. Nonetheless, local officials should be aware of the range of possible outcomes in their communities following an extreme natural hazard event, and they should be alert to the likelihood that what occurs after the event will depend to a considerable extent on what happened before it.

Dimensions of Demographic Change

Every disaster-stricken community has some temporary and long-term change in the number and kind of residents living there. People whose homes are badly damaged or destroyed arrange to live somewhere else—with family or friends, down the street, across town, out of town, or out of state depending on individual circumstances and options—until they can find more permanent housing (Comerio 1998). After Katrina, displaced New Orleans residents who were unable to return to their homes for weeks or months moved everywhere. Some moved to nearby Jefferson Parish to the west or across the Mississippi River to the south. Many moved to Baton Rouge, 80 miles to the northwest. Some moved to Houston, Texas, 350 miles to the west. Others moved all over the United States.

Several dimensions of population change may occur in both the immediate aftermath of an extreme natural hazard event and during the weeks and months during which communities attempt to rebuild and recover. The most obvious of these is a change in the total number of persons residing in the community. In recent disasters, the population changes in New Orleans associated with Hurricanes Katrina and Rita were widely reported in the popular media. There are, however, more subtle dimensions of population change that bear consideration: initial displacement, net changes in population numbers, the proportion of the community population that may move away, changes in demographic composition of movers and stayers, and changes in household composition, including household dissolution.

Initial Population Displacement and Repopulation

It is useful to look at the experience of communities that suffered disasters to see how their respective populations changed just before and immediately following the emergency period. In August 1992, Hurricane Andrew ripped across the southern tip of Florida with winds up to 175 miles per hour. Smith and McCarty (1996) conducted field and telephone surveys in the southern half of Dade County where most of the damage occurred. They interviewed 5,310 persons living in Dade County at the time of the hurricane. In the southern half of Dade

County (including Homestead and Florida City), 60 percent reported their home was either destroyed or suffered major damage. More than half the South Dade respondents moved out of their homes. Based on their data, Smith and McCarty estimated 353,000 were displaced from their homes. Of those living in the southern half of the county, about three-fourths remained in Dade County and about 9 percent moved to Broward County (north of Dade County). A similar proportion moved somewhere else in Florida, and 8.3 percent moved out of state. About two-thirds of the displaced residents had returned to their pre-hurricane residences, but, of those who had not returned, more than 90 percent who had not returned to their pre-hurricane residences did not plan to return to them. Smith and McCarty (1996) concluded that "it appears that most of the temporary population shifts caused by the hurricane had come to the end within 2 years" (p. 273). Unless they have strong economic or emotional ties to their community, one warm and sunny Florida community might be perceived by those displaced by a hurricane to be about as good as another. Moreover, some communities are less likely to be destroyed by a hurricane than others are, at least in the minds of the residents or evacuees. We interviewed some younger people who left Florida altogether simply to live and work elsewhere. "It wasn't all we had hoped for, and the hurricanes are simply too much to deal with. There are other nice places that don't have them." These individuals considered themselves mobile and acted accordingly.

New Orleans' Katrina experience was even more dramatic. The 2000 Census of Population reported that New Orleans had a population of about 485,000. McCarthy and his colleagues (2006) estimated the population in December 2005, 4 months after Katrina, at about 91,000. They also estimated that 1 year after the storm and ensuing flood the population had increased to about 198,000 (p. xii). Parts of the city with higher elevation and less damage repopulated much more quickly than low-lying areas. The low-lying areas were populated before the storm by households with, on average, lower incomes than households in higher areas, and the damage in the low-lying areas was more devastating.

In New Orleans, population estimates continue to be fraught with potential error, in part because many people continue to move in and out and around within the city, so the population is in flux. And because much of the city's housing stock remains damaged, homeowners who are unable to return to their damaged homes full time may still spend considerable time at their properties, repairing them or preparing them for repair or sale. Other homeowners continue to live with family and friends in the city or nearby parishes while they wait to fix, sell, or demolish their homes and start anew. As of March 2008 (2 years and 7 months after Katrina), 71.8 percent of the households in the city were actively receiving mail (Plyer 2008). By 2010, New Orleans' population had climbed to about 334,000, or about 80 percent of its pre-Katrina population. It appears that New Orleans is unlikely to return to its pre-Katrina population within the next decade or so.

We have conducted longitudinal studies of 16 communities that experienced floods, earthquakes, wildfire, hurricanes, or tornadoes. Every one of them experienced short-term population declines just before, during, and immediately following the natural hazard event. One-fourth of them experienced long-term population decline, usually because the local economy could not sustain the preevent numbers. Communities that had experienced population increases prior to the event and that had more vibrant economies typically rebounded to preevent levels within a decade of the event.

Changes in Demographic Characteristics

It is not simply the absolute number of persons in a community that changes before, during, and after an extreme natural hazard event and community emergency. Often, the event triggers changes in the characteristics of the population.

The city of Homestead became a lot less middle class when Hurricane Andrew struck and continued to change demographically thereafter. Days before the hurricane struck, the Air Force closed Homestead Air Force Base permanently and a large portion of Homestead's middle-income households left, moving to different Air Force bases. As the emergency ended and recovery efforts began to dominate, the U.S. Department of Housing and Urban Development provided resources to build apartments, primarily in the form of Section 8 rental assistance vouchers. Since so many of the preevent residents did not return, advertisements for the assisted housing drew many poor from northern Dade County. Consequently, in the years that followed, the population that left was replaced by low-income households, the heads of which had fewer job skills and far less income than those they replaced. Then, about a decade after the hurricane, when Miami spread south to the northern border of Homestead, almost 10,000 homes were soon built near highway and toll way interchanges for households with higher incomes, and once again, the demographic composition of Homestead changed significantly.

In Northridge, California, about 20,000 mostly middle-aged, middle-class persons of European descent left after the 1994 earthquake and were replaced in the first couple of years primarily by persons of Latino and Korean descent. Many of these persons retained much of their ethnic identity. With the change in population, small businesses changed, too. Many small businesses owned by persons of European descent were replaced by other small businesses owned by persons of

Latino or Korean descent. The community changed irrevocably, even though it looks generally similar to the preevent community.

Before the 1999 flood that almost completely inundated Princeville, North Carolina, Princeville housed about 2,000 people. A year later, the population was less than 900 (Brown 2001). By 2006, the population was back to preflood levels, but most of the people there were not the same people who lived there before the flood. Much of Princeville's single-family housing was replaced by public housing projects that attracted people from other areas and changed the characteristics of the community rather dramatically.

In New Orleans, the city's demographics have been dramatically altered since Katrina. Prior to Katrina, about two-thirds of the city's population was African-American, whites comprised about 28 percent of the population, and Hispanics and Asians accounted for most of the remainder. The population of African-Americans seems to have declined radically, as evidenced in a recent election in which the majority of voters were white and elections for the city council resulted in a white majority for the first time in over two decades. In general, it appears that New Orleans is becoming a "smaller, whiter city with a much reduced black majority" (Nossiter 2007). The city is also seeing an increased number of Hispanic residents, many lured by the prospect of recovery construction jobs.

Some communities experience very little change in community demographics following the emergency. Los Alamos, New Mexico, lost about 5 percent of its housing units in the 2000 fire, but the dominant employer, the Los Alamos National Laboratory, survived and continued operations despite having lost a few buildings. As a result, most of the people in the 400 destroyed houses did not leave; instead, they found other places to live in or near Los Alamos—perhaps because employment in the community remained stable and because federal aid for replacing lost housing was generous. Similarly, Grand Forks, North Dakota, retained its general population numbers and characteristics after the Red River flood in 1997.

Proportional Change in Population

It is common sense, but sometimes forgotten: It is not just the absolute number of persons who move away from a community that makes a difference in the recovery challenge. Rather, it is the proportion of the population that leaves that is important. Having as many as 20,000 people move from Los Angeles does not generate nearly the challenge that losing 10,000 residents does in Homestead, Florida. Similarly, the demographic makeup of those who leave makes a big difference. If those who depart represent a random mix of persons from the community, this is significantly different from a situation in which most of those who leave the community have the highest skills, income, and means of coping with the natural hazard event.

SOCIAL AND PSYCHOLOGICAL CONSEQUENCES

It's a never-ending nightmare. It never goes away.

—A Northridge Earthquake survivor

Perhaps the most overlooked and understudied part of disasters has to do with individual, family, and community social and psychological well-being. Following the initial shock of injury or death to friends and family, and of damage to the built environment, people try to make sense of what happened and find ways to deal with it (Figure 4.5). We have grouped our observations in communities across the country into several broad categories: (1) expectations about the aftermath, (2) cohesiveness and divisiveness, (3) individual mental health issues, and (4) community healing.

Expectations

The social and political consequences of disaster are not easily predicted, but they seem to follow a general pattern. In almost all communities we studied, as the immediate emergencies have been addressed and people are cleaning up and making repairs, there seems to be a generally expressed optimism that "This is just a bump in the road, and we'll soon be back where we were before it happened" or "We'll be back bigger and better than ever." We have not heard this from everyone, but we have heard it from most local elected officials and many residents, even in places that suffered almost total devastation. We could not tell how much of what we heard was rhetoric born of belief, heartfelt hope, or sheer desperation, but it suggested an expectation that things in the future could be much as they were before the event. It may be that no one wants to appear on television glumly predicting, "We will never be able to recover from this."

In the cleanup, fix-up period early in the aftermath, expectations about a return to normalcy are typically bolstered by cooperation and mutual assistance. Neighbors help neighbors. We often heard, "We've never seen anything like it. This disaster brought everyone together." This sense of community is further enhanced by a swell of volunteers

FIGURE 4.5   Lakeview neighborhood, New Orleans, March 17, 2007—
Humor is a well-documented means of dealing with psychological stress.
(Photograph by Lucy A. Arendt.)

who come to the community to give comfort and to help with clearing debris and rebuilding. But except in New Orleans, where volunteers
continued to arrive more than 3 years after the flood, volunteers usually
begin to drift away after a few weeks or months, and residents may feel
left largely to themselves.

Later in the aftermath, individuals start to define, usually quite subconsciously, a "new normal" to replace what they had defined as normal before the event. At the same time, individuals, organizations, and
groups find that their concerns and agendas are not shared universally
in the community. Other people have other interests, which sometimes
conflict. Preevent agendas for the city council and nongovernmental civic
groups go by the board as the meetings are dominated by postdisaster
problems and concerns. Traditional processes may be short-circuited.
People who were rarely or never involved in political exchange join the
fray in order to get their issue addressed.

Early in the aftermath, community and local government expectations about state and federal assistance are sometimes unrealistic. Even following a Presidential Declaration of a disaster, the federal government does not provide disaster funds to communities without strings attached. The funds are typically project based and designated for specific uses. Most of the grants are for brick-and-mortar projects. The federal government does not provide grants to cover local government operating expenses; it provides loans for that purpose. Moreover, federal programs are not particularly flexible; one size is usually expected to fit all, and every dollar spent must be accounted for.

As issues in the community move to the governmental agenda, unrealistic expectations are sometimes placed on local officials. For these local professionals, who are dealing with problems they have never before faced, added stress comes from elected officials and community groups who want the problems solved "Now!" In some communities, this results in frequent turnover in key positions. We do not want to reference specific communities, but in some that we visited, the positions of city manager, chief financial officer, and building official turned over almost annually for several years after the disaster. The combination of long weeks, political pressure, and no time for personal lives gets to be too much. People leave of their own accord or are fired.

After a few weeks, residents who had been focused on the losses to the built environment and on injuries to people they know begin to sense the losses to the social, economic, and political community, although few ever put it into those words. Expectations begin to change. The "feel good" period of cooperation and support starts to fade. People in every community get discouraged. In New Orleans, for example, virtually every locally generated evening newscast, even 2 years after the flood, contained flood-related stories and not many of them were particularly pleasant. Add to that the plight of so many people who are making mortgage payments on a house they cannot live in, as well as payments on the home somewhere else they established after the flood. Living in a small trailer parked on one's driveway for a week is an adventure. For 18 months, 2 years, or more, it is a continual, dreary reminder of one's plight. Faced with daily reminders of the extreme natural hazard event and dwindling attention from outside the area, people begin to wonder if they have been forgotten.

We found that while the length of the coming-together, "feel good about ourselves" period varied by community, the period tended to be one that people remembered fondly for years after the event. In nearly all cases, however, it dissipated before the cleanup was complete. Early in the aftermath of a disaster, the community often shifts from a period of collaboration and cooperation to a period of political conflict about who gets what and when. In some cases, the conflict is exacerbated by preexisting community tensions. Equity and fairness issues almost invariably arise among those who suffered losses and those who did not; those with losses sometimes group themselves in terms of who lost the most. Along the Mississippi Gulf Coast, in the wake of Katrina, some people referred to themselves as "slabbers"—people whose homes and belongings were swept away completely by the storm surge, leaving only the foundation slabs. In some communities, an "us versus them" mentality may develop among victims toward "nonvictims"—those who did not lose as much and who may be receiving more in the way of assistance than others think they are entitled to. Except in New Orleans, we did not see or hear of anyone overtly playing the "race card" in a public forum. We did not find many systematic policies or practices that directed benefits primarily to one racial or ethnic group at the expense of others, but we did encounter a few.

Individual Mental Health

In our earlier research in disaster sites, we did not plan to look at issues of postdisaster mental health (Alesch et al. 2009). But when we asked people, "What happened?" many made it abundantly clear that long-term psychological stress and often clinical depression were serious problems for them. The stress and depression made it difficult for some to recover personally, even after a decade or more. These problems rose to the community level as psychiatric services were stretched to the breaking point. Interviews with hospital personnel in New Orleans, for example, were routinely punctuated with concerns about the relative dearth of available psychological services. "What we really need, right now," they said, "are more psych beds. These folks are ending up in our emergency rooms, unable to get the care they need and complicating the care available for others."

Men, women, and children experienced the emotional stress and psychological problems. We heard about marriages that ended within a year or so of the disaster as a direct result of behaviors by one or the other partner in the weeks and months following the disaster. In most communities, we interviewed people who said that they were being treated for psychological ailments, disaster-related depression, and anxiety even 5 years after the event; some respondents reported having been in treatment for 6 or 7 years postevent, and some had attempted suicide. Many times, people we were interviewing broke down in tears, even though the actual disaster was 5 or 6 years in the past. It was painful to interview them, knowing that there was little or nothing that we could do, other than listen.

An analysis of our interview notes suggests that long-term adverse psychological effects are related to an individual's and family's resiliency and to the extent of their losses and the disruption to their "life trajectories." A few of the local officials we interviewed reported that the local government had made counseling services available for "a month or two" after the disaster but that very few people took advantage of them. Unfortunately, in many cases, the problems do not develop or emerge until later, when little help is available. Posttraumatic stress does not follow government-imposed timelines and we suspect that posttraumatic stress disorder following extreme natural hazard events is much more widespread than it is thought to be.

Consistent with our observations about psychological health, C. J. Huff, the school superintendent for Joplin, Missouri, observed that 1,400 students in his district were still being treated for varying degrees of posttraumatic stress disorder more than 2 years after a devastating EF5 tornado battered Joplin. Asked for the advice he might offer to the people of Moore, Oklahoma, traumatized by their own EF5 tornado in 2013, Huff said, "The buildings will get rebuilt, but you need to take care of the people" (Brooks 2013, para. 6). Staying with the story of Joplin, Missouri, Morris (2011) described children trying to "play" through the fear associated with their most terrifying moments. Four months after the tornado, Morris (2011) wrote,

> Just months ago, 3-year-old Allie Stout was cowering in a hallway beneath her parents—and a violently flapping mattress—as the monster tornado ripped her house apart. In seconds, Allie's world flipped upside down: room gone, toys gone, parents hurt, dog missing. Weeks ago, she was still "playing tornado" all the time (para. 2) ... "It's nothing for us to go back into her room and hear her telling her 'babies' that it's time to take cover," (her mother, Tiffany) Stout says, "and they have to lay down on the floor and put their hands over their heads and hold on tight, pray—pray for God's protection and pray that they make it through the storm." (para. 5)

Those who knew the preevent community will, most likely, try initially to replicate at least some parts of it in the postevent reconstruction. This usually begins with an attempt to rebuild or replace destroyed physical structures and artifacts with copies of the old ones. Reestablishing landmarks and familiar spaces helps considerably with some aspects of recovery for those who lived there before the disaster. Cox and Perry (2011) studied the importance of place as it relates to people who experienced the destruction of their communities by a Canadian forest fire. Their findings afford insight into why people try to reestablish the familiar setting of the preevent community. "Some residents faced the material loss of houses, businesses, and jobs, but even those who had not suffered direct material losses faced the loss of many of the routine and familiar aspects of their lives. For many residents, the fire resulted in an increased sense of vulnerability and an ongoing sense of uncertainty" (Cox and Perry 2011, p. 399). To the community residents who have survived a disaster, rebuilding familiar places can enable a sense of reclaiming one's "home" and asserting control over uncertainty. Familiar places help a community to "feel" like home; they represent shelter and continuity of social relations. They are a symbolic extension of one's self, home, and work.

We have concluded that depression and other psychological illnesses likely exacerbate the challenges associated with recovery. After all, a person who does not want to get out of bed probably does not care about reclaiming his or her home. Our findings are consistent with those of Bolin (1993), who examined the various impacts of the 1987 Whittier Narrows earthquake in Southern California, including psychological impacts. He found that "victims with higher levels of loss, fewer resources for recovery, and fewer social supports appeared to report higher anxiety and depression levels" (Bolin 1993, p. 83).

One of the most emotionally difficult parts of our research was listening to parents tell us about the disaster effects on their children. Some people reported that they and their children had difficulty sleeping in the months following the disaster, and that the children were particularly hypersensitive to unexpected noises or weather changes for as long as 5 years afterward. In one community devastated by a tornado, a teacher told us, "For the past 3 years or so, whenever the children look up and see low-hanging, dark clouds forming, they stop whatever they are doing and run for home." One woman told us about her grandson who, as an infant, was pulled from his second-story bedroom by a tornado. He suffered brain damage from his fall, and for the entire family, every day is a reminder of the disaster. Several years after a tornado hit a community, we were interviewing a local official and were interrupted, "Please wait," he said. "This is my son on the phone. He is at the community swimming pool and it looks stormy. He wants to come home right now, and I'm going to go pick him up." We waited.

We heard the same thing from parents in earthquake country. "Ever since the earthquake, every time there is even a little shaking or there is a strange noise, the children get wide-eyed and look for security." Another woman told us that her children could not sleep through the night for months and months after the earthquake, and that the lasting effects of the earthquake on the children contributed directly to the end of her marriage. In Tarboro, North Carolina, a not-for-profit group from the community arranged a way for children to talk through their fears and concerns stemming from the flood that inundated their city. The group contracted with an organization from Colquitt, Georgia, called the Swamp Gravy Institute. An art service organization and the consulting and training arm of the Colquitt/Miller County Arts Council, the institute held sessions with children in Tarboro to have them share and role-play their experiences during and after the flood in an attempt to facilitate their ability to cope.

FEMA and the Department of Health and Human Services provide limited funds to support assistance and counseling to individuals experiencing mental health problems caused or aggravated by an extreme natural hazard event or its aftermath once a Presidential Disaster Declaration (also known as a Stafford Act declaration) has been issued. FEMA (2012a) describes the process by which a Presidential Disaster Declaration is made: "Once a disaster has occurred, and the State has declared a state of emergency, the State will evaluate the recovery capabilities of the State and local governments. If it is determined that the damage is beyond their recovery capability, the governor will normally send a request letter to the President, directed through the Regional Director of the appropriate FEMA region. The President then makes the decision whether or not to declare a major disaster or emergency."

The governor of a state impacted by an extreme natural hazard event "may request Disaster Case Management in one of two ways: (1) as part of their Request for a Presidential Disaster Declaration that includes Individual Assistance, or (2) via a written request to the FEMA Federal Coordinating Officer (FCO) within 15 days of the date of declaration" (FEMA 2013a, p. 6). Disaster Case Management (DCM) entails the creation of a Disaster Recovery Plan by a case manager for an individual disaster survivor. The case manager serves as a "single point of contact to facilitate access to a broad range of resources" (FEMA 2013a, p. 6). The purpose of the DCM program is to facilitate a "whole community approach through funding to support voluntary, faith-based and non-profit organizations" (FEMA 2013a, p. 6). The goal is to "ensure holistic services to disaster survivors" (FEMA 2013a, p. 6).

The program provides for up to 24 months of service, with the possibility of a 90-day extension (FEMA 2013a, p. 27). Importantly, not all disasters are issued a Presidential Disaster Declaration, and for those that are not, a local government must look to its state or use its own resources to help people deal with disaster-induced mental health problems. The need for counseling and mental health care, in our experience, may not even be evident until much later than 15 days after a Presidential Disaster Declaration that includes individual assistance and may go well beyond the maximum 24 or even 27 months. We believe that it would be prudent for local government officials, perhaps through their statewide associations, to work with state mental health officials to develop a care policy and funding provisions well before the next disaster, and to recommend continuing evaluation of federal policy regarding time limitations in light of data on psychological and other care needs in the aftermath of a disaster.

Community Social Healing

Community catharsis is necessary. Virtually every community we visited conducted a memorial on the first anniversary of the disaster. Most memorial events include prayers for those killed or injured and for a brighter future. Permanent memorials take different forms: some communities erect a plaque in memory of those who died or simply in memory of the event. Others create a monument, a park, a statue, a facility, or some other brick-and-mortar edifice. Grand Forks, North Dakota, erected signs on vacant lots indicating what used to be there (see Figure 4.6). Gulfport, Mississippi, created a quiet place in a park near the beachfront and a monument containing items found in the rubble from the retreating storm surge. In the Internet age, many communities have established Web sites and blogs commemorating their experiences with photographs and text. The photographs and blog spots established in the wake of Katrina, for example, number in the thousands and catalog the hurricane's devastating effects on Louisiana and Mississippi.

Frankly, we, the authors, do not know much about community healing processes. We are not even certain about what "community healing" means. We are inclined to think that it means creating a collective

FIGURE 4.6   Grand Forks, North Dakota, May 19, 2004—The citizens of Grand Forks created memorials indicating where destroyed structures, such as the Security Trust Company, stood before the Red River flooded the town in 1997. (Photograph by James N. Holly.)

memory of the disaster and, then, finally being able to move on collectively without having the disaster in the forefront of conscious daily thought. We have found that, as years pass, individuals we talked with changed their stories somewhat. The changes appeared to us as though a community storyline had developed among those who experienced the disaster and who talked about it with others many times. The stories we heard 5 and 6 years after the event seemed rehearsed and as though the separate stories we had heard within 1, 2, or 3 years following the disaster were being melded together into a single story that becomes part of community lore. Our experiences with listening to people's stories and observing changes within those stories are consistent with research findings from Schiller and her colleagues (2010). They assert that memories are reshaped and rewritten every time we recall an event, a process they call "reconsolidation." Hence, survivors of extreme natural hazard events will replay their experiences and update them as time goes by and as their understanding of the events changes.

CHAPTER 5

Impacts on Local Government

I haven't been home except to shower and change clothes for more than six weeks. I sleep, eat, and shave here.

Midlevel municipal manager in city hall

National policy is clear: local government is expected to take the lead in community recovery. That seems entirely appropriate because local government is closest to the disaster and is really the only unit of government that can piece together the assistance from the outside into a cohesive and coherent approach to community recovery. Unfortunately, it turns out that local governments are often hard hit themselves by the disaster, making it difficult to reestablish themselves to undertake the often challenging responsibilities for recovery. Local government facilities and local government employees are part of the community, and therefore as likely to be affected by the disaster.

Local governments are brought to their knees more often in small and midsized communities than in large ones. This is mostly because large communities rarely experience extreme natural hazard events that devastate the entire community. It is more often the case that the extreme natural hazard event yields adverse consequences for part of a large community. This matters, since larger communities tend to have more local government staff members, thereby distributing the postdisaster workload. In addition, those same staff members are likely to live throughout the larger community, and so there is again a reduced likelihood that all of them will have had their personal properties affected by the disaster. Thus, the impacts described in this section are more likely to be applicable to smaller and midsized communities than to megacities like Los Angeles.

WORKLOAD AND EMPLOYEE STRESS

Extreme natural hazard events trigger exceptional workloads for public employees. These heavy workloads, which are periods of high stress, begin as the extreme natural hazard event occurs and extend through emergency response, initial recovery efforts, and long-term recovery efforts.

Anyone who has had experience in the construction of local government facilities understands that building, repairing, and restoring water treatment and distribution centers, wastewater collection and treatment centers, schools, hospitals, bridges, and other facilities are time-consuming, complex, and difficult tasks. Even when methods such as design-build contracting are employed, complex projects typically require years to move from preliminary design through permitting, construction design, contracting, site approval, and the like before construction can begin. Imagine a local government having to repair or build multiple facilities all at once following severe damage from an extreme natural hazard event. The workload can be truly staggering, even for the most effective local government, especially when the need is urgent and when other communities are in the same predicament and are competing for available contractors and labor. If the disaster is regional, building supplies and materials, labor, and managerial talent will be in short supply and will increase in costs—often dramatically.

Add to this the homeowners and business owners who want to repair, rebuild, and reinhabit or reopen quickly, and who need permits, inspections, and licenses as well as an enormous amount of information on any number of issues. Then add the massive workload of internal paperwork and accounting needed to apply for state and federal disaster assistance. This workload, which is already overwhelming, is then often compounded by the need to work in offices that have been damaged, or to make do with temporary quarters that are never quite adequate, that do not have needed files available, and that have temporary computer systems in place through which needed information is not easily accessible.

It isn't pretty. It isn't fun. It is hard, demanding, and exhausting work. Most of us have not been trained for working under these stressful conditions, and we have not had much experience dealing with the enhanced variety of challenges. Yet time and again, we saw local officials facing these very challenges and doing their best to serve the citizens who need them.

The workload does not diminish for local government after the immediate need to put out fires, rescue those who were trapped, recover bodies, and provide temporary emergency services to survivors. It just shifts to other arenas. Even before the debris is removed, local government finance, planners, and public works staff face mountains of paperwork that are required to apply and account for federal financial assistance. Project worksheets must be completed, requested data that are not readily available must be found, complex financial arrangements must be made quickly, and plans for housing and other needs of the community must be quickly developed. The pressure stems from (1) having too many tasks to do, (2) in too little time, (3) with insufficient information and resources to gather the needed information, and (4) with competing priorities causing conflict among key stakeholders (e.g., individual taxpayers, business organizations, local politicians). It is a perfect storm of excessive stress, the kind that inevitably leads to burnout (Schaufeli, Leiter, and Maslach 2009). Work overload is a well-documented source of psychological stress and burnout, with their attendant outcomes of increased dissatisfaction, reduced organizational commitment, increased intention to quit, increased absenteeism and turnover, reduced performance, increased deviant behavior, and a variety of physiological ailments (Finney et al. 2013).

At the same time, as noted earlier, the staff is handling increased demands for permits and inspections. Following Katrina, as shown in Figure 5.1, demands for building permits in Biloxi increased fivefold almost overnight, from 1,000 to 1,500 in each fiscal year (FY) between 1999 and 2005 to 5,000 in fiscal year 2005–2006 (City of Biloxi 2008).

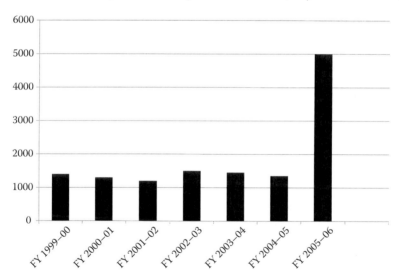

FIGURE 5.1 Building permits issued in Biloxi, Mississippi, from fiscal year 1999–2000 through fiscal year 2005–2006. (From the Comprehensive Annual Financial Report, City of Biloxi, Mississippi, Fiscal Year Ended September 30, 2006.)

Local officials find themselves dealing with two sets of demands at the same time: the routine local government functions that continue and the new set of disaster-related activities. The demands are intense, and they continue for months without letup. After a while, the adrenaline associated with the initial emergency period is gone, but employees must labor on. Dealing with people from state and federal granting agencies is not easy; in the case of large disasters, the federal government brings in temporary help who are not always well informed. We often heard local officials say, "Ask the same question of five of them and get five different answers," or some version of that statement. New staff members rotate into the community, requiring the added load of starting up with a new staff member. Rules and regulations for various federal programs are often complex and change almost continually. Frustration often builds among the local, state, and federal officials, sometimes boiling over into outright conflict.

THE BUILDING DEPARTMENT AS AN EXAMPLE

Initial Inspections

Local officials reported that their building and health departments had massive workloads for months and even years following an extreme natural hazard event. In most communities, the first set of demands grew out of the need for prompt inspections.

In the case of earthquakes, inspections were needed to ascertain whether buildings could be occupied. Green tags were given for structures that were available for immediate occupancy, yellow tags for buildings requiring repair, and red tags for buildings that were unsafe for occupancy. The need for the inspections and inspectors is well known in California, so there are arrangements for large numbers of inspectors from other jurisdictions to supplement the local staff. Even though the need is well understood, organizing people once they arrive is a logistical challenge under the best of conditions. It is even harder when people are exhausted and working away from their usual desks and offices. Building owners, managers, and tenants want into their buildings as soon as possible, and yet inspections are necessary to ensure life safety. Local officials must proceed systematically and with attention to safety first; this can lead to demonstrations of anger and frustration on the part of the people who "just want to get into their building and see what's what."

Flooded areas and places struck by tornadoes and hurricanes usually require building inspections, not only to ensure that the structures are safe for occupancy but also, when warranted, to search for bodies (see Figure 5.2). When the number of structures is large, as was the case

10/08/2005

FIGURE 5.2 New Orleans, Louisiana, October 8, 2005—Flooded homes in New Orleans are marked by search and rescue teams. (Photograph by Lucy A. Arendt.)

in New Orleans, where 80 percent of the city was under water after Hurricane Katrina, the demand invariably exceeds the number of staff members available from the local governments. In those cases, inspectors must be brought in from elsewhere, and they usually need training to become familiar with local code variations and idiosyncrasies.

Contractor Licensing

Most local jurisdictions require that contractors be licensed in that jurisdiction to do business there. After an extreme natural hazard event, the demand for contractors often greatly exceeds the number of contractors licensed in the jurisdiction. Tensions arise when building owners are eager to begin repairs and the contractors they want to use are not licensed in the community. However, local building departments are reluctant to waive the licensing requirement because they want to guard against unreliable contractors who flock to disaster sites hoping for work. Trying to serve the public by tending to its needs both speedily and with its protection in mind is a severe challenge. The strong desire for action can overwhelm people's ability to understand the need for cautious decision making. It is situations like this where people become frustrated by bureaucratic red tape, often neither understanding nor caring that the red tape may save them from being exploited by the contemporary version of a confidence game.

Local jurisdictions rarely work out policies for handling licensing procedures under emergency conditions in advance; they usually wait until after the disaster happens and unhappy people are lined up at city hall complaining to council members and the mayor or chief administrative officer. By this time, there is an almost endless list of other issues to deal with, staff members are already fatigued and tired of sleeping in city hall, and there is no time to work out a policy that has been thought through carefully. A similar problem is faced by hospitals having to quickly credential doctors and other hospital staff under emergency conditions. Even when policies have been worked out in advance, it still takes time to actually go through the processes. Paradoxically, the greater the demand for speed because of the extent of the disaster, the greater will be the challenges meeting the demand in a timely fashion.

Permits and Construction Inspections

In the late aftermath of a disaster, local building officials are almost always besieged by property owners wanting permits to repair and improve their property. In virtually every community we studied, the demand for permits and construction inspections overwhelmed local staff members. At the same time that other local officials are beginning to get some relief from the emergency burdens imposed by the disaster, the workload for building department staff is usually increasing. Turnover rates in building departments seemed particularly high during this period as staff members were either burned out or deemed inadequate by higher-level officials.

A few local governments we studied established priorities for inspections. Facilities that were needed in the community got priority inspections by local and, as applicable, state inspectors. These facilities included restaurants, hotels and motels, and hospitals, health care facilities, and other critical or chronic care facilities. Setting and articulating priorities seem almost essential to facilitate rebuilding and recovery. Helping people to understand where they stand in relation to the list of priorities is one of the many essential components of effective communication in a crisis (Massey and Larsen 2006).

Requests for Exemptions, Waivers, and Variances

In virtually every community we studied, we found that the number of requests for exemptions and waivers from zoning and building regulations increased significantly after an extreme natural hazard event. Perhaps the most common waiver requests involved requirements that were triggered when repairs or improvements exceeded some fixed percentage of the building's value. For example, many jurisdictions require that if repairs or improvements exceed 25 percent (or some other percentage) of the building's value, the entire building must be brought up to current building and specialty code standards. That may entail meeting the requirements of the Americans with Disability Act and making electrical and plumbing changes. Because building owners want to get their buildings back in use quickly, they may pressure local officials to waive those requirements or, more subtly, to estimate damage at less than the specified percentage. Requests may also be made to waive contractor licensing requirements; zoning, setback, and side yard requirements; and virtually any other regulation that stands in the way of a quick repair. Local officials reported being torn between the need to get buildings back into use quickly and the desire not to recreate the structural vulnerabilities that contributed to losses in the first place.

In some places, rebuilding may be substantially delayed while various stakeholders wrangle over proposed changes to land use regulations—changes that often have material implications for homeowners and small-business owners who are compelled to wait until the dust clears, lest they find out that their renovation or rebuilding does not meet some altered code or regulation. An example from New Orleans pertains to the requirements to raise homes above some identified height. As described in a *Washington Post* article:

> "Substantially damaged" houses in the area now must be raised, often three feet above the ground. But the requirements contain enormous loopholes, and there is a huge financial incentive to avoid them. Raising a house (above the floodplain) can cost upwards of $50,000, especially for the modern suburban homes built on concrete slabs in some of the most flooded areas. The federal government offers grants of as much as $30,000 for repairs, but in many cases much more is required. "The vast majority simply do not have the financial resources to rebuild differently," said Greg Rigamer, chief executive of GCR & Associates and a consultant in the rebuilding. Residents could avoid having to comply with the new guidelines by getting permits before the rules were enacted locally—thousands in New Orleans did—or if their houses were determined to be less than 50 percent damaged by Katrina. Many homes, even those that took on 10 feet of water for weeks, have been designated beneath that threshold, including hundreds whose owners appealed larger initial damage assessments.

> **Whoriskey 2007**

Other common requests for variances come from homeowners seeking extensions to the length of time they can keep their temporary homes parked on their lots. It is common for the vehicles to remain on home-owner lots for years, particularly when the homeowner was uninsured or underinsured, or when the demand for contractors far exceeded the supply. Local officials have to make difficult decisions with the homeowner on one side and vocal, unhappy neighbors on the other. Trailers in front of homes, diesel generators running loudly at all hours—this is typically not what neighbors have in mind when they think about their neighborhood returning to normal. The last FEMA trailer ("temporary housing unit") associated with Hurricane Katrina finally left New Orleans on February 12, 2012—approximately 6 1/2 years after Hurricane Katrina devastated the city (Burdeau 2012).

UNMET EXPECTATIONS AND NEW ROLES

In most cases, elected officials and department heads are typically just as inexperienced in disaster management as are lower-level local government employees. Lack of experience necessitates on-the-job learning, however difficult that may be. Role conflicts are likely to arise as department heads feel that others are infringing upon their turf. Accustomed to working in "silo" environments to administer their programs, these managers often find themselves being asked to work cooperatively with others to solve complex problems. Doing so requires learning how to communicate with and appreciate the skills of and the values held by different departments. This is no easy task in good times; it is even more difficult under pressure.

Sometimes decision makers may feel that progress is not being made quickly enough or that the outcomes of actions are not entirely satisfactory. Elected officials, feeling pressure from constituents, may have unreasonable expectations about the pace of recovery and about what local government staff is able to do about it. The perceived need for speed may overwhelm the actual need for critical thinking and decision making. Local government staff will need to find ways to "better manage community-level decision making" (Rubin et al. 1985, p. 35) in order to expedite the speed and quality of community recovery.

To meet the public's demand for near-immediate action, elected officials may make fundamental attribution errors (Buchanan 2011), assuming that others are personally responsible for any mistakes that are made, discounting the role played by external factors such as other agencies' requirements, ready access to needed data, and even simple misfortune. They may also fall prey to self-serving bias, accepting responsibility for their own successes while attempting to deflect blame for their own failures. However, neither pointing fingers nor taking credit for early successes helps the process of recovery. Rather, each response focuses attention away from needed problem solving.

CONFLICTING DEMANDS BETWEEN HOME AND WORK

In addition to the increased workload and the new problems that emerge daily, many public employees must confront the personal, inner conflict between the need to help strangers and the pressure to help their own families at home. These employees are expected to remain at their posts as needed during emergencies. Some—emergency managers, sworn public safety officers, utility workers, medical personnel, and chief executives—know that they will be required to stay and understand what is expected of them. Others—for example, buildings and grounds staff, building officials, financial personnel—are less likely to expect to remain at work but may find themselves called upon to stay or to report for duty as the storm winds up or winds down.

Yet like the citizens they serve, these employees are also very likely to have homes that have been damaged or destroyed and families who have most likely been adversely affected. Depending on whether there was any warning of the extreme natural hazard event, emergency and relief workers may not have had an opportunity to communicate with their family members to learn where they are, whether they are prepared, and what they might need. For employees who have not consciously signed on for such duty, it is difficult to literally work, eat, and sleep at city hall for days or weeks, and to come home, if indeed there is a home, for only a change of clothing and a quick hello and good-bye. Nor is it easy for their families.

In virtually every city we visited and studied, public employees stayed at the job, eating and sleeping at their workplace for extended periods of time while their families and their homes had to wait until everyone else was taken care of. They did so without thanks from the community, and often without extra pay or almost always without bonuses. In New Orleans, there is evidence that some public employees left their duty stations without authorization. That behavior by public officials is reprehensible, but it is also extraordinarily rare in most jurisdictions (Kushma 2007). Most public officials—and their families—sacrifice beyond the basic call of duty in the event of a disaster.

CONSEQUENCES OF EMPLOYEE STRESS

In many of the cities we studied, we were told, "Oh, he (she) doesn't work here anymore. Left a couple of weeks ago." Local government employee turnover in the 2 or 3 years following an extreme natural hazard event was significantly higher than we had originally expected. City managers, finance officers, and building officials seem to be particularly vulnerable. The pressure that local elected officials experience regarding the pace of recovery and the problems that are still unsolved is often passed on to government employees, who are doing their best against sometimes almost insurmountable obstacles. Frustration mounts and greener fields beckon. The appeal of a new job in a new city can be especially powerful for those employees whose homes have been damaged or destroyed and whose families have had to relocate. Once children are enrolled in new school districts, it becomes increasingly difficult to say no to job prospects in a new place.

Often local government employee performance declines in the face of extreme and prolonged stress, especially if employees have minimal experience dealing with a given set of stressors and their affective commitment is low. Individuals who have experience dealing with disasters, especially experience that has been generally positive, will often perform well despite high levels of experienced stress. Likewise, individuals who have a high degree of affective commitment to their organizations and communities, such that what ties them to their organization and community is a strong and emotionally based belief in the organization's and community's values, will often perform well despite debilitating levels of stress. Our observations on stress, experience with stressors, and performance for local government employees in the wake of a disaster mirror findings in other industries where stress is high. For example, Hunter and Thatcher (2007) found that the relationship between stress and performance was positive for bank employees with higher levels of affective commitment and higher levels of experience. Similarly, Peisah and her colleagues (2009) found that older doctors with more experience had significantly less stress and burnout than their younger peers. Finally, Finney and her colleagues (2013) concluded that correctional officers "experience higher rates of job stress and burnout that stem from organizational stressors, leading to negative outcomes for not only the correctional officers but the organization as well" (p. 1).

As individuals acquire more experience with a given set of stressors—in this case, extreme natural hazard events—they develop coping mechanisms that enable them to perceive the stress as manageable, thereby allowing them to stay focused on performing their responsibilities. The more they are able to stay focused on their tasks, and not on their stress, the higher their performance tends to be. It should be noted that even under high levels of stress, government employees typically perform at admirably high levels in the wake of disaster.

Employees faced with the same, seemingly intractable problems day after day can experience burnout and look for an escape. Sometimes employees are fired, but many more leave their job for a place where they think people will appreciate their work and where the stress will be more manageable. Simply put, the skills used to perform local government jobs transfer to other fields of employment, many of which do not require people to deal with hordes of dissatisfied community members or constant visible reminders of their own devastated lives.

We think another possible reason for high turnover is that disasters sometimes generate a high demand for scapegoats, and there is only a limited supply of targets. Elected officials are often better at finding fault than they are at finding solutions, so it is far better to blame federal, state, and local government workers for not meeting expectations than it is to blame the voting public—or themselves, for that matter—for voting down proposals to spend money that would have been used to mitigate the natural hazard event before it occurred.

DIMINISHED REVENUE BASE

Along with its facilities and infrastructure, a local government's revenue base is often devastated by an extreme natural hazard event. A local government is, of course, deeply concerned about developing and maintaining a tax base to generate the revenue that enables it to do what needs to be done. Decades ago, local governments generally depended primarily on revenues from the ad valorem ("according to the value") property tax base. Although today they have a more diversified stream of income on which to rely, much of that stream may be reduced or eliminated, at least for a time, following an extreme natural hazard event. The impacts that extreme natural hazard events may have on various local government revenue sources often surprise people, though not in a good way. Since local government taxation practices vary widely among the states, our discussion is kept at the general level except for specific illustrations.

Revenue Base as a Combination of Sources

It is not so much that one element of the tax base is diminished. It is that the extreme natural hazard event has the potential to diminish most of the local government's sources of revenue. The individual tax bases are linked to one another. Damaged real property is likely to lead to lower revenues from property taxes, sales taxes, tourism, and user fees.

For example, Biloxi's local government relies heavily on three sources of revenue: property, sales, and gaming taxes. The gaming taxes come from a number of casinos located in the city. The City of Biloxi experienced a significant decline in property tax revenue in FY 2006 and FY 2007 following Hurricanes Katrina and Rita in 2005, as shown in Figure 5.3. By FY 2009, property tax revenues had rebounded to pre-event levels. Sales tax revenues remained relatively constant through the period. Since some of the city's casinos were heavily damaged by

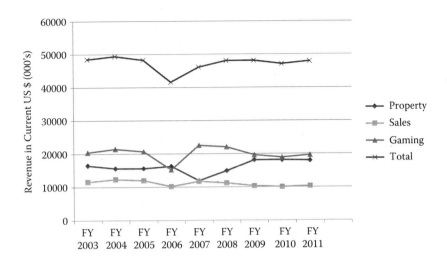

FIGURE 5.3 City of Biloxi, Mississippi, municipal revenues from property tax (ad valorem tax), sales tax, and gaming by fiscal year, 2003–2011. (From the City of Biloxi, Comprehensive Annual Financial Reports, 2003–2011.)

Hurricanes Katrina and Rita, revenue from gaming declined substantially in the following year, but rebounded quickly and, then, following national trends, declined gradually through FY 2010. By FY 2011, total revenues from the three revenue sources approximated that of pre-event levels.

In contrast, the City of Gulfport's revenue from three sources actually rose in the year following Katrina (FY 2006) because its retail center received little damage from the hurricane and served the needs of people replacing goods and repairing structures. Property tax and gaming revenue fell, as in other communities with extensive damage, property tax revenues in 2012 almost reached pre-Katrina levels, and sales tax revenues declined to levels one might project had the hurricane damage not occurred. Figure 5.4 tells the tale.

Sometimes the drive for enhancing local government revenue conflicts with other important community goals. In Escambia County (Pensacola), Florida, for example, the need for revenue for basic operations sometimes conflicts with the desire to make the community safer against extreme natural hazard events. The county is relatively poor except for areas near the shore: it owns much of Santa Rosa Island and its beautiful white sand beach on the Gulf of Mexico. A large proportion of the island is within the federally owned Gulf Islands National Seashore; however, Escambia County owns Pensacola Beach, which

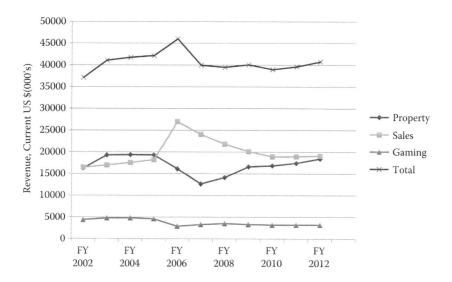

FIGURE 5.4 City of Gulfport, Mississippi, municipal revenue from property tax (ad valorem tax), sales tax, and gaming by fiscal year, 2002–2012. (From the City of Gulfport, Comprehensive Annual Financial Reports, 2002–2012.)

comprises much of the land outside the park that is available for development, and it leases that land to people and corporations that build on it. Because it is legally prohibited from levying taxes on real property located on Pensacola Beach, the county depends on head, bed, and sales taxes collected there to shore up its revenue needs. Its revenue stream would benefit greatly if the older single-family homes and rental units destroyed by recent hurricanes were replaced by larger hotels and resorts, and despite the reality of occasional devastating hurricanes, developers want to increase density along the white sand beaches. Thus, we expect that Pensacola Beach will be much more densely developed over the next few years than it was before the string of hurricanes that leveled so much of it, because of the need for local government revenue and the desires of profit-minded developers.

Ad Valorem Property Tax

Local governments typically levy ad valorem property taxes on real property, personal property, and business personal property. Real property refers to land, including not only the face of the Earth but everything of a permanent nature over or under it, such as structures, minerals, and timber. When Hurricane Andrew struck Homestead in August 1992, the city and the surrounding area suffered massive property damage. Direct damage from the winds and water was estimated at $25 billion.

Andrew's impact on southern Dade County, Florida, was extreme from the Kendall district southward through Homestead and Florida City, to near Key Largo. Andrew reportedly destroyed 25,524 homes and damaged 101,241 others. The Dade County Grand Jury reported that 90 percent of all mobile homes in south Dade County were destroyed. In Homestead, more than 99 percent (1,167 of 1,176) of all mobile homes were destroyed. The *Miami Herald* reported $0.5 billion in losses to boats in southeast Florida (Rappaport 1993).

Not all extreme natural hazard events wreak damage that is so extensive, but many result in damage to a major proportion of the community. In 1998, a tornado damaged or destroyed 44 percent of the buildings in St. Peter, Minnesota, including every building on the campus of Gustavus Adolphus College. In Montezuma, Georgia, the entire central business district was flooded for days. When that much damage is done to real property in a community, it will undoubtedly be reflected in the assessed valuation of real property in the local jurisdiction. Whereas the impact on the property is immediate, the impact on local government tax revenue may not be. Most jurisdictions base their ad valorem real property tax for the current year on the value of the property assessed the previous January. Thus, there is essentially a 1-year lag between when the value of a property is assessed, when the tax is levied, and when the taxes are due. That means that tax collections in the first year following the disaster usually do not reflect the loss to the tax base, particularly if the taxes have been accumulated in escrow by mortgage holders. If the taxes have not been held in escrow, hard-hit property owners may be unable to make the tax payment. After several years of nonpayment, the municipal or county jurisdiction will be able to foreclose on the property, but that may not be desirable in the quest for recovery.

Local governments take various approaches to valuing property following an extreme natural hazard event. Communities that have been flooded may be a little slow to reassess property where structures have not been washed away or destroyed, so assessed property values remain static until repairs are completed. In jurisdictions where the real property has burned to the ground, blown away, or collapsed from earth movement, property values are typically adjusted more quickly. Local tax boards of appeal are inundated with complaints if they do not make tax adjustments for properties that are no longer there as of the January assessment date.

There are a few anomalies. In some Florida Gulf Coast communities, prices for shore side and near-shore property have been known to increase rapidly immediately after devastating hurricanes. By demolishing and blowing away older, smaller buildings and other low-density uses, the hurricanes effectively cleared the way for larger and more expensive structures, including condominium projects and hotels. In one location we found small residential lots along the shore where only the concrete slab remained; these lots were for sale with some having sales prices listed at $2.5 million.

Personal property consists of such things as furniture, fixtures, plant equipment, office equipment, machinery, boats, aircraft, mobile homes, and recreational vehicles. A key characteristic of personal property is that it can be moved without damage to either itself or the real estate to which it is attached. Many states and local governments impose ad valorem taxes on personal property, whether it is owned by individuals or businesses. If you traveled the Gulf Coast after Hurricane Katrina, you would have seen how the personal property tax base fared: boats were found upside down 2 miles from the nearest water, recreational vehicles were crushed and some had been dragged out to sea, and flooded automobiles were abandoned everywhere (see Figure 5.5). A massive proportion of the personal property tax base of state and local governments had been destroyed. The effects of the loss of the real and personal property tax bases can have a devastating effect on community revenue for years as businesses and individuals work to repair, rebuild, or replace what was damaged.

FIGURE 5.5   Biloxi, Mississippi, September 3, 2005—Damage and destruction to houses and boats. (Courtesy of FEMA/Mark Wolfe.)

(Usually) Centrally Collected and (Usually) Locally Shared Taxes

State governments routinely collect some taxes and distribute them to local governments; collection and distribution are based either on where the revenues were generated or based on a formula intended to promote income equity among jurisdictions. Sometimes local governments levy income taxes, but they can rarely collect them; sometimes they are able to enact an "add-on" to a state sales tax and get that money transferred back to them. Some kinds of business personal property are taxed by the state, and the funds are allocated among the local governments in approximation to the amount of business the enterprise does within the local jurisdiction. Revenues from legalized gambling casinos and activities are often garnered by the state and allocated among jurisdictions in one or another way. Some enterprising local governments tax gambling in their communities to generate revenue that is, they hope, mostly from tourists.

State school aid comes from centrally collected and locally shared tax revenues. It is usually allocated based on the school census that each U.S. school district conducts at some time early in the fall semester, as specified by each state. School districts that are hit by disasters and lose a substantial number of students, even if only temporarily, can find themselves in desperate financial straits unless the state adjusts the formula to hold them harmless for some period. Similarly, if state aid to a general-purpose local government is formula based, the local jurisdiction may find itself in serious jeopardy financially.

To the extent that sales taxes are returned to communities that generate them, the damage caused by an extreme natural hazard event can have a devastating effect on retail sales within a community for an extended period. Luxury items that generate higher sales tax tend to be relegated to the bottom of individuals' shopping lists after a disaster, at least until they have had the opportunity to replenish their basic supplies (e.g., food, clothing, home goods). Even when consumers continue to spend in the jurisdiction, they are likely to shift a greater proportion of their expenditures to items that may be excluded in their state from sales taxes (e.g., food or clothing).

Tourist Taxes

Tourist taxes consist of levies on the kinds of things that tourists need when they visit a community: rooms, restaurant meals, rental cars, and almost everything else that can be conceivably taxed in an attempt to "export" revenue generation to nonresidents.

But the tourists stop coming when the beach is littered with debris left by the hurricane, when the hotels and motels are destroyed, and

FIGURE 5.6   Biloxi, Mississippi, May 15, 2006—Destroyed by Hurricane Katrina's storm surge, the Treasure Bay Casino and Hotel awaits restoration. (Photograph by James N. Holly.)

when the casinos are gone (see Figure 5.6). In short, they stop coming when the things that would attract them are no longer there. For communities that rely heavily on tourism as a primary economic driver, getting the tourist-attracting amenities back in place and advertised is critical to their economic well-being and to the financing of local government. When tourists are unable to stay at what may have been a "favorite" recreational destination, they will find new places to take their families and spend their money. Once established at their new favorite getaway, it may be almost impossible to lure them back to where they used to vacation.

User Fees and Utility Charges

User fees include fees for local government utilities; charges for necessary and optional services; charges for the use of government-owned facilities, such as community centers and park shelters; fees for recreation activities; and fees for individuals and businesses for licenses and permits. Such fees have become a major source of income for local governments. In 2004, the Wisconsin Legislative Audit Bureau conducted an extensive analysis of user fees by Wisconsin local governments; it reported that, collectively, local governments in that state charge more than 500 separate user fees and that revenue from those fees in 2001 totaled 21.1 percent of all local government revenue in Wisconsin (Joint Legislative Audit Bureau 2004).

As previously reported, Homestead, Florida, operates its own electric utility, generating, distributing, and selling electricity. When it is economically advantageous to do so, the utility buys power. Prior to Hurricane Andrew, the municipal electrical utility was a major source of revenue for the municipality, but the hurricane winds snapped off virtually every power pole in the city. The utility had employed far too few people to replace the poles and to quickly rewire virtually the entire city. External help was essential, but the task was still enormous. During repairs and the rebuilding of the city—a time when the city desperately needed revenue—revenues from the utility dropped significantly because it was a long time before it was able to deliver electric power again to those buildings that were still standing.

EXPENSES AND SHORTAGES

We need the employees, but we had to lay them off. No money.

—Local government official in a devastated community

A chief executive told us it was necessary to lay off a significant number of county workers in the wake of the disaster, just as those workers were needed the most to deal with enormous, recovery-related workloads. Expenses were soaring, revenues were plummeting, and the county simply could not meet the payroll. This county suffered more than most from skyrocketing expenses and major revenue shortfalls, but essentially every jurisdiction we studied had a similar story.

Expenses Rise Rapidly

Local government must be able to function to help the community recover. The services they provide must be restored and operating at least at some temporarily acceptable level of service and reliability. Schools and government-owned hospitals must be returned to operating condition, staffed, and equipped to carry on, along with city hall and critical facilities. Streets and highways must be cleared and reopened; bridges may need to be repaired or replaced. Even if only a portion of the community were damaged, the undamaged areas would still require the services they have come to expect from local government, even while the damaged sectors require extraordinary efforts.

Staffing demands for local governments typically increase during the aftermath of a disaster: employees must perform the regular, routine array of duties to undamaged parts of the community at the same time that they are struggling to put the machinery of local government back together and dealing with an increased demand from citizens for services. Homeowners and business owners need permits and building inspections; contractors from outside the city want to be licensed to work in the jurisdiction. All of this extra work costs money for which the local government, most likely, did not budget. Besides overtime pay and temporary employees to meet the extra workload, the extra costs show up as rental costs for temporary working space and equipment lost in the event, material for repairs and reconstruction, and even supplies that may have been lost. The cost of materials and supplies tends to increase after a disaster, as higher demand coupled with reduced supply leads to higher prices. And all these disaster-related expenses must be accounted for.

Some expenses, such as those for normal government operations, are not reimbursed by the federal government, except up to about $5,000. The local jurisdiction can apply for loans to cover those expenses, but the federal government expects to get that money back. If revenue shortfalls are severe for an extended period, the loans are difficult to repay. This is especially a problem for jurisdictions with large numbers of lower-income people, high service demands, and inadequate tax bases.

Some expenses, such as clearing debris from roads designated as state highways, will most likely be paid for by the state government unless the state undertakes those activities itself. Sometimes other local governments, operating under a mutual assistance pact or simply good will, may provide services at little or no immediate cost to the local government in which the disaster occurred. Those governments can invoice FEMA for their costs, as long as the helping jurisdiction has appropriately accounted for those costs.

Even when a local government expects federal reimbursement for disaster-related costs, the service must be paid for before reimbursement can be sought. Thus, local governments invariably find themselves facing a bridge financing problem. Somehow, they have to be able to carry themselves financially until the earmarked check comes in from Washington. And that could take a long time, especially when the money flows through the state government and not directly from the federal government into the local jurisdiction's accounts.

Meeting the Immediate Need for Cash

Most local governments do not maintain large balances in their checking accounts. Funds are invested and drawn upon as needed through the fiscal year. Local government finance officers are responsible for ensuring that funds are available for immediate needs, such as payroll and regular expenses, but also for managing cash flow to ensure that as little money as possible sits idle. Thus, even under the best of circumstances, local government officials have to hustle to free up funds to meet immediate needs in the wake of a disaster. Those funds may be obtained through reserves, insurance, loans, and institutional arrangements within states. With scrutiny, regulation, and interest in cash flow leading to lower reserve levels, many local governments can find themselves in near-impossible or impossible financial straits after a disaster.

Reserves, Insurance, and Loans

Some local governments are fortunate to have significant reserves, although, as mentioned, local governments are often not allowed to set aside significant amounts of money "just in case." Reserve funds are usually earmarked for some specific purpose, such as debt repayment, facilities improvement and replacement, and accrued employee sick leave and vacation. Following disasters, communities with reserves often borrow from those reserves to finance operations and help rebuild necessary facilities. That is, the local jurisdiction borrows from itself, with the expectation that either the loan will be repaid from federal grants (for those expenditures that are eligible for federal reimbursement) or over time as the revenue situation improves. The laws on what can be done with reserves vary from state to state, so local officials should determine what their state allows.

We encountered a few local governments that actually had disaster insurance. Disaster insurance is not always available from commercial sources—at least not at a price that local governments are willing to pay. Consequently, local governments that are insured are usually insured by "pool" policies that are created by a group of local governments themselves. Local governments contribute to the pool, and they draw from the pool when they have losses. Stuart, Florida, for example, was able to pay for a substantial part of its hurricane losses with proceeds from its pool insurance.

"Biloxi hit the jackpot when 2 months before Katrina the city spent $92,000 to purchase $10 million worth of business interruption insurance to cover lost casino revenues" (Gillette 2006, para. 1). Biloxi's mayor, A. J. Holloway, is said to have taken out a business interruption insurance policy on the city's casinos because the casinos provided, directly and indirectly, a major share of Biloxi's revenue. The city made only one or two premium payments before Katrina's storm surge struck, putting the casinos out of business for some time. As of July 2006, the city had collected $7.5 million from the insurer, which helped considerably in covering costs incurred from the storm surge and flooding.

Communities sometimes find themselves in the market for commercial loans immediately after the disaster and during the lingering aftermath. Our interviews suggest that, most often, local jurisdictions deal with banks or credit unions that have a serious stake in the community in that the financial institutions either are locally owned or have a long history of community involvement. It is typically to the advantage of such institutions to have the community and the local economy recover quickly. We saw at least one instance in which a local bank worked with the local government for more than a decade until that government regained its financial footing.

The federal government is also a source for operating loans. The Department of Homeland Security, through FEMA, will provide a community with a loan through its Community Disaster Loan Program (FEMA 2013b). Under extraordinary circumstances, these loans may be forgiven. The big problem for local government is that the financial emergency usually exceed 25 percent of the local government's operating budget and is almost always in excess of $5 million. It would be prudent, then, for local officials not to count on federal loans for much help in getting through the financial crisis.

Institutional Arrangements within States

Florida pioneered an approach to help local governments with their revenue needs following disasters. After Hurricane Andrew, the state helped jurisdictions in Dade County recover some of the sales taxes they would have received had it not been for the hurricane (Florida Legislature 1993, p. 11). Rebuilding efforts in south Dade County generated significant sales outside the damaged area, where sales tax revenues rose in excess of what they would have been had the hurricane not occurred. For 3 years, the state sent those excess sales tax revenues to stricken local governments in Dade County. It was a good start except that, from the standpoint of Homestead, Florida City, and other south Dade jurisdictions, 3 years was not enough time for them to recover to the point where they were able to generate sufficient revenue to operate at an acceptable level. Too often, people greatly underestimate the time needed to achieve even a minimum level of recovery.

Nonetheless, it seems entirely reasonable for local jurisdictions to prevail on governors and legislators to create programs in which unexpected revenue gains from disasters are used to provide assistance to the disaster-hit localities. Similarly, if neighboring communities, such as in Biloxi or in Baton Rouge, are burdened by persons displaced by the event, they, too, should receive a share of the unexpected revenue gains to help offset their increased costs.

A second way that states can help municipalities is to enact "hold harmless" laws for other centrally collected, locally shared revenues, particularly when the distribution of those revenues is formula driven. In just a few states, for example, school districts that suffer large and immediate reductions in school enrollment after a disaster are protected from rapid reductions in state aid for schools. The laws vary, but the general idea is that the state, in allocating aid, uses the previous year's enrollment figures, thereby providing assistance to a district that has been affected by the disaster. If the population loss is more or less permanent, annual reductions in assistance are phased in gradually until the district has balanced its resources (i.e., schools, teachers, staff) with its enrollment.

FUNDING FOR LONG-TERM RECOVERY

Federal Contributions and Grants

In September 2009, a Long-Term Disaster Recovery Working Group was established by the U.S. Department of Homeland Security and the U.S. Department of Housing and Urban Development at the behest of President Barack Obama. The Working Group's overall charge was to develop operational guidance for recovery organizations. This led to the creation of the National Disaster Recovery Framework (NDRF), "a guide to promote effective recovery, particularly for those incidents that are large-scale or catastrophic" (FEMA 2011a, p. 1). The NDRF "also focuses on how best to restore, redevelop and revitalize the health, social, economic, natural and environmental fabric of the community and build a more resilient Nation" (FEMA 2011a, p. 1). Clearly, the challenges faced by the United States in the wake of Hurricane Katrina prompted a high level of collective introspection by the individuals serving in the Department of Homeland Security, the Federal Emergency Management Agency, and the U.S. Department of Housing and Urban Development. Perhaps the most significant revelation of the post-Hurricane Katrina attempts at community recovery was that, despite the substantial array of federal, state, and local programs and services available to individuals and communities, better coordination between and among agencies, departments, divisions, and so on was needed if communities were to recover as quickly and as effectively as possible.

The National Disaster Recovery Framework shares a number of key words that indicate the enhanced understanding of the need for coordination. Phrases like, "scalable, flexible and adaptable coordinating structures" and "best practices" abound throughout the document (FEMA 2011a). The framework's focus is alignment of key roles and responsibilities; it is not intended to create or require additional layers of bureaucracy that might inhibit rather than enable community recovery. It identifies nine Recovery Core Principles: (1) Individual and Family Empowerment, (2) Leadership and Local Primacy, (3) Pre-Disaster Recovery Planning, (4) Partnerships and Inclusiveness, (5) Public Information, (6) Unity of Effort, (7) Timeliness and Flexibility, (8) Resilience and Sustainability, and (9) Psychological and Emotional Recovery (FEMA 2011a). The framework gives communities dealing with the aftermath of disasters a means for organizing their recovery efforts. The importance of this assistance cannot be emphasized enough, as the reality for many communities dealing with large-scale or catastrophic disasters is that these events are low-probability events with which relatively few community members may have any experience. The learning curve is often incredibly steep for these communities; the National Disaster Recovery Framework can help expedite and integrate the community learning.

Despite the technical assistance provided by FEMA, it is not responsible for fully financing a community's long-term recovery. Under the Stafford Act of 1988 (the amended Federal Disaster Relief Act of 1974), it is responsible for providing funds sufficient to rebuild local government facilities to where they were before the event. Although we have yet to see an instance in which the rebuilt facilities are not far superior to those that were destroyed, FEMA nevertheless has no mandate to facilitate the long-term recovery of the community *system*, including its economic base. Fortunately, the Department of Housing and Urban Development (HUD), the Economic Development Administration (EDA) of the Commerce Department, and the Farm Service Agency (FSA) of the U.S. Department of Agriculture (USDA) do have responsibilities for long-term community recovery, and all three provide significant amounts of funds for approved projects intended to stimulate local recovery.

The municipalities that fared best in receiving financial grants from federal agencies like FEMA, HUD, EDA, and the USDA shared several important characteristics. First, almost all of them hired, contracted with, or designated a very bright, aggressive person or persons to learn all that was needed to know about available federal programs and eligibility requirements. Second, they ensured that they were well versed in program requirements and regulations. Third, their local officials were adept at quickly drawing up sensible, readable project proposals to the various granting agencies. Fourth, each successful jurisdiction had staff designated to do little other than work on grant applications and administration, a job that was considered to be just as critical as bringing the water purification and distribution system back on line. Fifth, the jurisdictions did not blame the federal government or individual federal officials for their problems and for seemingly unnecessary red tape; instead, they worked with individual federal officials to provide the required information quickly and accurately. If they found a particular official hard to work with or unreasonably demanding, they did what was required anyway, at least until that official was replaced. Finally, successful local governments had sophisticated accounting systems in place that enabled them to track every dollar spent—to show work orders, bid sheets, time cards, and all other documentation required by the federal government to ensure reimbursement. Moreover, their records were sufficient to accommodate the needs of federal auditors who invariably arrived years later: municipalities told us of project files that were not audited until up to 7 years after the project and of files not closed until almost 10 years later.

Local governments without high-quality accounting systems and staff found themselves in trouble at almost every turn. Some cities were forced to return large amounts of grant money given to them because they failed to comply with the regulations. The time required to fend off the auditors was, we estimate, much more than the time required to do it right the first time.

Technical Assistance

Technical assistance is important to augment local talent and specific knowledge about methods and sources of additional financial assistance. Local governments are individually responsible for developing the strategies and action plans that will help their communities work toward recovery, but several states provide exemplary technical assistance to local communities in that effort. Florida, which did very little to assist local governments in the wake of Hurricane Andrew, has since become the national leader in providing technical and financial assistance to local governments in communities that experience disasters. Minnesota and Georgia also provide superior assistance to communities that ask for help in developing and implementing recovery strategies.

Rebuilding the Tax Base

Of course, long-term recovery of both the community and the local governments serving the community requires either rebuilding or developing anew a base of wealth, income, and business activity that is adequate to provide the needed revenue for collective action. Unless that is accomplished, when the federal aid ends, the community and the local government will wither. The interdependent nature of a community's tax base with its infrastructure, school system, health care system, and more cannot be overstated. Attracting high-quality business and good paying jobs to any community depends on many community characteristics, not the least of which is a collective belief that the community is an ongoing concern, that people intend to stay and make the community vibrant, and that the decision to locate in a given community will yield a return on investment better than a decision to locate elsewhere.

CHAPTER 6

Community Disaster Recovery
Definition, Processes, and Obstacles

WHAT CONSTITUTES COMMUNITY RECOVERY?

We have employed theoretical constructs from general systems and self-organizing systems theory in an attempt to understand how communities change through time, what happens when a community system experiences a major disturbance, and how a disaster unfolds. Based on field research, we have described the real problems that arise for real people in real places. Here, we focus on what constitutes community disaster recovery.

Not all communities recover from natural disasters. On rare occasions, the community simply ceases to exist following the extreme natural hazard event. The death of a community comes suddenly when the consequences of the natural hazard event are so extensive and intensive that, as in the case of Pompeii and Herculaneum, the community is destroyed and the site is abandoned. A more drawn out community death spiral may develop in instances when the natural disaster is sufficiently damaging as to exacerbate adverse preevent conditions such that the community system becomes unraveled and entropic; in the end, it simply fails to effectively function or to reestablish its ability to function and therefore gradually sinks into oblivion.

A Few Important Distinctions

One should not confuse community recovery with recovery at each of the several levels of recovery that might occur throughout the community. At the individual level, those who were injured physically or psychologically or who lost all or most of their possessions will be working at their own

FIGURE 6.1   Chalmette, Louisiana, March 11, 2007—The family whose home once sat on this slab no longer plans to live here. (Photograph by Lucy A. Arendt.)

recovery. Some will succeed relatively quickly, others will achieve recovery only many years after the disaster, and still others will fall short of success (see Figure 6.1). Families will typically experience or share the losses that individual relatives, friends, and neighbors suffered. Depending on the nature and extent of their injuries and losses, some will recover and, for the most part, put the disaster behind them, at least the physical manifestations thereof. Others will not. Until they die, they will measure their lives in terms of "before it happened" and "after it happened."

Some businesses will fail, sometimes dragging their owners' personal fortunes down with them. Some owners, managers, and employees will find new opportunities and flourish. It is important to remember that, frankly, "community recovery" does not require that the supermarket you own reopens, operates profitably, and that you recover your losses. What really matters for community recovery is that the community contains the minimum number of functioning supermarkets needed to support the

Chalmette is the parish seat of St. Bernard Parish, adjacent to Orleans Parish in Louisiana. The pre-Hurricane Katrina population of Chalmette was 31,910 at the 2000 census. The 2010 census reported that Chalmette had 16,751 people, a decline of 48 percent from 2000 and 2010. The number of housing units declined 38 percent from 12,896 in 2000 to 7,947 in 2010.

postdisaster community population. The fact that it is not your super-market may have implications for reestablishing linkages and for personal recovery, but that, as it turns out, is of little concern in terms of community recovery, pretty much regardless of your own personal tragedy. While the overall community as an open system achieves synergy through its parts (individuals, individual entities, etc.) it appears that the parts can change—as long as they perform required functions in appropriate sequences.

Individuals understand this phenomenon, even as it may pain them to say so. Like organizations, communities survive beyond the "turnover" of some individuals as they "recruit" new individuals, families, and organizations. New individuals, families, and organizations may have many characteristics in common with those who have left, or they may not. New neighbors replace the old, and new patterns of interaction—hopefully functional—replace what had been. Assuming that the community has a critical mass of individuals, families, and organizations to sustain it, it will go forward, even with an entirely new "cast" of characters. New people may bring fresh ideas; these ideas will be incorporated into the existing community fabric or they will alter it. In at least some cases, fresh ideas will enable a community to perform more effectively than it had in the past; in other cases, fresh ideas may lead to retrenchment or collapse.

In addition to not focusing on the fate of particular individuals or organizations, one should not confuse community recovery with reestablishing precisely what the community was prior to the extreme natural hazard event. Depending on the extent of initial and cascading consequences, what remains might only be fragments of the predisaster community. By that, we mean that many of the preevent residents and businesses may be gone, the demographics might be quite different, the economy may have changed, and familiar landmarks may have disappeared. Along with those changes, relationships among the resident population and organizations and between them and the outside world may have changed. The community that develops after the disaster may be substantially different from the one that existed before the event. It may be so different from the preevent community that it constitutes what may be best described as a different community on the site of the original community.

Depending on the extent of the consequences, new relationships must be forged and new community processes developed. These, we argue, will be formed as a primarily self-organizing process. That said, help from outside the community can enable and catalyze its recovery.

The Post-Katrina Emergency Management Reform Act of 2006 stipulated major changes to the Federal Emergency Management Agency (FEMA) within the Department of Homeland Security. The overarching goal of these changes was to improve FEMA's preparedness for and response to catastrophic disasters. The National Disaster Recovery

Framework (FEMA 2011a) was one result of the Post-Katrina Emergency Management Reform Act. As mentioned previously, the National Disaster Recovery Framework (NDRF) was a collaborative effort by the Department of Homeland Security/FEMA and U.S. Department of Housing and Urban Development. Without question, the development of the NDRF represented a major paradigm change and policy shift, in that it explicitly recognized the complexity of community recovery.

The National Disaster Recovery Framework is not a recipe for recovery; it is a "planning and capacity building recovery support function" (FEMA 2011b, p. 3). In addition to recognizing that community recovery is complex, the NDRF also recognizes that coordination is essential to facilitating positive outcomes. This is revealed in the NDRF's description of the "Outcomes for the Economy Recovery Support Function." It reads:

> Through a coordinated effort that draws from resources of Federal departments, agencies and services, the Community Planning and Capacity Building RSF (Recovery Support Function) provides expertise to ensure:
>
> - Enhanced interagency coordination of resources, requirements and support for building community capacity and community recovery planning.
> - Increased community self-reliance and adaptability.
> - Hazard mitigation and risk reduction opportunities have been integrated into all major decisions and reinvestments during the recovery process.
> - An improved planning process that ensures more effective and efficient use of Federal, State, nongovernmental and private sector funds.
> - Communities are able to shorten the timeline and improve specific recovery outcomes through more effective decision making and management.
> - Integration of socioeconomic, demographic, risk assessment, vulnerable populations and other important information into recovery planning and decision making activities.
> - Increased community-wide support and understanding of sustainability and resiliency principles applicable to the opportunities presented during disaster recovery.
>
> **FEMA 2011b, p. 4**

Recovery Occurs When All Key Functions Are Being Performed Adequately

Some define recovery as having been achieved when the community develops to levels of system performance that are likely to have been achieved had the disruption not occurred. Some are eager to measure the extent to which "the character of the system" has been restored. Others define recovery by comparing characteristics of the community in terms of the number of residents, jobs, and firms both before and after the disaster. When the numbers after the disaster match or exceed the numbers before the disaster, they declare the community "recovered." Certainly, these are the metrics that the average person often asks about when wondering aloud whether a given community has "recovered yet." We are often asked, for example, whether New Orleans has recovered since Hurricane Katrina. What people want to know is whether the houses have been rebuilt where they were swamped by floodwaters, whether the people have returned, who lives there now, and so on. Describing the evolution of the community's recovery interests many people less than does knowing the "state of the numbers" today.

For us, however, recovery is not achieved when all the damaged or destroyed physical artifacts of the community are restored or replaced unless, of course, the initial damages to the community are so slight or the community is so robust that consequences are limited to the physical damage and there are no cascading consequences. Rebuilding or replacing aspects of the built environment is always necessary, but only rarely sufficient for recovery (Alesch and Siembieda 2012). This is because the physical artifacts of the community, for the most part, do not perform the primary functions of the community; often, they simply provide the places in which many of the activities take place that actually build the relationships, adapt to challenges, and, ultimately, perform the functions and relationships essential to the community system. Some infrastructure actually contributes greatly to engaging in those activities by providing power, water, and other metabolic functions.

Nigg (1995) notes that "if one takes (the) perspective that community recovery can be equated with outcomes in the built environment solely, the sociological significance of what really transpires in the post-disaster experience is missed." Recovery, she suggests, "is not merely an outcome, but rather it is a social process" (p. 2).

In the aftermath of a major perturbation resulting in disaster, the early and instinctive actions of the individual elements of the community, including local government, are to scramble to maintain or restore the most visible elements of the system and the system itself to the status quo *ex ante calamitus* so as to preserve what they consider the community's essential characteristics. The visible aspects of the community system may be considered in the same way that the visible portion of an iceberg may be considered; the part we can see is important, but its importance is dwarfed by what lies beneath the water's surface.

This behavior is consistent with the notion that the basic principle of adaptation to disruption is the preservation of the basic system. The key is that the system changes, sometimes almost imperceptibly, as the self-organizing actors and elements within the system take actions to retain their individual viability within the overall system. The community system itself does not make choices intended to achieve dynamic homeostasis: it is, after all, an inanimate social construct. Corporate systems, for most practical purposes, have unitary decision makers (an owner, a board of directors, etc.) who make decisions concerning adaptation and systemic change to preserve the essential characteristics of the firm, or, at the least, its profitability.

Even so, the essence of a corporate system is not determined solely by actors atop the hierarchy. To think otherwise is to buy into a form of autocratic mythology. Rather, the most effective organizations "match cycles of autonomous and induced strategy processes to different forms of strategic dynamics; ... the role (therefore) of alert strategic leadership is to appropriately balance the induced and autonomous processes throughout these cycles" (Burgelman and Grove 2007, p. 965). In other words, organizations sustain themselves over the long run if they appropriately balance direction from the top with autonomous behaviors whose origin is throughout the organization. This notion of alternating the locus of strategic action is captured by the clever title of Burgelman and Grove's (2007) article: "Let Chaos Reign, Then Rein in Chaos—Repeatedly: Managing Strategic Dynamics for Corporate Longevity."

Whether discussing a community or a complex organization, the cumulative actions of (most) members of the community or organization system reflect or constitute efforts to maintain a level of stability (perhaps best described as functional disequilibrium) of the overall community system, including adaptation leading, ultimately, to a system with many changed characteristics. From an evolutionary perspective, most days in the life of a community will be witness to small changes for the community, some of which will represent large changes for individual actors (e.g., due to births, deaths, illnesses, job promotions, relocations, and so on). Other days in the life of the community—the days when an extreme natural hazard event occurs—will represent large changes for the community overall and some significant portion of the community's individual actors. This "punctuated equilibrium" model (Gersick 1991) helps us to see that while community change is ongoing, it is most noticeable when it is preceded by a major perturbation that punctuates the community's normal equilibrium.

We have come to define community recovery as having occurred when the individual actions by community residents and organizations, taken together, result in full (or near full) functioning of the community. By including "near full functioning," we are recognizing that many communities, including those that are considered whole and that have not dealt with an extreme natural hazard event, do not necessarily function as optimizing entities. If disasters occur when a community can no longer perform its critical functions, then recovery occurs when the community is able to perform those functions at adequate levels.

"Adequate levels" implies that communities, like individuals, engage in "satisficing" rather than "optimizing" behaviors (March and Simon 1958; Simon 2000) when making decisions that affect the collective system. Actors within the system operate under conditions of bounded rationality; they do not possess sufficient cognitive resources to make purely rational decisions, so they choose the best of what's available—often what's most obvious, apparent, or known. Actors within the system cannot evaluate potential outcomes with sufficient precision, rarely if ever know the relevant probabilities of outcomes, and possess limited—even reconstructed—memory. It should be no surprise, then, that faced with a novel situation (an extreme natural hazard event), most actors within the system tend to rely on the "tried-and-true" and seek the relative stability that characterized the community before the event.

For all practical purposes, we have adopted an amalgamation of work by Mitchell (2004), Verhoef and Nijkamp (2004), and Renschler and his colleagues (2010) to think about community functions. We apply those views to evaluating the health of a community system. If performing the critical functions at an acceptable level describes the community before the disaster, and failure to perform one or more of the functions means the community has suffered a disaster, then it follows that recovery means that that community has re-realized its ability to perform those functions.

Presumably, this also means that the community has achieved some level of long-term sustainability and viability in the postdisaster context, even if the character of the community system is either somewhat or considerably different from that of the preevent community. Communities are unable to sustain themselves without interaction with other communities, but recovery implies that the community has become self-sufficient in that it does not require continuing significant subsidies from the state or federal government. Recovery also implies that the community is likely to be self-sustaining over some extended period in the near future.

Unfortunately, we do not yet have an adequate set of metrics that enables us to state unequivocally when community recovery has occurred or even how close a community is to full recovery. We believe that when a community is recovering, that recovery advances in fits and spurts, and proceeds unevenly across the spectrum of critical community functions. This aligns with the model of punctuated equilibrium described by Gersick (1991), who asserts that periods of inertia and action are typical as groups move toward some goal. In this case, the goal is recovery of the community system. In the immediate aftermath of an extreme hazard event, and after the debris has been cleared, we would expect a high level of energy around the issue of community recovery. Key stakeholders will come together, promoting their vision of the steps needed to reestablish the community. After the initial burst of energy, the punctuated equilibrium model would suggest a period of inertia; this does not mean that nothing is happening to move the community forward, but that the energy level and attention to action is not as high, not as engaging, as in the period preceding the inertia. In this way, the community moves toward its recovery in fits and starts or may become stuck in inertia.

We previously referenced Mitchell (2004) who specified various functions that communities perform. He listed material and economic, metabolic, learning, performance, creative expression, and regulatory. We also referenced Verhoef and Nijkamp (2004) who listed what they perceived to be the primary roles (or functions) that communities perform: shelter, religious, cultural, political, economic, engineering, and networking (p. 90). Another framework relevant to our discussion is that developed by Renschler and his colleagues (2010). They describe seven community dimensions that together enable community resilience: population and demographics, environmental/ecosystem, organized governmental services, physical infrastructure, lifestyle and community competence, economic development, and social-cultural capital.

We used the conclusions of all three sets of authors to forge what we think is an operational list of functions for those concerned with either studying or facilitating community recovery. Our list consists of the following requisite functions:

- *Communication*—The communication function includes providing means and opportunities for direct interpersonal contact, electronic two-way communication (telephone, Internet, social media, etc.), and print and broadcast (newspapers, television, radio). Performing the communication function(s) requires physical infrastructure, software, trained staff, and maintenance.
- *Cultural, performance, and creative expression*—The cultural, performance, and creative expression function includes the ability to engage in activities that extend beyond meeting the "bread and butter" social experiences, access to the performing and visual arts, and opportunities for self-actualization. It includes the lifestyle and community competence dimension described by Renschler et al. (2010).
- *Material and economic activity*—The material and economic function of the community centers on the acquisition of raw and semifinished materials and the production and marketing of goods and services in the community.

- *Learning*—The learning function consists of formal and informal means for primary, secondary, and higher education as well as for lifelong learning and training.
- *Transportation and distribution*—The transportation and distribution function consists of providing the means for intra- and inter-community mobility, shipping, commuting, and related activities.
- *Metabolic activities*—Providing metabolic infrastructure includes structures, processes, and staffing to provide health care, power generation and distribution, providing a potable water supply, providing for solid and liquid sanitation, and all the related activities supporting the ability of community members to perform other functions.
- *Political*—The political function is the means employed to determine governing policies, practices, and the allocation of public resources within the community.
- *Public safety and regulation*—The public safety and regulatory function provides security for members of the community and helps to prevent activities and behaviors detrimental to the community. The function includes police, fire, public health, and related activities. Renschler et al. (2010) reference this as part of their organized government services.
- *Shelter*—The shelter function relates primarily to the provision of housing but extends to providing appropriate structures within which various other functions are primarily performed.
- *Social, symbolic, and religious*—Social, symbolic, and religious functions include the access of residents and visitors to places and activities that fulfill social needs, symbolic expression, and the performance of and access to religious rituals and events. Renschler and his colleagues (2010) describe this in the context of social-cultural capital.

Each of these functions/dimensions must be restored to the extent that it is operating sufficiently (adequately) to meet individual, family, and greater community needs for the community to achieve recovery. Using the model of bounded rationality described by March and Simon (1958), one might say that a formal declaration or perception of community recovery depends on a critical mass of the community saying that the community is once again "good enough." Trying to "optimize"—or as may be understood in the context of community recovery, to return everything to precisely its *ex ante* state—will most likely lead to frustration and a collective perception of failure. It is not possible to return everything to its previous state, and, as Simon (2000) says in talking about the limits of human rationality, "preoccupied with attaining the optimum, you won't get even an acceptable result" (p. 26). In other words, "optimizing is the enemy of Satisficing" (Simon 2000, p. 26). Spending time and money chasing an elusive state of being that cannot be caught will result in decisions that impede recovery rather than facilitate it.

In American society, most of these functions are performed by a mix of governmental, not-for-profit, investor-owned organizations, individuals, and clusters of individuals. Following the initial consequences of a natural hazard event, the allocation of activities to repair, replace, or even operate the various elements required to fulfill the functions might be different from the preevent allocation, at least temporarily. Local government, particularly, is called upon to take the lead in community recovery: a role for which few local government officials are prepared and for which there is certainly no cookbook.

COMMUNITY RECOVERY PROCESSES

We are not the first disaster researchers to observe that self-organization of complex systems is relevant to community recovery. Comfort (1994), for example, noted, "Self-organization is potentially important in explaining the processes of change and resistance in large, interdependent systems, which often precipitate disaster by their inability to adapt their performance appropriately or in time of avert known risks" (p. 393). So, too, did Koehler at about the same time. Koehler, in fact, explored how those concerned with disaster recovery can learn from chaos theory and related concepts (1995).

Initial consequences from extreme natural hazard events vary greatly. Other things being equal, our experience is that the greater the proportional damage to the natural and built environments and the more deaths and injuries that occur, the more likely it is that cascading consequences will result from the event and the more difficult recovery will be. The greater the damage to the built environment, and the more people whose health is affected by the disaster (as a percentage of the overall population), the more likely it is that the community's collective coping mechanisms will be undermined as the demands of the postdisaster situation quickly swamp the community's ability to address problems.

Not all extreme natural hazard events, particularly those on the "not-very-big" end of the spectrum, generate significant cascading consequences, but some do. Others, likely to be in the "low probability/high consequence" range of the scale almost inevitably generate significant cascading consequences. If the initial damage is slight and there is no significant diminution of the community's ability to perform all its critical functions, then what happens is generally not a disaster and the recovery process usually requires little more than repairing or rebuilding parts of the damaged community's structural artifacts. In such cases, the local "disaster" may, in fact, simply be a bump in the road and things may, in fact, return to approximate preevent normality in a relatively short time.

However, when initial damage to either the community's built or natural environment or cascading consequences from the event seriously diminishes the community's ability to perform its critical functions, then the recovery challenge and process are more complex and demanding. It is more than a bump in the road. Eventually, a new normal will emerge and the community will be different from what existed before. When the initial and cascading consequences are significant, then recovery requires restoring or reestablishing the full array of critical community functions. Accomplishing that is neither easy nor inexpensive, so recovery is not always assured.

The challenge is to get to a new normal that is generally acceptable ("good enough") to the community's residents. Recovery from a significant community disaster is anything but orderly. Prior to the extreme natural hazard event, the healthy community is in functional disequilibrium, not in equilibrium. It is sufficiently stable to perform its functions, but with enough disequilibrium to generate adaptation to many changing circumstances. During and following the extreme natural hazard event, the order that exists within a system in dynamic homeostasis can devolve into pandemonium or even approach total chaos.

We would expect self-organization to arise from postevent chaotic conditions, but that does not mean what results from spontaneous self-organization will be desirable to the community's residents. Triggering positive, functional self-organizing community recovery from a serious community breakdown depends, of course, on the extent to which it approaches chaos. Chaos has a specific meaning to mathematicians, so it is more appropriate to say that if the disturbance is sufficiently large, then the "useful disequilibrium" of the preevent community may degenerate into pandemonium or near-chaos following the event.

When a community begins its recovery process, the outcomes may or may not be a desirable and adaptive community. The outcome might emerge as a downward spiral for the community or it may exacerbate an already existing downward spiral.

Recovery Processes: Like Preevent Community Change, But Accelerated and More Tumultuous

Community recovery rarely begins from complete dissolution of the preevent community. Even following terrible catastrophes, parts of the built environment remain. As long as some preevent residents remain, individual and collective memories and habits remain. Dynes and Quarantelli argue that how recovery proceeds is rooted in the social structure and fabric of the impacted society (cited by Nigg 1995). What remains forms the base from which efforts begin to replace or get by without elements and linkages lost in the disaster.

There is relatively little longitudinal research on how recovery processes proceed and play out in communities and even less comparative analysis of longitudinal recovery processes across communities, either within a single culture or cross-culturally. We do know, however, some things worth addressing here.

We maintain that all the functions communities perform must be operating before community recovery is complete. That having been said, there are obviously priorities. These may vary somewhat from place to place and from time to time, but ensuring the availability of the basics needed for daily life is always one of the highest priorities. Thus, high priorities are attached to those functions associated with shelter, food and water, medical care and public health, public safety, sanitation, transportation, and communication.

Critical infrastructure includes, among others, electrical generation and distribution; transportation including roads, bridges, and tunnels; communication facilities; and water supply and sewage disposal (see Figure 6.2). When it is at all possible, those responsible for such

FIGURE 6.2   Biloxi, Mississippi, May 8, 2006—Hurricane Katrina destroyed the Biloxi Bay Bridge, which linked the communities of Biloxi and Ocean Springs, Mississippi. Two lanes of the newly constructed bridge opened on November 1, 2007, more than 2 years after Katrina. The bridge was completed in April 2008. (Photograph by Daniel J. Alesch.)

infrastructure begin almost immediately to repair or replace what was damaged or lost. Often, the repair or reconstruction includes adaptations intended to make the new infrastructure less likely to be damaged in subsequent events. In the rush to reestablish those critical functions, communication and cooperation are very important, but sometimes it does not take place as well as it might. For those charged with building a new bridge in a new location to replace one, most of which is either at the bottom of the river or being salvaged, communication is extremely important. The bridge designers need to know what might be in the same location, but hidden at the bottom of the river or just below it. Building a new bridge on top of tunnels carrying water or sewage pipes or over cables lying on the bottom is never a very good idea, but responsibility for sewers and cables are likely to not rest with the bridge builders. Thus, when everyone is working urgently to put a critical facility in place and operating, conflict and delays sometimes occur. Intentions may well be good; what tends to interfere is the structure of the community whereby different subsystems (e.g., water, power) are administered by different agencies and organizations. Different agencies and organizations have their own strategic priorities, funding sources, staffing, jargon, and so on—all of which facilitate delays and distortions between agencies and organizations.

The community, as a holistic system, often does not recognize the human-imposed structure of subsystem maintenance. Whether we want the subsystems to interact or not, they must, in order to produce a functioning whole.

We have come to believe that the socio-economic elements and linkages heal, are repaired, or replaced largely on the foundations of what remains from the preevent period, building on memories of what was, who was involved, and what their respective roles and relationships were. The people who perform functions that are dependent on basic infrastructure services, but who do not need buildings built specifically to house their activities (at least initially) generally appear to get organized, heal, and resume their functions mostly on their own accord and timetable. Those that are successful combine what is remembered with adaptations to the new realities and in the new context. As time and resources permit, buildings and facilities appropriate to the various functions are constructed and the functions are performed in more suitable and familiar surroundings.

Sometimes, rebuilding takes longer than one might think, especially in the case of structures with important symbolic meaning attached to them, such as the World Trade Center towers. It appears to us that the more people or groups with somewhat varying interests are involved in deciding how to appropriately address the loss of a symbolic icon, the longer it takes to reach an acceptable accord and to begin design and

construction. This delay is consistent with delays suggested by the garbage can model of decision making (Cohen, March, and Olsen 1972).
In the wake of an extreme natural hazard event, a community may take
on at least some of the characteristics of an organized anarchy, in which
the community operates on "the basis of a variety of inconsistent and ill-
defined preferences, ... unclear technology, (and) ... fluid participation"
(Cohen et al. 1972, p. 1).

With different groups of stakeholders having varying goals, decisions about recovery may take what is perceived to be an extraordinary
amount of time. Decisions about public goods, such as iconic structures,
will wait until several streams come together in the garbage can (Cohen
et al. 1972): shared understanding of the problem, agreement on possible solutions, influential participants, and choice opportunities that
include space on decision-making agendas and needed resources. As
anyone who has ever worked in a university can attest, accommodating
the four streams can be a time-consuming process.

Why not simply delegate the decision making about rebuilding to a
small group of individuals or to local government officials, maybe even
a group of "community rebuilding" experts, if the normal process associated with a so-called organized anarchy takes so much time? Because
doing so would be inconsistent with the character of a community. For
better or worse, communities are the synergistic and holistic outcome of
multiple layers of stakeholders and their interests, and respectful hearing
and integration of their views is both necessary and time-consuming.
Artificially rushing the process is likely to yield dissatisfaction, as stakeholders perceive that their interests and values have been disregarded or
incompletely addressed.

As mentioned previously, it is important to understand that no one
entity is in charge of recreating the community: it remains as a self-
organizing system. Individuals and organizations make choices about
what to do, how to do it, where to do it, and when to do it, most often
having heard and interpreted cues and incentives from decision makers
in key roles and from those to whom they look for advice. Key decision makers create much of the context and provide many of the cues
that influence choices made by others both inside and outside the community: choices that will ultimately determine the community's postevent trajectory.

Specifically, local government officials make important choices that
influence the postevent trajectory. They communicate their expectations about the future of the damaged community, make decisions about
which public investments will be made, when the investments will be
made, and which behaviors will be encouraged and which will be discouraged in one way or another.

Key decisions are also made by individual investor-owned and not-for-profit organizations concerning the extent to which, if any, the future of their organization involves investing or reinvesting in the postevent community. The sum of individual actions concerning what to do, where to do it, when to do it, and how to do it in the weeks or months following the disaster have important consequences for the postevent characteristics of the community.

Dynamics of Self-Organizing Adaptation to New Circumstances

In our series of annual discussions with residents in postevent communities, we found that many residents of a community initially perceived even a major disaster as a bump in the road and thought that, before long, things would return to what they were before the event. Depending on the individual business owner or resident, it took as little as a few weeks or as long as 6 months or a year before he or she came to the realization that things would not return to what was before and that a new normal was emerging and would presumably persist for some time. When the realization was internalized, people changed their expectations concerning their future in the community. Even within the same neighborhood, we talked at length with people whose expectations ranged from a belief that they had to postpone retirement to some indefinite time, that they would have to move somewhere else, or that the disaster opened a door for them to pursue a new course, which would profit them both emotionally and financially.

Even as consequences continue to unfold, attempts to recover are made at many levels in the community. Individuals and households struggle to regain some approximation of what they perceive as normal. So do businesses, not-for-profit organizations, and governments. Their collective efforts comprise attempts at community recovery. Eventually, the new normal develops for each of the elements that make up the community. The community system, if it survives, changes and moves on.

Individual agents comprising the community obviously vary in their adaptability, ability to interpret the consequences they and others have experienced, and their willingness or ability to visualize alternative courses of action in response to what has happened and is happening around them. Some of the cues influencing household decisions about their subsequent behavior are obvious. If the organization in which a person is employed is destroyed, closed, or relocated, that individual agent is likely to try to identify employment options. If a family sees that a significant number of its friends and neighbors move away, it will consider this a cue when making choices about what to do next. When a significant number of residents choose to leave a community, unexpected systemic effects are likely to unfold. For example, we have seen otherwise undamaged restaurants and other kinds of businesses that catered to people who subsequently left town decline, and then close permanently, within a matter of a few months after an extreme natural hazard event. Dodging the initial bullet is not enough to ensure sustainable operations for any organization as consequences continue to unfold in the aftermath.

Some individuals find their choices constrained; they may have no money, no skills, strong family ties to a suffering community, and little understanding of what lies beyond their immediate world. One successful businessperson who was injured in the Northridge Earthquake told us, "The sensible thing to do is to move my business to another place with fewer earthquakes and closer to my suppliers and customers, but my wife won't leave because her family lives here." Others may have fewer constraints and perceive more options open to them.

In short, the recovery process consists of the choices and actions of individual private and public actors concerning their role, if any, in the community and, thereby, its ability to perform the physical, social, cultural, economic, and political functions that shape the postevent developmental trajectory. Eventually, if the community survives, a new normal develops for each of the elements that make up the community. The community system changes and moves on, having lived through the event perturbation and its aftermath.

Beware! Some Advice Can Be Misleading

Any number of publications exists concerning recovery. Most of them contain at least some information that should be ignored or, at the very least, taken with a large grain of salt.

Illustratively, contrary to the opinion of many, there is no standard recipe for recovery: every community and every disaster is unique and requires a unique recovery strategy. Does that mean that a given community cannot learn from others who have been through disasters? Certainly not. At the same time, individuals must keep in mind that they cannot replicate precisely the experience of one community in another and expect to have the same outcomes.

Second, we think it is misleading to think that there is a generalizable timetable for recovery. Some of those who have suggested there is such a timeline were generalizing from a small sample of similar communities with similar disasters. Recovery phases may be approximately the same, priorities for action might be similar, and some activities are essential in every disaster, but those living and working in a disaster site should not judge their progress against that of some other community that suffered the same or similar extreme natural hazard event. As previously stated, recovery depends in part on preevent conditions. Since no two communities are alike along all of the relevant scales, it should come as no surprise that no two recoveries will be precisely the same.

A third example is certainly misleading. Some "experts" have been known to advise communities and small businesses that they should reopen for business as soon as possible (see Figure 6.3). That makes sense if all of the pillars of business survival are in place, if the business plan still makes sense in the aftermath of the disaster, and if the owner can carry the small business until gross receipts and profits begin to

FIGURE 6.3   Long Beach, New Jersey, March 22, 2013—Businesses in Long Beach Township show signs of resiliency following the destruction left by Hurricane Sandy, as many of them return for spring. (Courtesy of FEMA/Rosanna Arias.)

approximate preevent levels. We have spoken with many small-business owners who wish they had known that. One interview stands out in our minds. After having visited a merchant several times over the period of several years, we asked how his business was doing. "Terrible," he said bleakly, "I have to gross about $130,000 a month to break even and for the last year or so, I've been averaging $80,000 a month." He had all the small-business pillars in place except for having a place to do business. By the time he found a building that met his needs, competition had taken all his customers. He, like many others who did not have all the pillars to support his or her business, might have done much better to examine their business plan, their market, and their real chances at success before unlocking the door and declaring themselves open for business.

Finally, community actors are encouraged to avoid making a blueprint for recovery. Blueprints are precise goals that can be achieved by taking well-specified actions in a well-specified sequence. That works in a deterministic process, but recovery is most certainly not a deterministic process. It is a stochastic process. There is no one best way to move toward recovery and to be able to reliably predict the outcome of individual actions taken in pursuit of recovery. The first reason for being unable to predict the outcome of a series of prescribed actions in a stochastic process is that virtually every action is fraught with ambiguity. With enough information, one could calculate the probability of each of a large number of outcomes, but there is never enough information to do that when faced with extreme uncertainty and, sometimes, virtual ignorance. This means that it is impossible to determine the outcome of a series of actions ahead of time. As mentioned previously, without information and without known probabilities, community actors will have to satisfice, making "good enough" decisions.

The second reason for not making a blueprint is that recovery is a large set of choices and chances. Choices are those things that the individual agents in a community make about what to do, where to do it, how to do it, and when to do it. Even pursuing a choice, once made, is risky. Just because you thought it would work does not mean it will work. Chance events are essentially outside our control. If they were under our control, we would call them choices. The chance events that arise are often big surprises and, even if they are not, the outcomes of those events can only rarely be reliably predicted.

WILL IT, CAN IT, EVER BE THE SAME?

To the extent that the natural hazard event results in a significant disruption in community processes and the performance of community functions, the community's return to what existed before is extraordinarily unlikely. It will never be the same: a river passing by is never the same as it was yesterday, but it often bears a close resemblance to yesterday's river. The community may become significantly different if the disruption is exceptional, just as a river would be significantly different if the event were to create, for example, a new channel for the river.

Like other communities that suffered extreme natural hazard events, Homestead, Florida, changed dramatically following Hurricane Andrew. The changes were a direct though not immediate result of the hurricane and choices made as it approached and after it struck. The closing of Homestead Air Force Base and an exodus of snowbirds fearful of more hurricane damage and attracted to other counties in Florida put a huge hole in the local economy. It led to a significant change in the demographic composition of the community as well. During the reconstruction following the hurricane, large numbers of persons of Caribbean and Latin American descent moved into the city. Their migration to Homestead was stimulated when the U.S. Department of Housing and Urban Development granted low-income housing assistance vouchers (Section 8 vouchers) to encourage and facilitate rebuilding apartment houses destroyed by the hurricane. The residents for whom they were presumably intended were no longer living there, and households from low-income areas of metropolitan Miami who were eligible for housing assistance moved into the units, considerably changing Homestead's demographics.

It seems obvious that New Orleans will never be the same as it was before Katrina. Moore, Oklahoma, struck by an EF5 tornado in May 2013 will be closer to the pretornado community than New Orleans will be to its pre-Katrina self, but even Moore will never be the same again (see Figure 6.4). This will be true even though it is likely that most of the residents whose homes were destroyed will rebuild. Most homeowners have insurance against losses from wind, but relatively few have hurricane, flood, or earthquake insurance. Moreover, housing is easily rebuilt and the path of the tornado, though devastating, did not destroy most or all of an economic, housing, or social component of the Oklahoma City suburb. People there will mark time in terms of before and after the tornado. On the other hand, Moore has suffered six tornadoes of EF2 or greater since 1999. That is probably just an unfortunate quirk, given that there does not appear to be a reason that Moore should experience tornadoes more frequently than other nearby communities should. Some people may come to believe that Moore is either unlucky or a tornado magnet and move elsewhere based on that belief.

Inevitably, new realities and new sets of relationships replace the pre-event realities and relationships as people adapt, leave, or are replaced by others. The physical evidence of the disaster gradually disappears, but some scars, mostly invisible, will remain. The community becomes

FIGURE 6.4 Moore, Oklahoma, May 22, 2013—Aerial views of the damage caused by the tornado that touched down in the area on May 20, 2013. (Courtesy of FEMA/Jocelyn Augustino.)

viable only when the adaptive behavior of the individual components comprising that community makes it viable. Inevitably, those individual components will comprise both preevent and postevent residents as well as outside actors including the local, state, and federal government.

VARIABLES THAT IMPEDE OR FACILITATE RECOVERY

We have said that the recovery process is uncertain and that it varies in every community. In the following pages, we describe some of the variables that generate that uncertainty.

Perceptions

Disasters may be viewed as "socially constructed" events. Objective measures of loss and consequences do not make a disaster a disaster, but collective interpretations of consequences do. That is why an airplane crash resulting in 300 lives lost (at once) is viewed by many as more tragic than separate automobile accidents that take 50,000 lives annually. Proximity, similarity, and national attachment are also important in perception. The loss of approximately 2,000 lives in Hurricane Katrina, for example, was seen as more devastating by some Americans than was the loss of 125 times as many lives during the 2004 Indian Ocean tsunami or the deaths of nearly 100,000 persons each in the 2008 typhoon in Myanmar and the Sichuan Earthquake in China.

The City of Los Angeles and Los Angeles County certainly did a lot following the 1994 Northridge Earthquake, but the efforts were generally limited to restoring services, repairing infrastructure, and assisting with repair and replacement of lost housing stock. Despite the enormity of loss from the earthquake, it did not threaten the solvency of local governments, nor did it pose severe threats to the continued viability of communities in the Los Angeles metropolitan area. However, in smaller cities that are not embedded in a megalopolis where losses are not large by regional or national standards, the consequences of an extreme natural hazard event are perceived as affecting almost everyone in the community and posing threats to continued community viability. In such cases, recovery becomes the issue on everyone's front burner. It dominates talk in the local breakfast haunts, the front page of the local paper, every nightly newscast, and every politician's agenda. It becomes the primary agenda item for individuals trying to figure out how they can collectively regain their community's status as a self-organizing system.

It appears to us that local governments take on a more activist role in disaster recovery when the event is perceived to very deeply affect a very large proportion of the community and when it is evident to local leaders that economic or social recovery is unlikely without aggressive and concerted action to facilitate or stimulate that recovery. Another factor affecting the level of proactivity on the part of local government seems to be the expected proactivity of business organizations. When businesses and other organizations are able to make a significant difference to the recovery effort, local government is either able to entirely focus on other issues or take a less authoritative role.

Community Disaster Resistance and the Nature and Scale of Initial Consequences

Obviously, the initial effects of extreme natural hazard events on communities vary considerably from place to place. Those initial effects vary in terms of the number of injuries and deaths of residents, the number of persons and households displaced from homes or the community, and the nature and extent of damage to the built environment, including physical infrastructure. We know, too, that the extent to which the event has an impact on each of these dimensions depends on the nature of the event itself. A pandemic or an incident such as that in Bhopal in 1984 might result in a large number of deaths and disabilities, but have virtually no effect on the community's physical or natural environments.

How much initial damage and the nature and extent of cascading consequences depends not only on the magnitude, proximity, and duration of the event, but also on how resistant the community is to those events. Contracting a disease is much worse for someone whose immune system is compromised, other things being equal, than it is for someone who is healthy and strong. It is the same with communities. Those built to resist or avoid the forces exerted by an extreme natural hazard event will fare far better than those that are fully vulnerable to it.

We could create a scale by which to classify the initial consequences of an extreme natural hazard event, but such a scale is not necessary for our purposes. It is enough to note that some extreme natural hazard events generate few if any deaths, little population displacement and then only for a short time, limited damage to homes and businesses, and all utilities are reestablished to everyone in just a few days. This might result in a minor disaster or perhaps a major inconvenience. On the other end of the spectrum, it is not at all difficult to imagine a disaster in which large numbers of people die; in which thousands of households are displaced from their homes and community for an extended period of time; in which damage to the built and natural environments is extensive, widespread, and devastating; in which public order and safety is hardly secured; and in which no one really knows or can estimate reliably when utilities and services will be reestablished. We choose to call this a catastrophic disaster; much like Katrina's consequences for New Orleans Parish. Most disasters exist within a broad spectrum between these endpoints.

Preevent Community Status and Trajectory

We have seen natural disasters occur in communities already experiencing a downward trajectory. Even before the event, those communities struggled to achieve social and economic viability and several of them struggled to adequately perform critical community functions. Over the years, Montezuma, Georgia, had lost its primary economic *raison d'être* as a social and commercial center serving an agricultural base surrounding the community. New kinds of crops, new kinds of agricultural machinery, and improved access to larger communities caused Montezuma's decline. If it were to flourish, it would not only have to recover from the damage inflicted by the devastating flood, but it would need to create a new reason for being. City leaders understood this and made a valiant attempt to generate a new trajectory for the community by turning it into a retirement community and a tourist attraction. Their challenge was not simply to restore community infrastructure and functions, but to alter a trajectory of long-term decline into a more favorable trajectory characterized by long-term viability. The efforts did not work as well as hoped.

Communities like Montezuma face challenges of recovering from two community disasters at the same time. For them, restoring the ability of the community to perform critical functions means creating a new trajectory, not simply working to restore a community with an existing desirable and functional trajectory. It requires recovery from a dual disaster: the disaster triggered by the flood truly exacerbated the disaster triggered by changing circumstance and inadequate means of coping with those changes.

Resiliency and Recovery

Resiliency is often used in concert with community sustainability (Mileti 2006). Resiliency is different from robustness or resistance: it is "the ability to prepare and plan for, absorb, recover from, and more successfully adapt to adverse events" (National Research Council 2012, p. 1). For our purposes, it is concerned especially with the ability of a community to rebound from both the initial and cascading consequences of an extreme natural hazard event. Ultimately, its focus is enabling recovery. Certainly, community robustness and resistance may be linked with community recovery. A community can make itself more damage-resistant; it can create institutions and processes that will help it rebound from disasters. For us, community resiliency is the quality of both its residents and its institutions to rebound and to recover from the harmful consequences of an extreme natural hazard event.

Resistance (or robustness), resiliency, and sustainability are words used frequently in conjunction with one another in the disaster literature. Sustainability is generally defined as the capacity to endure, particularly to sustain well-being over the long term. It is usually used in conjunction with balancing ecological, economic, political, and cultural interests as communities develop (Mileti 2006). "(T)he construct of resilience is generally understood as the capability of a community to face a threat, survive and bounce back or, perhaps more accurately, bounce forward into a normalcy newly defined by the disaster related losses and changes ... community resilience is ... a reflection of the people's shared and unique capacities to manage and adaptively respond to the extraordinary demands on resources and the losses associated with disasters" (Paton 2006; Norris et al. 2008, as cited by Cox and Perry 2011, p. 396).

Even resilient people and organizations can experience disruption and conditions approaching chaos in the aftermath of an extreme natural hazard event, especially when adverse effects are cascading through the community. The immediate consequences of the event can generate significant uncertainty in those who experience it. When sufficient numbers of residents (individual agents in the self-organizing system) find themselves in extraordinarily ambivalent situations within which preexisting decision criteria and behavioral cues no longer seem applicable, individual community functions may falter and no longer meet expectations.

In 2011, Cox and Perry explored resiliency and related social-psychological phenomenon in an article with the provocative title, "Like a Fish out of Water." In the article, they analyze disaster recovery in two Canadian communities that suffered from a disastrous forest fire. Their study highlights "the importance of the psychology of place to community and individual resilience which place is disrupted—not only through displacement, but as the result of the myriad economic, material and symbolic losses and changes associated with disaster events" (Cox and Perry 2011, p. 395). They suggest that people who return to their former home and community often become disoriented and have difficulty adjusting to the uncertainties associated with the destruction of a known environment.

In its 2012 report, entitled *Disaster Resilience: A National Imperative*, the National Research Council makes a critical point about the necessity of creating a culture of resilience. "Developing a culture of resilience would bolster support for preparedness and response, and would also enable better anticipation of disasters and their consequences, enhancing the ability to recover more quickly and strongly. Resilient communities would plan and build in ways that would reduce disaster losses, rather than waiting for a disaster to occur and paying for it afterward" (National Research Council 2012, p. 2). Culture is a function of the beliefs, norms, values, and ways of thinking and acting in a given community. Through both informal and formal means, communities enable and reinforce the beliefs, norms, and values that strike the majority of a community's citizens as appropriate and right.

One of the coauthors had an interesting conversation with a local government employee from a southern Wisconsin community during a workshop on community recovery. The woman shared her community's experience with a series of extreme natural hazard events. After experiencing one such devastating event, her community acted swiftly to enable its future resilience. Property taxes and other forms of revenue were increased to help fund building and other efforts intended to better prepare the community for future events. Leaders from throughout the community stepped forward to embrace and support efforts to build a strong community. An adjacent community, having experienced the same extreme natural hazard event as the first, reacted quite differently. Though some efforts were made to rebuild the community after the event, little effort was exerted on future resiliency. Instead, the community elected to do only what was absolutely required to restore aspects of the built environment. The woman describing her community's experience spoke with pride about her community's efficacy in moving forward, and her confidence that the community would be resilient in the face of an extreme event. She expressed doubts that the adjacent community would rebound well, and noted the general lack of confidence and collective optimism in the neighboring community. Evidently, experiencing an extreme natural hazard event alone is insufficient to motivate interest in resilience. Individuals and communities must also perceive the event to be potentially repeatable in order to fully learn its lessons.

For many individuals and communities, experience can be an excellent teacher. One illustration of the importance of having experienced disaster for those focused on resistance and recovery centers on a woman, Dorothy Zaharako, who came to Homestead to assist the municipality with its financial operations following Hurricane Andrew. She subsequently became the chief financial officer for the City of Stuart, Florida. There, she put into practice what she had learned in Homestead. Notably, she and officials from nearby communities created a hurricane insurance pool that served the city particularly well when it suffered moderate damage in 2004 from Hurricane Jeanne.

Available Resources

One wonders how communities will recover from disasters that take most or all of the people's and their government's resources. Many places in remote impoverished parts of poor nations were ravaged by typhoons and tsunamis in and around the Indian Ocean in recent years; they lost virtually all of their resources. Communities in the United States are fortunate that the federal government provides so much money for disaster relief and recovery, that private individuals are extraordinarily generous, that so many strong and generous nongovernmental not-for-profit organizations exist, and that, overall, the economy generates sufficient excess to provide assistance.

Sometimes, it seems to us that what local governments do in the attempt to foster community recovery is solely driven by the availability of federal and, to some extent, state monies for specific projects. Restrictive conditions are placed on the use of funds, presumably, for two reasons. The first is to encourage local governments to do particular things that seem to federal policy makers to assist in the recovery effort. The second, it seems to us, is that officials at a higher level of government distrust what officials at a lower level might do with monies given to them without having strings attached. The result of the tight strings on financial assistance is that it is left to local officials to cobble together a sensible, overall plan from a host of funding sources that do not, by themselves, encourage or facilitate the development of such an overall plan. It should be noted, though, that state and, especially, federal programs help fund activities that almost all local governments would have to undertake regardless of whether federal funds were available, including, for example, debris removal and repairing or rebuilding damaged public infrastructure.

Block grant funds from the Department of Housing and Urban Development provide a source of revenue for projects designed by the damaged community to aid in recovery. Because they are block grants, the funds may be used for any of a wide range of programs and activities. Creative local officials may use these funds to create synergies with projects from narrowly specified sources of assistance. Local governments are almost invariably extremely short of funds, and their revenue from local sources usually shrinks in the aftermath of the disaster, so block grants do seem to induce governments to do things they would not otherwise do or to substitute the block grant funds for money they would have spent on the funded activity so their funds can be put to another use. If a granting agency wants to help ensure that the grants do not simply replace money the local government would have used on the activity (thus freeing that money for other activities), then matching grants are preferable to block grants. Under most circumstances, matching grants induce additional expenditure by the recipient government.

Political Culture, Political Realities, and Political Practicality

"Political culture" is a term used to describe, among other things, how most of the people in a particular place tend to perceive the appropriate role of government and collective action. Within regions and states, and even within various parts of individual states, dominant ideological beliefs and pragmatic concerns about the appropriate role of government vary. The culture affects who is elected to public office, as well as the actions that states and local governments take or do not take to respond to disasters.

Variances in political culture means that some communities are more proactive toward hazard mitigation, more involved in postevent recovery, and more open to a wide range of recovery strategies. In a few communities we studied, local government used government resources to build subdivisions, acquire and sell lots for development, and even build and sell housing directly to end users. In other places, that role was left entirely to private business. Some states and communities enact stringent building regulations to help ensure the safety of residents, while a few other states do not even require that every general purpose local government have a building code. Similarly, government efforts to ensure compliance with codes vary among places.

Sometimes, political culture mixes with political reality. As mentioned previously, Florida City, Florida, is a small, predominantly African-American community adjoining Homestead. Florida City aggressively tried to attract business in the post-Hurricane Andrew months and years. It acquired building lots that Dade County had taken because of tax delinquency, improved the lots, and sold them to local families who qualified. The small city was proactive for a number of reasons. The mayor had been in office for many years and enjoyed the support of the city council. The political continuity of the council and the mayor positioned them to take bold actions. Many other communities do not have long-term incumbents with relatively little competition for elective office; in addition, they may be more politically divisive. In those communities, issues that divide constituents and office holders may reduce the likelihood of aggressive, sustained developmental initiatives.

Political practicality can also affect how much money becomes available to local government for recovery. Princeville, North Carolina, is a small community with an almost entirely African-American population. It was founded by freed slaves in the 1880s. It was badly damaged by flooding in 1999 (Brown 2001) (see Figure 6.5). The continuing struggle to make Princeville a viable, thriving community is a case study in how sometimes good intentions and lots of money are not enough to secure a community's recovery. Princeville received massive federal assistance. Unfortunately, the struggle to make Princeville a viable community was a daunting challenge even before the town was ravaged, especially since nearby communities were thriving and drawing away Princeville residents and money.

President Bill Clinton, while visiting Princeville following the devastating flood, promised that the federal government would rebuild the community. Presumably, the president wanted to make a statement about the commitment of the government to poor and destitute members of a racial minority. It also helped, however, that Princeville was small so, presumably, it could be rebuilt for a lot less money than it would take to rebuild New Orleans or even Homestead. Thus, substantial funds flowed into Princeville for a variety of projects, including public housing. The funding was not enough. Princeville's starting position was well behind the start line. Its economy had been in tough shape before the extreme natural hazard event. Existing drug and crime problems escalated with the introduction of public housing. New people who moved into the community had fewer skills. Projects were started and left unfinished. Many changes in the community have not been for the better.

The disaster served to exacerbate a preexisting set of conditions, and without a history of collective efficacy, the community could not achieve

FIGURE 6.5   Princeville, North Carolina, September 28, 1999—The muddy streets of Princeville, North Carolina, illustrate the destruction wrought by Hurricane Floyd. The resultant flooding of the Tar River led to the evacuation of residents. (Courtesy of FEMA News Photo/ Dave Saville.)

a functional level of recovery. As defined by Bandura (1997), "Perceived collective efficacy is defined as a group's shared belief in its conjoint capabilities to organize and execute the courses of action required to produce given levels of attainments" (p. 477). This collective belief focuses on the group's operative (functional) capabilities. Several factors contribute to the synergistic effects of collective efficacy, including the mix of knowledge and competencies possessed by community actors; how the community is structured; how well the community is led (by both formal and informal leaders); and how the community's members interact with each other (i.e., do they act to undermine or support each others' efforts).

The essential role of collective efficacy in community recovery cannot be overstated; it is the collective sense of "we shall overcome" with emphasis on both "we" and "shall overcome." Together, community members must have a high degree of confidence that they can transform their community into the community they want. An influx of money alone—even a great deal of money—does not a recovery make.

Creativity and Resourcefulness of Local Leaders

Some local officials and community leaders are simply more creative and resourceful than others when it comes to cobbling together resources from sources beyond what the local tax base generates. Vision, creativity, and persistence are powerful forces for garnering funds from diverse sources to help a community rebuild and revitalize. As referenced earlier, local governments that went out of their way in the aftermath of a disaster to hire people with special skills in putting together ideas and proposals usually were able to do more and receive more governmental assistance than those that did not. These local governments had the forethought and wherewithal to solicit help intended to garner even more help. They knew their limitations and sought to augment them.

CHAPTER 7

Facilitating Recovery

WHO'S IN CHARGE?

Municipal officials sometimes believe that they are in charge of community recovery. However, since the community is primarily a self-organizing system, local government is not really in charge. Local government has its role, of course, as do all of the actors and agents in the system. Local government is responsible for facilitating recovery by providing the support and incentives needed by residents and resident organizations to make appropriate choices about what to do, where to do it, when to do it, and how to do it. This, in and of itself, is both difficult and critical. Local legislative bodies are much more accustomed to adjudicating the disparate desires of constituents and to allocating resources to provide services than they are to developing, considering, and enacting policies on truly complex matters. The administrative arms of local government primarily devote themselves to delivering services, not to solving complex problems that cut across their respective departments and agencies. Local government is also responsible for coordinating many of the activities and projects funded by the state and federal government so that they contribute to recovery. Still, some state and federal agencies, such as the Army Corps of Engineers, act directly in the community and may or may not actively cooperate with local officials.

In that context, local government hopes to help move the community toward recovery, often while operating under conditions of great uncertainty about best steps forward and their execution. There is great unpredictability concerning the outcomes of choices. Progress proceeds in fits and spurts. Support waxes and wanes, as choices are made and supporters and detractors speak their piece. There is an element of path dependency so changing directions as new information or ideas arise is often difficult from both a practical and a political perspective.

Residents expect those in power and those in staff positions to know what to do, and to know the likely outcomes of their decisions. This expectation helps residents cope with the uncertainty and even fear that the disaster has provoked. Believing that "somebody" has things under control makes it easier to continue limping forward.

All this takes place while near chaos conditions may reign within some parts of the community system. Under those conditions, individual agents in the community find themselves making important choices under conditions of extreme complexity and uncertainty. To the extent that doing so is possible, local government acting to reduce some of the uncertainty and contribute to making wise choices can ease the community's recovery.

FIRST THINGS FIRST

Prompt and Effective Response

This book is about recovery, not about response during the emergency period following an extreme natural hazard event. Often, however, recovery is made easier than it might otherwise be when prompt and effective response during the emergency period reduces the potential of more cascading consequences.

Local government activities during and immediately after an extreme natural hazard event are usually driven and prioritized by what they see as necessary. In almost every community we studied, local government engaged in warning the population, helping with evacuation if necessary, sandbagging as floodwaters rose, rescuing those in need, detecting and suppressing fires, and working to ensure public safety. Local emergency management centers are activated and the local government goes on high alert. The government's activities can also include coordinating communication, controlling crowds, ascertaining damage, shutting down various public utilities to ensure safety, establishing crime scene perimeters, and dispatching rescue teams. Of all the things local government does in connection with a disaster, immediate response is perhaps what it does best.

Restoring Government Services and Repairing Public Facilities and Infrastructure

A second cluster of activities is often initiated almost immediately. Achieving an acceptable level of public safety and civil order is a prerequisite to recovery. This, of course, overlaps concerns that may have arisen during the immediate emergency. It can, however, as it has in New Orleans, become a long-term concern. The key point is that no one wants to invest in a community or in a part of a community where either they or their investment is in imminent danger of fire, flooding, massive traffic problems, violent and lawless gangs, or extensive criminal activity. Establishing basic public safety and rule of law is a prerequisite to the success of other recovery activities.

Other activities include removing debris generated by the extreme natural hazard event, repairing government-owned infrastructure, restoring public utilities, and restoring services for which the local government was responsible before the event. These activities signal the beginning of the recovery effort. Local government crews repair streets and bridges, they restore water purification and distribution systems, they put sewage collection and treatment facilities back into operation, and, if they own them, the local governments fix utility generation, distribution, and collection facilities or let contracts to private firms do so. Local governments typically do little or nothing to rebuild infrastructure or facilities they do not own, such as hospitals that are owned by not-for-profit or investor-owned organizations.

In some communities, which governmental entity—city, county, or state—removed the debris deposited by the flood or tornado from various streets in a community depended on whether the street was designated local, county, or state (see Figure 7.1). Sometimes, but not always, those arrangements were made before an extreme natural hazard event. It is, of course, better to work out who is to do what before the streets are clogged

FIGURE 7.1   Joplin, Missouri, June 7, 2011—Crews work to remove debris around Joplin, caused by the May 22nd tornado. FEMA commissioned the U.S. Army Corps of Engineers to oversee private contractors during the controlled debris removal. (Courtesy of FEMA/Steve Zumwalt.)

with debris. Officials in communities who had not worked out arrangements in advance reported to us that working out the details of who was responsible for what after the event was time-consuming and sometimes generated unwanted friction as people were operating under stress.

Often, local government officials had not considered the extent to which they were interdependent with other entities until they found themselves having conversations under duress. Although many local officials have become familiar with and participated in tabletop exercises to pinpoint communication and other issues during a potential crisis, very few had experience working through the level of detail associated with catalyzing their community's recovery.

Deciding which elements of the built environment to tackle in what order and for which parts of the local community is not easy. Whereas it may seem obvious that the first elements requiring attention will be those associated with power and potable water, it is not always possible to address these elements first. Streets may need at least partial clearing and buildings may need to be inspected before power can be restored. Officials may find themselves in the unenviable position of having to decide which parts of the community will receive services first as a function of guessing which parts of the community are most likely to be repopulated first. These guesses are not always accurate, and they are not always acceptable to affected residents. Residents of New Orleans' Lower Ninth Ward, for example, did not see their electricity reestablished until summer of 2006, more than 10 months after Katrina made landfall (Louisiana Justice Institute n.d.). As a result, residents of the Lower Ninth had to watch other neighborhoods begin the road to recovery while theirs languished.

Providing Short-Term Assistance to Individuals and Families

In concert with other public and private organizations, local governments provide short-term assistance to residents. They help recover the dead and provide morgues or temporary storage of the bodies so they can be identified. For the survivors, local governments help provide medical treatment, temporary shelter, food, and other necessities, including portable toilets (Port-A-Potties). The local governments usually receive help from nearby local governments, private utilities, state agencies, federal agencies, nongovernmental organizations (e.g., American Red Cross), and private individuals.

In some communities, private citizens provided hot meals to those who suffered losses or were working on the cleanup. "The power had been out for some time and the food in our freezers had begun to thaw," one small-town restaurant owner told us. "I would much rather cook it and give to those who need it than to throw it away."

Helping Residents Start to Recover: Essential Goods and Services Must Be Available

Some people can camp out for a while in the ruins of a community, but for sufficient numbers to return or to stay, essential goods and services must be available. Local government cannot be responsible for all these goods and services, but it can facilitate their availability. Some activities are more urgent than other activities and deserve a high priority in local government recovery efforts. In our studies, local governments learned that they must respond very early to the needs of disaster workers and remaining residents. That calls for special efforts to enable some restaurants to open or reopen by ensuring rapid response inspections and permits. Some gasoline stations and convenience stores have to be open to meet local needs.

Florida, learning from its hurricane experiences, requires gasoline stations to have power generators so they can provide gas when the power is out. Motels and hotels have to be available for disaster workers, news crews, officials from various levels of government, and others who need to be there. Pharmacies must be opened to ensure that those who need them can get their medications. Grocery stores must be reopened and stocked. It is important for banks to be opened earlier than one might think. It makes more sense to work hard to expedite the reopening of several hardware stores and building supply retailers than it does to help jewelers and other providers of luxury items reopen early, since what these organizations sell is not likely to facilitate early community recovery efforts. These businesses are better off either altering what they do to better enable the recovery process or waiting to reopen and drawing upon their business interruption insurance.

After the immediate emergency, recovery can begin when money is available both from within the community and from outside it. Local government needs upfront money to undertake essential tasks. It might come from reserves, insurance, loans, or grants, but without access to money almost nothing can be accomplished. Private organizations need money, too, if they are to rebuild, repair, replace, pay employees, buy supplies, and so forth. This includes both profit-seeking and not-for-profit organizations. Last, but not least, individuals and families need money to meet their immediate needs and to initiate their own recovery activities. Individual recovery efforts, of course, when taken in aggregate, are critical to community recovery.

FIGURE 7.2   St. Bernard Parish, Louisiana, 2005—Exterior of a branch bank destroyed by storm surge from Hurricane Katrina. (Photograph by Daniel J. Alesch.)

Having money available means that local financial institutions must be operating, at least at a makeshift level. People and firms need access to their accounts, and local financial institutions in the communities we studied worked hard to quickly open. We have seen financial organizations operating in warehouses, trailers, and make-do facilities when their regular buildings are unusable (see Figure 7.2). And, we have seen bankers in hip boots shoveling cash into biohazard bags for subsequent shipment, counting, and decontamination or replacement. While local government may not think first of helping financial institutions to quickly reopen, it should be clear that doing so will be a prerequisite to kick starting the community's recovery.

Ensuring Temporary Shelter

At the same time as basic services are being put back in operation, it is necessary to provide assistance to move people from emergency shelter to temporary shelter and then to permanent housing. The Federal Emergency Management Agency (FEMA) will meet some of the need for temporary shelter. Relatively low-cost hotel and motel rooms must be available, however, to meet the needs of those who are in the community temporarily for cleanup and construction. The community must move promptly to ensure the availability of housing that workers can afford and that is relatively convenient to workplaces if it hopes to attract a sufficient number of workers to help jumpstart the local economy. This need not be permanent housing in the community. If housing is available in nearby communities, businesses and local government can organize bus transport and car pools from neighboring communities for those who have jobs in the recovering community but who do not yet have housing in it. Permanent housing will eventually be provided to meet the effective demand.

It is possible that some larger employers will work with employees and prospective employees to create living arrangements that are suitable, at least, for the short term. In New Orleans, for example, most of the hospitals that reopened in the immediate aftermath provided temporary housing for their employees for months after Katrina. At least some of the hospitals that closed continued to pay employees for several months, even though the employees could not report to work. Doing so enabled employees to pay rent or mortgages. Employers and local government may find it useful to establish commuter buses to and from other communities if workers can find accommodations in those communities until more housing becomes available in the disaster community. Again, in New Orleans, several employers paid employees to commute from Baton Rouge each day, since housing accommodations with power, water, and sewer were difficult to secure in New Orleans.

Loans and small grants are generally available for homeowners to repair their homes. Some local governments bought land, created subdivisions, and sold houses on the private market; others obtained vacant lots and housing foreclosed for nonpayment of taxes, rehabilitated the housing, and sold it to persons who had lost their homes in the disaster.

Beyond assisting homeowners, the government's role in helping private parties restore productive parts of the community is limited to a few kinds of organizations. Illustratively, the federal government will provide funds to repair damage from extreme natural hazard events to hospitals owned by state and local governments and not-for-profit organizations. Sometimes, it will provide money to those hospitals for hazard mitigation. The federal government may do the same for privately owned hospitals if they are organized as not-for-profits. It will not, however, provide grants to investor-owned hospitals that provide exactly the same services and that are also required by law to serve uninsured and indigent persons.

Similarly, local privately owned, profit-seeking businesses with disaster-related losses are eligible for very little assistance except for Small Business Administration (SBA) loans. Often, we were told by small-business owners that they were refused assistance from local and national philanthropic organizations even in their capacity as a resident home-owner with substantial losses. Had they been employed by someone, they would have been eligible, but being self-employed, for some unknown reason, precluded them from benefits others received. This is especially problematic for community recovery, as small businesses comprise 99.7 percent of U.S. employer firms, employing 49.2 percent of individuals in private-sector employment (Small Business Administration 2012).

On the other hand, one class of business owners is eligible for a wide variety of federal disaster loans and grants. If the business is agricultural, more than a score of federal programs provide grants and loans to private, for-profit owners to cover direct losses from a wide variety of extreme natural hazard events. Presumably, the Congressional rationale is that privately owned, profit-seeking farming is more worthy of assistance than a privately owned, profit-seeking firm focusing on manufacturing or distribution, or even those that provide health care.

ASSESSING THE NATURE AND EXTENT OF THE CONSEQUENCES

Following an extreme natural hazard event, it is important for a local government to obtain and interpret information about what has happened to the local community and its dynamics. Local governments need to understand the disaster at multiple levels and from multiple perspectives, including those of individuals, neighborhoods, consumers and businesses, infrastructure, and organizations. They need to interpret massive amounts of disjointed information and work to understand what it means. What goods and services are not yet available? What is happening to housing and where are people living? What is happening with large employers? What specific needs do they have? Local governments need to seek deep understanding and to integrate information that makes sense with things that may not yet make sense.

It is also essential for local governments to look for systemic consequences to the community as they begin to manifest themselves. Systemic community consequences will not be as obvious in the immediate aftermath as injuries, deaths, and damage to buildings and other structures, but it is particularly important to identify, catalog, analyze, and address them. Addressing them is the key to recovery. There is always a temptation to think that the extreme natural hazard event happens and the consequences occur essentially immediately, and then you begin to address them. However, the consequences often continue to unfold over weeks and months. In that sense, the disaster is dynamic. Consequences unfold and sometimes do not give much warning. Since they continue to unfold through time, it is necessary to monitor the community regularly to watch for them as they appear and to assess how they are playing out. Almost every day, you'll say "Now what?"

As one example of consequences that tend to manifest over time, we share the perception of many in disaster-ravaged communities who have talked to us about the evolving needs for psychiatric care months and even years after an extreme natural hazard event. There are never enough in-patient beds, and there are never enough caregivers. Individuals may seem to be psychologically OK only to have a breakdown well after the initial debris has been hauled away. Staying alert for the signs of increasing demands for psychiatric and other care is just one of the many tasks to be undertaken by local government officials trying to facilitate their community's recovery.

This means that local officials have to find ways to identify consequences as they are unfolding. It requires continuing communication with people from throughout the community; the view from city hall does not catch everything that deserves attention. Community leaders, business owners and managers, managers of financial institutions, educators, executives in not-for-profits, citizens in the street, and officials in adjoining or overlapping units of government can all provide important intelligence on various cascading consequences and unanticipated events.

It is not particularly urgent for local officials to spend time thinking about ripple effects manifesting themselves in other communities. There is enough to do focusing on their own community. State and federal officials, however, should pay close attention to ripple effects. In New Orleans, a few of the hospitals that closed more or less permanently following the flood had been designated as the primary facilities to care for the indigent (e.g., Charity Hospital). Without them, the indigent sought health care at hospitals outside the community, hospitals not designated by the state to care for indigent people and for which there were no arrangements to reimburse them for those services. Similarly, cities like Baton Rouge that bear heavy burdens in the aftermath of disasters because they are inundated by those who leave disaster sites should not be obliged to carry that burden by themselves.

Local officials should make an effort to identify any ripple reverberation consequences beginning to manifest themselves in the community. If other places are taking on roles that had been carried out by your community, it may indicate the importance of taking steps in your community to cope with the potential loss of key functions and roles. For example, the community will want to decide the utility of maintaining its educational institutions and libraries, its fire and police service, its water and sewage systems, and so on. Whereas it may make good economic and political sense to retain these functions and services locally, it may also make sense to consider consolidating with other communities.

An intelligence function is also essential to identify and evaluate options and opportunities that may emerge in the community after an extreme natural hazard event. Under normal circumstances, it may be sufficient to wait for these things to come to the attention of local government through the normal course of business, but unusual times demand unusual practices. It is important for local officials to keep their finger on the pulse of the community more closely than ever in this difficult and critical time. Local government officials who are enmeshed in the community's fabric through its professional associations, churches, schools, sporting leagues, and so on will have greater opportunity to ground-truth what they are thinking and hearing than officials who isolate themselves from the community and its ongoing concerns.

ENSURE THAT LOCAL GOVERNMENT IS UP TO THE DEMANDS THAT WILL BE PLACED ON IT

Abraham Lincoln is said to have stated, "If I had eight hours to chop down a tree, I'd spend six sharpening my axe." This homey saying makes good sense. In the immediate wake of a disaster, local government administration is not routine. As the emergency begins to wind down, it is common for administrators to breathe a sigh of relief. Too early! The aftermath of the disaster will be even more complicated and trying than the emergency response. Local government will not be able to help very much with recovery unless it is operating effectively and efficiently. What follows is not a step-by-step checklist for getting local government apparatus in good working order or prepared to take on the massive task of recovery. Rather, it is a collection of things that we learned from officials with significant disaster experience.

Fortifying Accounting and Finance Systems

We found that some local governments thought they had adequate financial accounting systems and documentation procedures before the disaster, but then had serious trouble when state and federal agencies conducted their reviews and audits. Federal project funds flow into jurisdictions after a presidential disaster declaration, but after the money is gone and the projects are completed, the auditors arrive looking for documentation of eligible expenditures, looking for expenditures that are ineligible under the terms of the grants, looking to ensure that procedures were followed precisely, and looking for errors and mistakes made by local officials. Almost every local official told us that accounting and finance systems are put to the test in the aftermath. The federal government's program auditors will want (demand) complete records on how every dime was spent and compelling evidence that every dime was spent in compliance with program regulations. If they do not get that evidence, they will want to get some or all of the money back from the local government. Some local governments have found themselves facing the prospect of writing a large check to a federal agency.

It is not simple to keep track of expenditures in the aftermath of an extreme natural hazard event. Local government staff members find themselves dealing with situations they have not previously encountered, trying to do both the job they did before the disaster, and trying to deal with new complexities and tasks they have never done before. Moreover, most federal program rules are complex. Not all agencies employ the same procedures. In addition, federal agencies may hire temporary personnel in response to a specific disaster. These personnel are often less knowledgeable about rules and regulations than are long-time employees. This may explain why local officials in several cities told us they received contradictory information from agency personnel on successive days. Local government experiences varied. Some had wonderful experiences with federal officials and others did not. The lessons, however, are clear: from the very first day, make sure that complete record-keeping and accounting systems are in place.

As mentioned previously, some small municipalities hired one or more individuals and charged them with the responsibility of reading and understanding the regulations of every federal program with which the local government was or might be involved. In those cases, the local government had fewer difficulties over the long run. Grand Forks, North Dakota, had help from consultants setting up their systems and met federal expectations completely after they experienced catastrophic flooding in 1997 (see Figure 7.3). Even local governments with adequate systems sometimes found themselves answering questions from federal auditors 5, 6, or 7 years after the disaster. Local governments with insufficient systems spent years fighting federal efforts to recapture tens of thousands and sometimes millions of dollars.

Local governments benefit from having a chief financial officer on staff. The federal government does not advance funds; it reimburses local governments after expenditures are made. In some states, the federal money goes through a state government agency before it gets to the local government. Delays in reimbursement are common. Managing cash flow and arranging for bridge financing can become a staggering problem. Maintaining an overall view of local government finances and keeping the jurisdiction within safe financial limits requires more than accounting skills; it requires someone who understands finance, management, intergovernmental relations, and in general, how things work in a political system.

FIGURE 7.3   Grand Forks, North Dakota, April 1, 1997—Aerial of Grand Forks neighborhood flooded after the Red River floodwaters came through the town. (Courtesy of FEMA/Mike Rieger.)

Reducing Nonessential and Downright Irritating Bureaucracy

In government and other monopolies, there is sometimes a tendency to externalize costs to the user. For example, in some states the Department of Motor Vehicles is seen by residents as inefficient because it externalizes its administrative costs to the customer: You get to wait in line so that the agency does not have to spend more money on employees. Local government is sometimes in a monopoly position: Where else are you going to get a building permit? However, in the aftermath, local government cannot afford to generate additional frustration and animosity toward local government among residents who need help to speed their personal recovery. The residents should not have to bear the burden of unnecessary delays, costs, or hassle. Unnecessary procedural steps create more hassle and consequently, higher costs. Angry citizens will contact their city council members, who can make life extraordinarily difficult for local government staff members.

Florida City, Florida, a small, poor jurisdiction immediately adjacent to Homestead, struggled for a long time to build a viable local economy, even before Hurricane Andrew. As previously described, it developed a particularly useful approach after Hurricane Andrew. The mayor and his chief associates decided to slash red tape when dealing with firms that were thinking about locating within the municipal boundaries along U.S. 1 at its junction with the Florida Turnpike. Whereas some municipalities require prospective firms to meet with three or more committees and to comply with the conditions imposed by each, Florida City officials decided to simplify the process. The mayor and two department heads met with the prospective employer at a time and place convenient to the prospect. The three were empowered by the City Council to cut a deal with the prospective employer essentially on the spot. Prospective builders and employers liked the service and the speed of decision making. Eliminating the red tape worked well for Florida City, but the Florida City approach requires trust that the small team will work toward the interests of the community as a whole. Florida City's fairly homogenous demographics and political stability facilitated this approach.

Local government needs to recognize that it is very difficult to conduct business as usual in the wake of a disaster. While the usual expectation is that local government will create and adhere to standardized operating procedures that ensure stable and consistent outcomes, in the aftermath of an extreme natural hazard event, local government needs to play the role of catalyst. It needs to be responsive and flexible. It can return to managing in ways that promote consistency when the external environment has stabilized, at least to a manageable degree. The new job of local government is to get needed work done as quickly as possible and solve problems, not offer a complex array of services that generate paperwork. Because the overall job changes in the wake of an extreme natural hazard event, daily operations must change accordingly. It is far better to simplify them when you have time to give it serious thought; following a disaster there is not much time for contemplation.

Changing operations to be flexible rather than consistent can be very challenging for local government staff, most of whom are accustomed to their role as "rule keepers." They may resist attempts to add flexibility, arguing that maintaining consistency is the key to returning things to normal. The kind of person who thrives in a bureaucratic work environment designed to ensure fairness and consistency might understandably rebel when what they know is threatened. Leaders in local government agencies and offices will have to take on the role of persuading staff members that temporary changes are needed, and that the emphasis on consistent processing and attention to standard operating procedures will return when the community's recovery is underway. "Flexible, creative styles of problem-solving and decision making" (Rubin et al. 1985, p. 44) will facilitate recovery, rather than rigid, by-the-books fixation on standard operating procedures.

Local governments can do things to local businesses attempting to recover that are actually counterproductive. One of the most egregiously annoying municipal actions we encountered was in Northridge. There, the owner of a camera store at the heart of the damaged area reopened

his shop and was trying to accommodate the residents' demand for cam--
eras and film to document their losses. His street was blocked off by a
National Guard cordon, so he attached a small sign to a nearby cyclone
fence to help people find his shop. The City of Los Angeles ticketed
him and fined him $300 for posting an illegal sign. For years, he had
the same bitter complaint: "Here I am in the middle of a huge disaster
zone, trying to stay in business, generating sales tax revenue for them,
they've made it impossible for people to get to my store, and then they
have the gall to fine me!" Local government attention to rules that fit a
community that is not trying to recover can serve only to frustrate the
people who should be served by local government. Attachment to rules
when they are not sensible will not help a community return to normal,
though that may be the intent of those administering the rules.

Based on our research, we concluded that recovery requires a local
government to be flexible and adaptive; it must be able to do things it has
not done before and do things in ways it has never done them before. It
may be better to simplify processes beforehand than it is to waive them
or ignore them in time of crisis. In the aftermath, there are not enough
resources to do things that do not need to be done or to do things that
can be done more simply. Identifying the means for expediting processes
in advance of a disaster can ensure that careful thought has gone into the
streamlining of the processes and can enable a return to the status quo
when the time is right.

Ensuring Adequate Staffing

Municipalities almost always experienced staffing problems as they
worked toward community recovery. Staff members tended to become
exhausted from the long days, sleeping at city hall, worrying about
how they could help with recovery at home while being at work all the
time, and the 24/7 job that many lived with for months on end. They
needed backup. Second, local governments often found that they did not
have enough of some of the requisite skills needed to deal with the huge
and complicated load of rebuilding the community's infrastructure,
writing project proposals to state and federal agencies, and managing
complex projects. Some local governments hired high-level temporary
staff or consultants to help search for funding opportunities, develop
plans and proposals, set up accounting procedures, understand legal
implications, work with state and federal officials, and provide coun-
sel to harried elected officials and managers. Where we found a local
government that had done this, we found no one in that local government who regretted the choice. We found some instances in which the

individuals hired for the short term were still there years later and still helping with complicated recovery problems.

In small and midsize communities, it is usually necessary, following an extreme natural hazard event, to augment the staff for dealing with the combination of heavy workload and new challenges. Smaller local governments we studied typically lacked one or more skill sets or had inadequate numbers of people with those skills to accomplish the job. Many local governments needed help to evaluate and assess systemic community consequences, devise and evaluate strategies and programs, manage projects, work with granting agencies, and to track expenditures. Sometimes, help is needed for contracting with dozens of vendors to remove debris, repair facilities, and design and build new facilities. That work is demanding and time-consuming, and people can work overtime only so much before situational demands overwhelm their capabilities. It makes sense to contract with temporary help at this time.

Local governments that searched and recruited nationally for top-notch consultants usually fared better than those local governments that tried to make do with what they had. Good consultants are those who have been through disasters before, have a solid record of accomplishment of being helpful in other communities, are easy to work with, and are there when you need them. It is best to check with other local governments to learn about their experience with specific consultants or consulting firms. If you can see a problem coming, as in the case of major flooding on a long river, it makes sense to have made these inquiries before the flood-waters reach your community. Individuals who have professional contacts outside the local community can be especially useful during the recovery period, as they can seek assistance and resources outside the community.

It is important to remember that the federal government will cover the cost of people who are working on recovery, but it will not pay for people doing the routine business of running a city government. At least one local government we studied made the mistake of hiring everyone it needed for the extra workload as regular city employees. When the time came that the federal government would no longer pay for recovery workers, the city had considerable difficulty removing those employees from the payroll. Local revenue was inadequate to cover the operating budget with those employees on the payroll and trouble ensued. This adds to the argument favoring the employment of temporary and contractual staff.

Learn about Assistance Programs

Some local governments in our studies hired one or more individuals as consultants and charged them with reading and understanding the regulations of every federal program with which the local government was or might be eligible. Where that was done, the local government was usually successful in obtaining grants and assistance with less difficulty than communities that chose to rely on an already overburdened staff.

A host of assistance programs are available from federal, state, and private sources. Some of these are available to local government, but others are available to private and not-for-profit organizations. Rather than hoping that those nongovernmental organizations in your community find the right assistance programs, local officials can work to ensure that every person and every organization in the community understands which programs exist, eligibility requirements, basic rules and regulations, and how to maximize the probability of being successful. A clearinghouse function for such assistance programs might be established in city hall, on the city's Web site, or in cooperation with a not-for-profit organization within the community.

FEMA publishes guides to federal disaster recovery assistance programs and Disaster-Applicable Recovery Programs. Some of these programs provide money to mitigate future losses in the community from extreme natural hazard events; others provide funds for repair or replacement. Likewise, some provide funds to local governments; others provide loans and grants to individuals and to businesses. The local government that does not know which programs exist and their eligibility rules is very likely missing out on funds it can use for recovery or to reduce losses from the next extreme hazard event.

Creating a High-Level, Problem-Solving Advisory Team

Since childhood, most of us have been subjected to motion picture storylines in which a demented scientist or some mindless monster or force of nature threatens a disaster that will end life as we know it unless thwarted. A single hero or heroine, usually a reporter, faces the threat and saves the world while the rest of us, especially scientists and government employees, stand helplessly on the sidelines looking for all the world like deer in the headlights. In real life, teams comprising public employees, private organizations, and citizens with exceptional skills, dedication, and perseverance are needed to address extreme natural hazard events and their consequences. Real men and women, working collaboratively and over time, tackle the multifaceted issues associated with community recovery from extreme natural hazard events. Superheroes do not fly in and save the day.

The local government will need a high-level problem-solving team, a team that cuts across specialties and across departments to see the big picture and to understand how the parts fit together. This has to be a team of people willing to tell top leaders when something does not appear to make sense, people who have good ideas, people who can work together, and people who can handle responsibility. The team may comprise the department heads, but it does not have to do so. It might be an ad hoc group comprising the mayor, city manager, and two or three other individuals who are particularly competent.

The individuals who comprise these leadership advisory teams have to address some very difficult questions and tackle some very complex issues. Perhaps the first of these is to assess damage. Assessing physical damage is relatively easy compared with identifying the consequences that followed from the physical damage. Which components of the community were damaged? How badly? What other effects have spread or are likely to spread through the community? If the community suffered only losses to its built environment, then the challenge is to repair or replace those elements as quickly as possible. However, if adverse effects have already begun or if the community is faced with the prospect of addressing preevent problems as well as problems generated by the extreme natural hazard event, the situation is far more complex and demanding. The challenge of fixing long-standing problems exacerbated by the extreme natural hazard event is extremely tough and, sad to say, is sometimes virtually intractable.

DEVISE A LOCAL RECOVERY STRATEGY

In a disaster, local governments are usually called upon to orchestrate long-term recovery activities. What has to be done in each community to move toward recovery is largely contextual. It depends on what the community was like before the event, how much of what parts of the built environment were damaged or destroyed by the event, and on the nature and extent of consequences that are cascading through the social, economic, and political parts of the community. Some communities will simply need to try to reestablish the kinds of dynamics that existed before the event. Others will find themselves in the position of having to create a viable economy and social structure almost from scratch. Regardless of their circumstance, local officials will have to identify the problems facing the community and to decide what to do beyond the initial response to the event.

Virtually everyone who has offered advice on recovering from disaster urges local government to make a plan. Most will advise local governments to make a preevent recovery plan, as well. Planning is, in fact, crucial. The challenge is to take an approach to planning and to develop a set of plans that makes sense while still early in the aftermath of the disaster. What kind of disaster recovery planning makes sense? It is imperative that local officials understand the conditions under which those plans will be made and to remember how recovery proceeds.

Decision analysts talk about the need for different decision strategies when making decisions under various conditions having to do with what we know. These are conditions of certainty, risk, uncertainty, and ignorance. Policy making and planning can be viewed as subsets of decision making: (1) deciding on policies to guide the endeavor and (2) making plans on how to get from where you are to where you want to be. When your community suffers a significant disaster, is there any question where local leaders find themselves? It certainly is not under conditions of certainty concerning what will happen. Conditions are almost inevitably characterized by uncertainty, where probabilities of success and failure are unclear, and perhaps ignorance.

Under those circumstances, drafting "blueprints" for recovery is likely to be more dysfunctional than useful. Having land planners draft maps of what the community should look like 20 years hence is a lot like developing a 20-year community master plan for Berlin in 1930. Here are the simple facts. The municipality has a critical function but cannot determine the precise outcomes of the recovery efforts. Two things are vital to remember. First, the recovery period will be rife with unexpected events and unexpected outcomes from expected events. You will get some choices and you will experience many chances. Second, the community is, after all, largely self-organizing. Local government can guide, facilitate, coax, and even coerce. It can use its spending power to shape the context within which private decisions are made concerning the critical choices: what to do, where to do it, how to do it, and when to do it. It can incentivize some actions and deincentivize others. Ultimately, however, many of the choices will be made by people other than the individuals in local government offices and agencies.

A sensible approach to recovery planning is to begin with ascertaining what it is you would like to have happen and what you want to keep from happening. This can be accomplished by sitting in one's office and thinking about it, but a more useful approach is to involve others. Getting buy-in to a plan is easier when those affected by the plan participate in making it. Making a plan in a town hall meeting is not very effective. What is effective is soliciting ideas about desirable and undesirable features of the community that will emerge from the disaster and then, outside the town hall, converting those preferences into a statement of policies. No constituency should feel excluded. People who live in the community can sometimes be quite articulate about what they want and do not want.

Listening to key constituencies (e.g., property owners, business owners, teachers, municipal employees) and discovering their problems, concerns, and needs is far more fruitful than sitting around a table in city hall either assuming or guessing what they want. Local government officials add insult to injury when they impose their own priorities on constituents whose perceptions and expectations have been ignored. At the same time, it is vital to move the process along quickly enough so that delays do not become dysfunctional. Leadership advisory teams charged with moving the community forward must balance the benefits of participation with potential costs of the same.

Policies serve as guides for coping with uncertainty and ignorance. During recovery, decision makers will be faced with scores of important choices. A clear statement of policies serves as criteria for making choices about what to do and where to do it in the herky-jerky, tumultuous, and uncertain postevent period. Decision makers will also be faced with uncertainty about how some things are unfolding. They will also have to acknowledge their ignorance of phenomena yet to manifest themselves. How one decides a particular question will, almost invariably, have consequences for future decisions. At the same time, it is completely unreasonable to forestall making decisions that have to be made. It is important, therefore, to develop policies that can serve as criteria for helping to evaluate the alternatives when making decisions. We caution against making decisions before they are needed. By that, we mean that it is not necessary to decide on a location for the new library in town while the city is still under water. What is important is to define some criteria or policies that will be used to evaluate sites for the library (and other important structures) when the time comes to make that decision. Illustratively, it might be important to have the library on a main bus line, near the center of the community, and so forth.

Because making firm decisions today limits future options, it sometimes makes sense to take what we like to call a "soft path." Soft paths are solutions that are revocable. They sometimes involve using operating funds rather than capital project funds. Uncertainties can be resolved or sometimes may even resolve themselves over a short time. If there is a way, when faced with ignorance, to use a soft path it is often better than trying to change things once the concrete has cured. Committing too early to actions that are later regretted or overturned can exacerbate impressions that local government leaders are too quick to make poor decisions, and insufficiently thoughtful and open to stakeholder input.

As the emergency period recedes, the community needs a vision, policies, priorities, and a strategy for moving away from known evils to something better. Rather than a blueprint, local leaders are encouraged to devise a strategy. The strategy is a general guide on how to get from where you are to where you would like to be. It leaves room to adopt any of a number of potential actions within the general strategy, as it is necessary to adapt to changing circumstances. With a blueprint, a change in circumstance usually means having to recreate the entire blueprint, and under conditions of uncertainty and ignorance that is not the way to proceed. Recreating a blueprint is a costly and time-consuming way forward that will likely leave dissatisfaction and waste in its wake.

There will be some opposition to a strategy. One is that many people in the aftermath of disaster abhor ambiguity. Not having a detailed action plan for everything can be unsettling to some. The second big opposition will come from funding agencies. They want project plans that they can approve, fund, and monitor. The local leaders' challenge is to make certain those detailed blueprints can be devised so that they are compatible with all of the guiding policies.

Finally, a leadership advisory team might be created to conceptualize, outline, and evaluate the likely efficacy of various strategies for moving from where the community is to where it wants to be. This has to be done with the understanding that no community stops changing unless it is defunct. Thus, the strategy is really a general course of action, one that can be adapted as situations and needs change. The basic strategy is necessary to help ensure that the community can effectively use the resources it has to move the community toward recovery. The leadership advisory team should spend a considerable amount of effort over a relatively short time period trying to define a flexible strategy with a high probability of success.

Defining a flexible strategy with a high probability of success is, of course, easier said than done. Usually, it means not putting all one's eggs in a single basket unless it is absolutely necessary to do so. Single-industry communities are vulnerable in ways that multiple-industry communities are not. It means regularly and rigorously reviewing the strategy to evaluate the extent to which it is proving out. It means devising a strategy based more on facts and on careful assessment than on hope and intuition. It means being bold enough to capture people's imagination, but not so bold as to appear out of touch with reality. Mostly, it means surrounding oneself with smart people who are not reluctant to say the emperor has no clothes if, in fact, that is how they see it.

Whatever the basic strategy, reality testing is important. Too often, we have seen communities commit to a strategy that has only a slim chance of resulting in the desired outcomes. It is almost as though people think that believing in the efficacy of the strategy is enough to make it work. The "hope strategy" is not very good. It is extremely important to get objective, constructive criticism before committing to a course of action and then continue to get constructive criticism as the course of action proceeds. Of course, no one can ever tell in advance whether a strategy will work out as anticipated, but success is more likely if the strategy is revisited often to ascertain that it is generating the desired outcomes. Regular feedback and correction as needed together can greatly facilitate either achievement or alteration of desired outcomes.

It is not the job of a leadership advisory team to make the decisions about what to do. This group is essentially a policy analysis team: its job is to identify problems and issues, learn about them, analyze them, and to try to illuminate the consequences of various paths one might take so that the authorized decision makers can make choices that are more informed. The team should help authorized decision makers visualize an attainable future, define goals, and select strategies that are likely to be effective in attaining the goals.

Either this team or another must be responsible for appropriately sequencing and staging activities to meet current and emerging needs. It should identify critical opportunities for seeding in the community with projects and assistance to private groups to guide subsequent private actions. The city should institute a rolling plan that is updated as needed, at least annually, perhaps as part of the budget cycle, based on what has transpired.

As individuals, organizations, and government take action, contingent events will play out, conditions will change, and some uncertainties will be resolved as others emerge to take their place. New obstacles to goal attainment will appear, like unwanted epiphanies, demanding a change in order to achieve the goal. For example, until the factory opens, it is impossible to know whether a local employer will be able to make good on his or her promise to rebuild and reopen. Until former residents begin to return in numbers, it is not prudent to count on that happening. Until a firm commits to building in the community's new industrial park, it is not wise to assume that it will happen. Nothing is for sure and plans have to take that into account. Otherwise, communities will find themselves with problems like empty industrial parks around which they have created an infrastructure that is unneeded and wasteful.

Effective plans provide for branching into new directions at various junctures, depending on how things are going. Adaptation does not mean abandoning the plan and having to start again from scratch; it requires working with the reality of the situation to increase the probability of getting where you want to be. Thus, to be effective, planning strategies and programming activities have to be a continuing process, particularly in times of great uncertainty. It is critically important that some group in the community be responsible for continually monitoring the community to identify unexpected events and trends, and to assess how well the community's efforts are working toward recovery goals. Changes and adjustments will most certainly be required simply because none of us is omniscient; we are always faced with unknowns, unexpected or undesirable outcomes, or side effects from some action we take, or by actions taken by others that come as a welcome or unwelcome surprise. The law of unintended consequences is indisputable; unintended consequences will arise, no matter how carefully or deliberately we plan and make decisions. Human beings are boundedly rational (March and Simon 1958; Simon 2000); we can only access and evaluate so much data, and hence our decision making is necessarily probabilistic. Accordingly, we return to our advice that decision makers take the soft path as often as possible. Minimizing the number of dead ends in decision making should facilitate more positive outcomes than bad.

We have not said much here about traditional land use planning. Traditional approaches to community planning are inadequate for planning postdisaster community recovery. They can be, however, an important expression of those community goals that can be displayed on maps: land use allocation, distribution of facilities, and physical infrastructure. They are very much like a blueprint for a house. They show what it should look like, but do not say much, if anything, about how to get from a vacant lot to the final house with people living in it. They will help guide government decisions about where to put facilities and infrastructure and may be used to influence private decisions about where and where not to build.

The planning we suggest local governments embark upon embraces land use and facility planning, but it is much more. It addresses a broader array of goals and it is action oriented. It is devising a course of action that is intended to get us from where we are to where we want to be. It consciously addresses the existence of contingencies and unknowns, and anticipates the need to change and adjust in anticipation of events and in response to changes in circumstance. The kind of plan needed for post-disaster community recovery is different.

One phenomenon that we have observed is the interest by some stakeholders to "correct" all of a community's perceived problems in the wake of a disaster. After flooding devastated New Orleans, many spoke of the opportunity to "fix" the city's problems through government reforms of its educational, public housing, criminal justice, health care, and urban planning systems (Flaherty 2012). The outcomes of changes made to these systems have been mixed at best in the 9 years since Katrina. Too many decisions appear to have been made without input from continuing residents, including especially members of the African-American community and the poor. Instead, decisions appear to have been made in arguably paternalistic ways, for example, when minimally damaged or undamaged public housing units were torn down despite protests from residents (see Figures 7.4 and 7.5). In the aftermath, the city's housing authority has found itself administering more than 17,000 housing vouchers, almost twice the pre-Katrina amount (Flaherty 2012).

Examples such as these reinforce our advice that local government officials carefully consider the viewpoints of affected stakeholders before taking action. They also point to the need to make changes carefully,

FIGURE 7.4 New Orleans, Louisiana, October 8, 2005—The B.W. Cooper housing project, also known as the Calliope Project, was a complex of four-story buildings stretching along Martin Luther King Boulevard as it runs northwest out of the Central Business District. (Photograph by Lucy A. Arendt.)

after considering possible interdependencies. Rents in New Orleans, for example, escalated after Katrina, making it difficult for residents to live there. The housing issue was compounded by the slow return of industry, education, and health care. In the apparent rush to "fix" the city, planners and other well-intentioned "social entrepreneurs" (Flaherty 2012, para. 6) may have, in fact, slowed the rate of recovery for New Orleans.

ENSURE TWO-WAY COMMUNICATION

One of the most critical matters that has to be addressed extremely early in the aftermath is a community communication plan. Every community we studied had some way to communicate to the public during the emergency period. Every community we studied also attempted to communicate with the public about what was going on in the city during recovery, but only a few had plans and procedures for how to do so well. The following observations and suggestions stem from our conversations in those communities.

FIGURE 7.5 New Orleans, Louisiana, October 8, 2005—In the aftermath of Hurricane Katrina, most of the public housing in New Orleans was demolished, continuing a process started in the decade before. (Photograph by Lucy A. Arendt.)

Formal communication from local government to its constituencies serves both symbolic and substantive purposes. It is important for citizens to know that their local government is on top of things: operating, aware of what is going on, and doing what needs to be done. It is similarly important to know that there is a source of accurate, reliable information. As mentioned previously, when everything else is in disorder and chaos, people need anchorage. Some of that anchorage might be provided by local media, but after the emergency period, most of the people's information must ultimately come from the local government.

The substantive elements of communication from local government will change through time. Initially, the content will focus on what happened, where to get help, how to make contact with friends and family, and when and where certain events will occur. Later, the messages typically change to provide information to those working on their own recovery challenges, including specifically what local government is doing, and timetables for the availability and expected completion of various government tasks, such as the restoration of power, water, and sewage treatment; the reconstruction of infrastructure; debris removal and trash collection; airport opening; mail distribution; public events and meetings; where to go for information and help; and the like.

An important function of communication from city hall is impeding the rumor mill. Rumors are always rampant during and following disasters. Neighbors talk with neighbors and facts or half-truths become distorted, too often for the worst. Remember the telephone game where you whispered something into the ear of the person sitting next to you, then waited to see what message came back around the circle? Imagine that writ large and spreading, not in a circle, but in a growing wave across the community and then echoing back, badly distorted, through the community. Overcoming rumors is hard work and not always effective. It is best to try to nip them in the bud. Too often, while they may contain some element of fact or truth, rumors primarily convey the tacit theories of their "distributors." In other words, they represent what makes sense to the teller, based on his or her prior experience and set of beliefs about how the world works. The resident who distrusts government as a matter of course, for example, may see negative intent where none exists. The resident who imagines the worst-case scenario in all dealings may predict a recovery timeline far more pessimistic than reality might suggest.

Information must be seen as credible. The first step in ensuring information credibility is making sure that it is truly accurate, reliable, and accessible. A second step is making sure that the information comes from a credible source, one that is trusted. A third step in ensuring information credibility is making sure that any missteps are immediately recognized and addressed. Mistakes are inevitable; addressing them requires courage and diligence. Local government leaders must be willing to accept responsibility for errors in communication. Confessing to mistakes and communicating future steps to mitigate against mistakes will go a long way toward establishing trust and credibility with residents.

Remember what you already know: reporters do not always get it right. Providing written press releases is more likely to result in accurate reporting than hoping the reporter gets it right when he or she hears something in the hallway. After a disaster, reporters are likely to be pulled off other beats, like sports, to cover the disaster. They often have limited knowledge of the natural phenomenon and even less knowledge of how local government works. Like everyone, they are subject to their tacit theories and may therefore struggle to hear what local government is trying to say. Make it easy for them and better for yourself.

It is important to communicate with the full range of community constituencies, including local elected officials, department heads and employees, community residents, homeowners, business owners, state officials, federal officials, and media representatives. Some will require more frequent and more detailed communication than others will, but the messages must be consistent. The messages must also be tailored to the recipient. It should be evident that the more relationships established in advance of the extreme natural hazard event, the greater the likelihood that communication in the aftermath will be smooth and effective.

Typically, only larger local governments have one or more staff members trained to communicate effectively with the outside world or whose primary job is to provide public information. The only way to ensure that messages are consistent and accurate is to have a policy on who is permitted to talk with whom about what. Designate a principal contact point and explain the communication policy to all the staff. Depending on the circumstances, it may make sense to have several contact points, each with a designated area about which they are able to talk authoritatively. It may also be advisable to hire a communications consultant to help establish communication policies and practices, and to help with technical matters.

Communication has to flow from the city and to the city. Too often, we have seen situations in which local officials devised plans on how to help one or another group without ever talking with members of that group. For example, most local government administrators know little or nothing about small business, yet, in city after city, they sat in their offices, imagined what local small business people needed, and then devised programs that were either not useful or downright dysfunctional. Before local officials assume that something is needed or not needed, they must sit down to talk with the people who are going to be affected to learn what is likely to be effective or detrimental.

Similarly, local government must communicate simply and in a timely fashion with community members who need information about local government's plans and timetables before they invest money in rebuilding or changing what they do and where they do it. This is easier said than done. Still, community members should not have to listen to dysfunctional rhetoric (e.g., "We're going to rebuild [insert name of place] just as it was") in place of concrete plans. Rhetoric ultimately angers people, especially when they rely on promises that can never be fulfilled. Eventually, many people will take their money and leave the dysfunctional community, exacerbating the recovery situation.

There are many options for getting needed information to people on a timely basis. Some school districts have automated telephone, text, or e-mail systems that advise parents that school will be cancelled or delayed because of a blizzard, ice storm, threat of severe storm, or even during human-initiated threats. After disasters, some local governments set up Web sites where people can get timely, reliable information. These are sometimes part of the local government's regular Web site; otherwise, the official Web site provides a hyperlink to a different site dedicated entirely to community disaster and recovery news. Hospital officials we interviewed in the course of our research tell us that it is often useful to have the Web site generated in another community so that, if power is disrupted in the local community, the site is still operable. For those who remain in the community, simple forms of communication can be best. For example, posters on information kiosks located in well-traveled areas can be an excellent way to update people on community happenings.

The choice of how to communicate will vary. During the emergency response, police cruisers with loudspeakers may be the most effective means. When basic utilities are beginning to come on line, radio and television make sense. Posters and billboards are useful, especially if local print media are not able to print and distribute papers. Face-to-face community meetings in neighborhoods are an important means of maintaining communication and a sense of connection for residents. In recent times, social media such as Twitter and Facebook have played an increasingly important role during both response and recovery. For example, in the midst of the January snowstorm in Atlanta, citizen and consultant Michelle Sollicito created SnowedOutAtlanta, a Facebook group intended to help stranded motorists locate help (Garner 2014). By the end of the storm, the Facebook group had grown to more than 56,000 members.

It is important to set up communication processes before the disaster. If local officials wait until after something happens, mistakes will be made, time will be lost, and information will not get to those who need it. People should know where to look for information before an extreme natural hazard event; they should not have to go hunting after the fact. Doing so only adds to their uncertainty and anxiety.

CHAPTER **8**

A Recovery Starting Point

The key challenge in recovery is to bring people, housing, and jobs together in the community so that a critical mass is achieved that will build upon itself. People, jobs, and housing are prerequisites to the healing or rebuilding of the social community. Depending on the extent of damage to social, cultural, and economic elements of the community, it may take years to redevelop them, but housing, jobs, and security are prerequisites.

Recovery is not a sequential "fix one sector completely and then move on to the next one" kind of activity. Some functions require that other functions be attended to before it is possible to address them. Others have to move along in tandem, changing and adjusting to changes in one another. Having said that, it is important to point out that none of them has to be completed before work can proceed on the others. Each functional sector has to be addressed sufficiently to permit others to catch up and then they can each be advanced more after that. Local administrators will likely lie awake nights struggling with the chicken-and-egg problem: "How can I get either in place without the other being in place first?"

Essentially, the local leaders' challenge is to jumpstart the process so that private interests get sufficient positive cues to invest their energy and resources into taking additional, subsequent steps. Once private interests are confident that the community is on course to recover, they will be more likely to take a risk by investing in the community. In addition to stoking private interests' confidence in the community, local government must also facilitate the provision of basic items considered by many to be the foundation for successful communities (e.g., utilities, infrastructure, schools, health care, business districts, affordable housing, appropriate recreation facilities). Once private interests have begun their return or new entry into the community, government must then work to continue to provide appropriate cues as to what is acceptable and what is not, including where to build and what to build.

Consequently, it is necessary to do a careful, thoughtful, and accelerated assessment of the community's present state and its likely future. As observed by Rubin and her colleagues (1985), "Communities with leaders that have a vision of the community's long-range economic development can be expected to fare better during recovery" (p. 38). To that end, and as mentioned previously, local government must establish a reliable intelligence function. What was the most likely future for the community had there been no disaster? What would it take to get the community on a positive trajectory? What "critical mass" of what kind of resources would be required? What is happening to similar communities across the country? Have any had the kind of success your community would want to emulate? This is not easy work. It demands a level of addressing reality that many in the community would rather avoid. Hoping for the best or imagining it will happen is often substituted for hard-nosed thinking. Again, it is often useful to get outside help to see the community as it is, rather than as we remember it with selective recall or as we wish it were. The problem is that no one wants to bring bad news. Consultants, and state and federal officials are usually optimistic to a fault. Who wants to be the messenger who says that the best thing to do is to fold your tent and move on? Probably no one. Who wants to be the messenger who says that the bustling downtown you remember from the 1960s is never coming back, at least not the way you remember it? Again, probably no one. Nonetheless, it is possible to get people with a stake in the community to develop a realistic appraisal of the community's future.

One approach to working with community people, and perhaps the simplest, is a SWOT analysis. What are the community's strengths, weaknesses, opportunities, and threats? But do not make the mistake of thinking this analysis can be performed in an hour or two by a large group over coffee and doughnuts down at the schoolhouse. Too often, we have seen organizational and government officials conduct SWOT analyses and develop "strategic plans" in an afternoon with a group from the community or the organization. That is good for show and may even provide some insights, but it rarely results in adequate analysis or realistic planning. That requires serious thinking by skilled people over whatever time is available and not just shooting from the hip. Similarly, if local leadership has some strong ideas about what to do and simply uses the group planning as a charade, the more savvy people in the group will notice it in a heartbeat and any good will that might otherwise have developed will be turned into negative response.

Following a careful assessment of where the community is at this time, one must then address an even more daunting question: What's possible for the future? Frankly, we have not seen any community that tried valiantly to transform itself into something radically different from what it was before the disaster actually achieve the desired transformation. In looking at those that tried it, however, we do not know what could have been done differently to effect something that would have more closely approximated the desired transformation. We concluded that it is extremely difficult to make the community into something that it was not, even in a decade of effort. Frankly, when many of the same people come together as have been together before, they have a tendency to think the same way, consider the same issues, use the same resources, and lo and behold, achieve the same results. This may be why some communities continue to hold out for the thriving "downtown" of yore. "Maybe if we tried harder, this time it would work."

Doing the same thing repeatedly and expecting different results is said to be the definition of insanity. If people know this (and it appears that this is an oft-quoted quote), then why do they do it? Many factors influence our perceptions and decision making, including cognitive biases (Stanovich and West 2008), past experience (Juliusson, Karlsson, and Gärling 2005), age and individual differences (Bruine de Bruin, Parker, and Fischhoff 2007), and belief in personal relevance (Acevedo and Krueger 2004). Cognitive biases, in particular, influence people by causing them to overrely on expected observations and previous knowledge, while disregarding information or observations that are perceived as uncertain or inconsistent with expectations, without consideration of what's really happening. We struggle to recognize our own preferences and biases, and it is difficult for us to see how they color our thinking and decision making. We do not want to believe that the desired outcome is beyond our reach; we believe that we can achieve the reality we want, because we want it so badly.

We do think that it is possible for communities to position themselves for transformation, but whether transformation can actually be achieved depends on many things coming together over a period of years. That certainly does not mean it cannot be done. As World War II ended, Las Vegas was virtually nonexistent. Low taxes, massive private investments from a wide variety of sources, and a primary industry based on entertainment and lasciviousness can do a lot to grow a city. Not to mention a strong desire on the part of several influential people (e.g., mobster Benjamin "Bugsy" Siegel, a member of the Meyer Lansky crime organization). On a more positive note, the Marshall Plan helped restore war-torn Europe into an economic powerhouse in a relatively short time. Still, one could argue that many of the requisite pieces had existed prior to the Depression and World War, enabling the prosperous society that eventually developed.

The most promising approaches we have seen build on what is already working in the community, augmented with new components that have the potential for fostering further development. St. Peter, Minnesota; Biloxi, Mississippi; and a few other communities have taken that approach with some success. St. Peter has positioned itself as a community that is complementary to nearby Mankato. It offers affordable and quality housing to individuals working in Mankato where such housing is scarce. Biloxi was having some success with casinos pre-Katrina. Rather than seek some other form of industry, Biloxi has chosen to facilitate the tourism industry by supporting additional casino development. In both cases, both communities elected to pursue a trajectory that included services that were in demand (i.e., housing, casinos).

At the same time as looking to see what might be done, it makes very good sense to learn what should be done to ensure that recovery actions lead to a community that is more resilient, less exposed, and less vulnerable to subsequent events. All of this requires specifying some general goals or performance characteristics of the community as it moves toward recovery.

The community goals definitely should not be to rebuild exactly what was there before the disaster. If the pre-disaster community was vulnerable to this disaster, chances are that, if it is rebuilt just as it was, it will be similarly vulnerable to a subsequent disaster. The challenge for local government and community members will be to build a better, more resilient version of what existed prior to the extreme natural hazard event, while taking into account the community's essential nature and core competences. Building hazard mitigation into the community recovery plan is an extremely important goal. Books such as *Holistic Disaster Recovery: Ideas for Building Local Sustainability after a Natural Disaster* (Mileti 2006) provide guidance on how to build resiliency into a community through hazard mitigation.

SHAPING THE POSTEVENT COMMUNITY TRAJECTORY: REBUILDING OR RESTORING THE ECONOMY

Most local governments we studied worked to put things back the way they were before the disaster. A few local governments, however, took a different view. The communities intent on creating a more viable community than existed before the event made large emotional and financial investments in community economic infrastructure, usually supported financially by state and federal grants in aid. Some of the proactive communities were more successful than others were. Frankly, most of the local governments that worked hard to reshape the community's trajectory were the ones where the preevent community trajectory was not particularly desirable. Typically, their local economies were declining or had not been developing at a pace or in a hoped-for direction. The efforts were not driven as much by community "boosterism" as by a deep concern for the future well-being of residents and an acknowledgement that, without a successful intervention, the future was not bright. In many of these cases, local leaders hoped that the disaster would provide an influx of federal money and thus an opportunity to propel the community into a more favorable trajectory by establishing a vital economy and a viable community. The case of New Orleans appears to fit this description, as previously described. Prior to Katrina, New Orleans had issues with poverty, crime, housing, its educational system, and more. While the jury is still out, New Orleans seems to be limping along rather than flourishing in the aftermath of Katrina, a victim of its many failures long before the hurricane and subsequent flooding swamped the city.

Chickens and Eggs

Bringing workers back to the community makes little sense unless there are jobs waiting for them. Right after the extreme natural hazard event, there is often a shortage of service workers in restaurants and lodging establishments and in demolition, cleanup, and construction (see Figure 8.1). Some workers take on those as temporary employment while looking for work that is more suitable. They need the income and the

FIGURE 8.1 New Orleans, Louisiana, October 8, 2005—Signs promoting cleanup and construction services litter the neutral ground of New Orleans in the aftermath of Hurricane Katrina. (Photograph by Lucy A. Arendt.)

shortage of workers often pushes up wages in them. Long-term recovery will not occur, however, until stable employment separate from the "employment of recovery" is available. This poses a chicken-and-egg problem. Employers may be willing to reopen only if there is an adequate workforce and labor may return to the community only when jobs are immediately available. In these cases, local government may be able to help find a solution.

Helping to ensure the availability of sufficient numbers of housing units at affordable prices will greatly facilitate attracting new workers and making it possible for residents who left the disaster scene to return. In the short term, that means getting temporary housing on site or bringing workers to the community from other communities in which they found housing. Over the longer term, much more can be done to assist with housing. In Florida City, for example, the city bought and was given lots. The city then went into the home-building business. It sold the homes it built for an affordable price and gradually left the home-building and selling business. In East Grand Forks, the city built a subdivision for new housing.

It is probably unreasonable to assume that large numbers of workers will return to a badly damaged community until schools and other family-oriented facilities are back in operation. While we usually expect those who evacuated the community to make the round trip and return, they do not always come back. They need one or more good reasons to return. If they find a better life in the community in which they found temporary shelter, they may not come back. This may be especially true if their home community has been subject to multiple extreme natural hazard events over their lifetime. Rebuilding one's home and life once is probably enough for most people; doing it multiple times requires an attachment to place that few people may feel, depending on how deep their family's roots are in a given community.

Living in a trailer when one has become accustomed to a house may be acceptable in the short run. In the end, however, homeowners will want to live in a dwelling they can improve and mark as their own. Living with extended family, likewise, can be a workable housing solution in the short term, but eventually people want their own domicile returned to them. Perhaps especially in the United States, having one's own home is a symbol of emancipated adulthood. Asking people to continue living in a community where they feel as though their living space is not their own is a sure way to dissatisfaction and a desire to live elsewhere. Thus, local government will want to facilitate housing for its residents, knowing that doing so is the key to many other elements of community recovery.

Local Support for Small Businesses

A few local governments helped businesses get back into business by facilitating permit applications and health inspections, targeting businesses that had to open as soon as possible. Most midsize and smaller communities we studied attempted to provide modest help to other small-business owners as well. Often, this was the result of the Chamber of Commerce or a local banker advocating for help to small businesses. The assistance usually took the form of small loans. The loan programs usually offered some kind of subsidy, including low or no interest, deferred repayment, and possible forgiveness of the principal. Local banks sometimes subsidized the interest rates themselves.

In the communities we studied, help for local businesses usually came from local government and was funded, one way or another, through a combination of Department of Housing and Urban Development (HUD) Community Development block grants, private donations, and actions taken by local financial institutions. Many local governments did little or nothing to assist local businesses with their financial needs arising from the disaster. Most local governments have very little experience helping local businesses remain in business in the community or getting back on their feet after a community disaster. They are more likely to have more experience trying to attract new businesses and industry to the community, so that is what they did. Too often, when confronted with problems, we do what we know how to do rather than doing what needs to be done.

The loans to small businesses always had some strings attached. Usually, the business had to agree to do business within the local jurisdiction for some number of years to earn loan forgiveness. Owners who took the loans sometimes found the strings attached to the loans to be particularly burdensome, despite their initial attractiveness. For example, it rarely makes sense to stay in an existing business location if no one else is there. The local jurisdiction may want to revitalize its fading central business district by requiring borrowers to do business there, but the owner usually just wants to start making money again.

One of the authors had the good fortune to meet with a small-business owner as he was relocating his inventory from a block of businesses that had been cordoned off by the local officials after an extreme event. When asked his plans, the business owner indicated that he had found a location to lease that was open for business and that was surrounded by other businesses that were also open. The owner indicated that while the move was sad—he had been in his location for more than a decade—it was also necessary for his business' survival. Local governments must be quick to understand the importance of creating destinations, especially for consumers interested in retail products and services. Likewise, they need to understand the importance of colocating businesses and their suppliers, to the extent that doing so is practical.

Businesses may be ineligible for financial assistance from state and federal agencies, depending on their financial history. A small business may not even be eligible for a loan from the Small Business Administration (SBA). And since SBA loans are typically predicated on business income before the disaster, they tend not to reflect the prospects for the business after the disaster as the postevent community changes. Accordingly, some small-business owners who got an SBA loan reported to us that repaying the loan had become a major burden.

The Small Business Administration is authorized to make loans to homeowners, not-for-profit organizations, and businesses, regardless of size, in areas covered by a federal disaster declaration. Three kinds of loans are available: physical disaster home loans, physical disaster business loans, and economic injury business loans (Code of Federal Regulations, title 13, section 123.5). The loans are made at lower interest rates than typical of private financial institutions. SBA loan criteria include "reasonable assurance that you can repay your loan out of [sic] your personal or business cash flow, and you must have satisfactory credit and character" (Code of Federal Regulations, title 13, section 123.6). SBA practices may vary somewhat from disaster to disaster: "Since SBA cannot predict the occurrence or magnitude of disasters, it reserves the right to change the rules (in the disaster loan program) without advance notice, by publishing interim emergency regulations in the Federal Register" (Code of Federal Regulations, title 13, section 123.1).

The SBA makes significant investments in disaster areas in the form of loans to homeowners and businesses. Nonetheless, some of the owners we interviewed had complaints about the loan programs. Since the loans are made primarily based on the business before the extreme natural hazard event, and because business conditions after the event are often quite unlike those before the event, the loans sometimes became an albatross for them instead of the hoped-for solution to their problems. For those seeking loans of at least $14,000, the SBA requires that business owners "provide available collateral such as a lien on the damaged or replacement property, a security interest in personal property, or both" (Code of Federal Regulations, title 13, section 123.11). We heard numerous complaints from small-business owners who availed themselves of the loan programs that the loan program made it virtually impossible for them to make changes to their business that were necessary to adapt to new circumstances. Some people claimed that the SBA had "sold their loans" to private firms and that it was impossible for them to get partial releases of collateral pledged for their loans. SBA officials have told us that the SBA does not sell its loans. We did not investigate the claims of the business people to fully understand the problems they were encountering. Rather, we were concerned with people's perceptions, since it is those perceptions that drive behavior, regardless of their accuracy.

Alternative Strategies Used to Rebuild the Local Economy

Not all community economies unravel following an extreme natural hazard event. Unfortunately, particularly for communities not favored with a great location, desirable amenities, or the other magnets that attract economic activity, extreme natural hazard events often create or exacerbate very serious economic problems for months, years, and even decades following the extreme natural hazard event. The malaise or decline is a consequence of the extreme natural hazard event and of the dynamics of economic and sociocultural development and change.

The challenges of establishing or reestablishing a viable economy that might be sustained over an extended period are enormous: across the country and internationally, everyone else wants the same thing and is competing for it. A significant part of the challenge is that the local economy is truly self-organizing and, to a very considerable extent, outside the ability of local officials to influence very much, much less to manage. Individuals and individual firms make choices about what to do and where to do it. In communities that are off the beaten path and that have lost their locational or amenity advantages, locals are faced with the extremely difficult challenge of creating a new *raison d'etre* for the place—one that is a magnet sufficiently strong to bring development.

Instead of, or in addition to, helping individual businesses, local governments sometimes attempt to use the disaster as the launch point to make long-term improvements in the community economy. As described earlier, this is most likely to happen in communities that were having economic problems before the extreme natural hazard event or events. When state and federal money is available for rebuilding and for economic development projects, the local governments are inclined to try to have the resources to do so.

SEVEN STRATEGIES

We found that, collectively, local governments seem to select from among seven basic strategies in an attempt to foster postdisaster economic development. We review each of these strategies on the next several pages.

Do What We've Always Done

One popular approach is to continue to do what the local government was doing before the event. That usually comes down to attempting to attract business and industry by (1) advertising the attractiveness of the local community, its location, local amenities, and the sterling workforce; and (2) offering incentives such as free land or buildings, tax abatements, and the like. The popularity of this approach is demonstrated by the massive number of largely vacant municipal industrial parks across the United States.

The problem is that these activities usually attract mobile industries, industries that can pick up and move quickly and that are likely to leave town when the incentives run out. We used to call it "chasing smokestacks" or "chasing shoe factories." While people no longer want smoke stacks and very few shoe factories exist in the United States, there are footloose industries that tend to move from place to place in search of tax breaks, low taxes, and low cost labor. If your community is in trouble, they may be a lot better than nothing, but usually not for long.

Recreate What Used to Be

It appears that many local officials hold in their hearts a passionate conviction that there should be a central business district in their community: a place where people shop, do business, and gather. Historically, the core of the city was where one found the cathedral, the markets, the banks, and the castle. Vibrant central business districts in midsized cities are now largely historical artifacts, replaced by suburban malls that follow sprawl and strip malls along major thoroughfares. Even so, many local governments still try to bring them back, trying to breathe life into central city corpses. They forget that these central business districts died for a reason (or for several reasons): parking fees, lack of interesting consumer destinations, lack of proximity to housing, lack of iconic eateries, higher crime, and so on. As long as community residents are content with the often-suburban options that have replaced the central business districts, they are unlikely to patronize the central business district, no matter the money pumped into it.

For example, although Grand Forks, North Dakota, and East Grand Forks, Minnesota, did a mostly superior job of recovering, and accomplished much that other places might well want to emulate, they each spent a large amount of grant money trying to recreate central business districts that were largely moribund before the flood. Retail businesses had been moving away from downtown and toward the edge of town where the people lived. Grand Forks spent an enormous amount of money provided by the rest of us through the federal government to rebuild something that was not working before the flood, and it is not working much better now. Across the river in East Grand Forks, the city helped move a popular restaurant and bar a couple of blocks north and about 20 feet vertically. That worked out well because the move made the successful business more attractive. However, when the city bought a small downtown shopping center and converted it into a place it could lease out to small businesses, it did not work out as well, because the customers still went primarily to the new, auto-accessible shopping areas on the city's periphery.

Frankly, using "free money" from the federal government in an attempt to recreate a vibrant central district makes more sense than trying to use money scraped from the local tax base. In some ways, it is a "no-cost" approach to financing a project with considerable appeal, but a low probability of success. On the other hand, there are opportunity costs. Those monies might have been spent to make considerable progress on other local problems and concerns. It is essential that local government decision makers not be swayed by nostalgia and a longing for a time that may have little in common with the present.

Following the fire, Los Alamos, New Mexico, also attempted to revitalize its central business district. Downtown Los Alamos faced two challenges. Los Alamos is basically a one-business town, that being the Los Alamos National Laboratory. The lab had recently gone to a four-day week and had built a new cafeteria onsite for workers. There was also a newly improved highway down the mountain to Santa Fe, which brought that city a lot closer to Los Alamos, at least in terms of travel time. Whereas Los Alamos lab employees previously had mostly eaten lunch and shopped in downtown Los Alamos, they now ate at the new cafeteria at the lab on their workdays and went to Santa Fe on their long weekends to do much of their shopping. The city used the fire as a focal point and lever to try to revitalize downtown businesses, but it could not change the proximity to Santa Fe or the food at the lab facilities. Individuals' habits had changed, and having a new central business district would not prove sufficient to change their daily behaviors.

A Great Leap Forward

Of all the cities we studied, we were most impressed with Homestead, Florida's, bold approach to economic recovery after its triple disaster. Hurricane Andrew essentially flattened the city, driving out many of its residents. Closing Homestead Air Force Base drove out many more residents. Finally, at least locally, the North American Free Trade Agreement (NAFTA) is thought to have had a major adverse impact on the area's agricultural economy. Local officials thought hard about how to use Federal Economic Development Administration funds to launch Homestead into a new economic orbit. The strategy seemed sound, but it has not worked out as hoped almost a decade and a half later, despite massive amounts of federal assistance to the city.

The city focused on creating attractive facilities and amenities to bring business and retirees to the community. As previously mentioned, one project was a major league spring training facility. Just before Hurricane Andrew struck, the city had completed an $18 million spring training center for a major league baseball team, the Cleveland Indians. The Indians had decided to move to Florida after a half-century of conducting spring training in Arizona. After the hurricane essentially destroyed the facility, the city quickly rebuilt it, using federal grants and insurance money. The park was opened in 1993 and refurbished in 1996, but the Cleveland Indians had already moved to Chain of Lakes Park near Orlando and were not about to move again. Homestead is now the owner of a large baseball facility with faded and peeling paint that does not see much baseball (see Figure 8.2). As described by Veiga (2012), the stadium has been "a headache for city leaders ever since Hurricane Andrew struck" (para. 1) ... "the salmon-colored structure that held so

FIGURE 8.2 Homestead, Florida, June 15, 2004—Peeling paint and corroded pillars bear witness to a community's dream to sponsor spring training and other sporting events at the Homestead Sports Complex, destroyed by Hurricane Andrew in 1992 and rebuilt but never used for spring training. (Photograph by James N. Holly.)

much promise for the city became known as the 'pink elephant.' It was costing the city, too—up to $500,000 a year, at a time when Homestead was on the edge of bankruptcy" (para. 39).

A second major facility built by the city was the Homestead–Miami Speedway, intended to cash in on the popularity of NASCAR. The track is doing fairly well, hosting, as it does, a solid program of racing. Unfortunately, a lawsuit initiated after the city had developed the track resulted in a Florida Supreme Court decision that led to the city having to pay ad valorem property taxes to Miami–Dade County on the assessed value of the facility. That created an unexpected and significant drain on the city's finances just when local officials were looking forward to a significant cash infusion to the community and to the city treasury.

The third effort involved the development of a very attractive and well-developed 280-acre industrial park complete with infrastructure. Local leaders had hoped to convert the former Homestead Air Force Base into a commercial airport to facilitate trade with Latin America. The park was developed in collaboration with the Rockefeller Group Development Corporation. However, the base now serves as home for military reservists, so the city has no commercial airport, and the industrial park remains largely vacant nearly two decades later.

All this effort and money failed to do for Homestead what its location near Miami has brought about. After more than a decade of unrealized hopes for revitalization, Homestead is now growing. Miami has expanded southward. Homestead was the next available area for housing, so people from Miami are turning Homestead into a bedroom community as thousands of new homes have been constructed since 2003. It reflects a fundamental change in Homestead's historic role in south Dade County, as well as a new trajectory. This has generated major increases in the local tax revenue but done little to improve local employment options.

Transformation

A few cities have tried to transform themselves following a disaster. One story is particularly illustrative. Montezuma, Georgia, is a small town on the Flint River in south-central Georgia with about 3,400 residents. It is located about 50 miles south-southwest of Macon and about 16 miles from the nearest access to Interstate 75. Montezuma was created when a railroad was built to cross the Flint River at that location and to serve the surrounding agricultural area. It continues to serve this role, but as highway access to larger towns improved over the years, the larger towns took market share from the community.

Montezuma's local government continually works to attract employers to the area. Low-cost labor is available, but it is mostly unskilled and undereducated, and there are many locations with better access to the interstate highway system. Local officials have struggled to find ways to make Montezuma attractive to both industry and to retirees but without great success. Local merchants originally relied on local trade because they were conveniently close and did not face competition from national and retail chain stores. As that competition emerged and became strong, most locals remained in business by providing exceptional customer service or by extending credit to those who might otherwise have difficulty obtaining it. Even so, with good highways leading to Perry, 25 miles away, and to larger cities farther north on the interstate toward Macon and Atlanta, large chain stores increasingly drain away local business.

Montezuma flooded in July 1994 because of heavy, persistent rains produced by Tropical Storm Alberto. Small earthen dams creating farm ponds along Beaver Creek failed under the deluge and water ran overland into downtown Montezuma. The old core of Montezuma, dating to the 1850s, was built in "a low swamp in the midst of a dense thicket of woods" where the railroad crossed the Flint River (Macon County Chamber of Commerce 2013, para. 1). Being in the lowest part of the town, the old business core had also borne the brunt of floods in 1902, 1929, and 1948.

Following the overflow of Beaver Creek, business owners watched as the Flint River rose and as water sheeted into the city from higher ground. The levee built by the Army Corps of Engineers in 1956 stood strong, holding the sheeting water in the central business district. The Flint River reached its highest crest in recorded history, about 35 feet. The water, muddy and colored by the red clay typical of Georgia, remained in the business district for 6 days, trapped by the levee as the flood swept downstream (Macon County Chamber of Commerce 2013).

The Corps refused to permit city officials to breach the levee to drain the downtown, but rumor has it that a local official drained the town center by cutting a hole in it with a backhoe under cover of darkness. In any event, the downtown drained, leaving the entire urban business center muddy and shop inventory destroyed.

City officials tried to look on the bright side: the flood was an opportunity to get help and resources to rebuild the central part of town and, perhaps, to reestablish it as a place to go, to shop, and to attract tourists. The plan was relatively simple. The old business core was picturesque but generally neglected. Local officials reasoned that they could redo the old historic core and create a magnet for retirees and tourists. The community is close to Andersonville, the Civil War prison site and home of the National Prisoner of War Museum, which draws a relatively small but reliable number of visitors annually.

The city worked with representatives from the State of Georgia who helped rehabilitate the business district into a quaint replica of what it had been many years before. With help from the State of Georgia Historic Preservation Division, the city was able to acquire title to the facades of commercial buildings in the old central commercial core and then repair them, paint them in complementary colors, add attractive street architecture, and create a pleasant place for shopping and visiting. Old style street lamps were installed. Cozy open spaces were created. Pavement was replaced. Statues and monuments appeared and trees were planted.

Unfortunately, the community has yet to realize the hoped-for resurgence. The rejuvenation of the business district did not generate much in the way of new employment, the tourists never came in the numbers hoped for, and neither did well-off retirees. By 2004, many of the downtown merchants were barely hanging on. Some had closed and left their buildings vacant or were replaced by marginal establishments aimed at lower-end buyers. The wonderful paint jobs are peeling and the dream may be fading. The population has declined over the past decade.

The Montezuma effort did not attain the hoped for long-term community resurgence but not because the local officials did not develop a thoughtful plan for transforming the community. The city was hampered by considerable poverty in the area, a largely uneducated workforce, and few employment opportunities for locals. National trends make it tough for small or isolated towns to survive. Unfortunately, Montezuma did not develop a big enough magnet for tourism, shopping, and retirement living to overcome the basic problems of the community and the immediate region. To further compound the problem, the construction projects took more than a year, during which access to downtown and the shops there was extremely limited and inconvenient. Consumers change habits when confronted with "hassle costs"; if reasonable substitutes are available (e.g., other shops, located elsewhere) and switching costs are perceived to be low, consumers will stop visiting shops that were once more accessible.

Working with the Market

Florida City, located immediately adjacent to Homestead, was also devastated by Hurricane Andrew. Florida City is smaller than Homestead and primarily home to African-Americans. Before the hurricane, it was a poor community with relatively few employment opportunities; about 40 percent of the households lived below the poverty line. After Andrew, Florida City was largely in the background as assistance poured into Homestead; however, Florida City had two advantages over Homestead. The first was location. Within Florida City's boundaries lies the intersection of the Florida Turnpike and U.S. Highway 1. Second, the city had a very stable local government. The mayor had been in office for many years, as had several members of the small city council.

We reiterate details of Florida City's story to illustrate anew the value of working with the market. Following the hurricane, large retailers began visiting the area because U.S. Highway 1 is one of only two routes to the Florida Keys and there are virtually no large building sites between Florida City and Key Largo, 30 miles to the south. The mayor and his staff assessed the situation and made a prudent decision: Florida City would simplify approval processes when a firm thought it might want to locate along the highway near the toll road terminus. The mayor and two or three other city officials would meet anytime, anywhere with prospective businesses. They would be able to cut the deal with the private firms in a single meeting and the decision would stick. Rather than having to appear before five or more committees over a series of weeks or months, the business representatives could meet once and be assured that the deal would be approved. We are inclined to think that Florida City was able to implement that strategy because it has a long-time mayor and stable city council. If local politics are factious, that is not reflected in the long incumbencies of local officials. The community was thus able to empower the mayor and top local officials to focus on reducing the hassle factor for businesses. It worked.

Between its location advantage and the streamlined approval processes, Florida City attracted two big-box retailers to its jurisdiction within 2 years of the hurricane. The new buildings augmented a small tax base and the box stores provided many jobs. Though the jobs were mostly at or near minimum wage, they afforded employment to many who had little employment history, few skills, and limited mobility.

Building on What They Have

Three communities we studied provide good examples of bringing about economic recovery by building on the assets the community had prior to the extreme natural hazard event and that largely remained following their disasters. St. Peter, Minnesota, is a community of about 10,000 people located in South Central Minnesota. Founded in 1853, it is one of the state's oldest cities. It is surrounded by rich farmland and serves as an agricultural-business center. It is also home to Gustavus Adolphus, a small liberal arts college, and to a state hospital. Minnesota Highway 169, which runs through St. Peter, connects it with Minneapolis-St. Paul, about an hour away, and with Mankato, 20 minutes to the south.

On Sunday, March 29, 1998, an EF3 tornado caused severe damage to the community (see Figure 8.3). The tornado had a particularly wide swath, up to a mile and a half wide in some parts. It damaged or

FIGURE 8.3 St. Peter, Minnesota, March 30, 1998—Many historic buildings in St. Peter, including the one shown in this photo, were heavily damaged by the unusual EF3 tornado. (Courtesy of the National Oceanic and Atmospheric Administration/Department of Commerce/Amy Card.)

destroyed 40 percent of the homes in the community, many buildings in St. Peter's downtown commercial area, and every building at Gustavus Adolphus College. Fortunately, Easter break at the college began the day before the tornado struck so the campus was essentially vacant when the storm struck and no one was killed or injured there. Because the warning sirens worked, only two people were killed despite the ferocity of the storm. The town was without water, sewer, or electricity for nearly a week. Damages in the small town were estimated to be $300 million to $500 million.

Funds from the Federal Emergency Management Agency helped considerably with covering the cost of rebuilding and repairing infrastructure. The city was insured against tornado damage and its insurance company gave the city a "down payment" of $1 million dollars to start repairs. Repair of privately owned property was greatly aided by the fact that a large proportion of property owners were insured against wind damage. Gustavus Adolphus College was insured but also received considerable financial disaster assistance from its alumni, greatly facilitating rebuilding and improving the campus. Students, too, helped greatly with cleanup at the college and in the community.

The community suffered mostly initial consequences. There were relatively few systemic community consequences. Neither the economic nor the social fabric of the community was severely damaged.

Furthermore, much of what the community achieved in the months and years after the tornado was already in the works or in the planning stages before the tornado struck. St. Peter's Comprehensive Plan, developed 3 years before the tornado, had roots in a document prepared for the Chamber of Commerce 20 years earlier. In his introduction to the 1995 Comprehensive Plan (City of St. Peter 1995, p. 4), Bob Moline wrote:

> This comprehensive plan can provide a framework for continuing the story, setting the most general of limits, laying down some rules, ground rules, so to speak. It offers a suggestion here, chosen direction there, and organizes the continuing conversation because in one sense the plan is never "finished." It serves as a friendly guide; follow it but make adjustments depending on the flow of the shaping forces and events.

Local officials did not hesitate, nor did they wait for help from a federal agency. Though the 1998 tornado shaped some aspects of St. Peter's future, the existing plan and vision for St. Peter was the touchstone of the recovery process. In the spring of 1999, St. Peter hosted a 3-day visit from the Minnesota Design Team (MDT), a volunteer group of architects, landscape architects, urban designers, planners, and other experts in design and community development that has been helping communities around Minnesota to develop shared visions for improving their physical and environmental design since 1983.

As a precursor to the MDT visit, St. Peter's officials were asked to identify the three most important problems the community faced. They identified recovery from the tornado, defining a common vision for the future, and acquiring resources to meet the vision. When asked to anticipate the problems St. Peter would face in 10 years, they responded with a short list:

- What do we do with an older downtown area that is changing from storefront to service-based business?
- How do we balance economic growth and need for housing?
- What can we do to make our landscape and river an asset to our community?

When asked to "describe the three best opportunities for your community today," their response was:

- Our ability to make changes with deliberate forethought after the tornado.
- A great spirit of cooperation within the community and its groups.
- The chance to put new infrastructure in the ground that may impact our community's long-term future.

Like most places, the early emphasis of St. Peter's recovery process was repair and reconstruction of municipal facilities, utilities, and infrastructure. Fortunately, a significant part of the cost for a new library had already been willed to St. Peter by a benefactor, so a new library would have been built even if the old one had not been destroyed by the tornado. The community center was also destroyed by the storm, but a new facility had already been planned and the early insurance payment (along with a grant and additional city borrowing) advanced the construction schedule. On the other hand, a municipal affordable housing project was delayed a year or more because St. Peter's priorities became reordered. Upgrading the city's electrical power generation plant was in the planning stages before the tornado and, after 5 days without power, the upgrade project gathered new support. The city also added a fiber optic capability to its infrastructure and moved power, phone, and data lines underground.

The municipal government, the nearby Minnesota State hospital, the local college, and the people of St. Peter established a level of collaboration and interaction that has continued since the storm. In the 2004 Comprehensive Plan (City of St. Peter 2004, p. 7), local officials looked back at the recovery period, noting:

> In the aftermath of the 1998 tornado many previously held ideas and thoughts about our community were brought once more to the forefront, to be weighed against the current reality and our wishes for the next 20 to 30 years. These ideas were challenged based on the hope that the tornado, which brought tremendous devastation, also brought a clean plate, that golden opportunity to rethink the past thoughts and make sure they match our current hopes.

Biloxi and Gulfport, Mississippi, appear to have also taken appropriate steps to rebuild their local economies following Hurricanes Katrina and Rita by building on what they had before and what remained after the devastating hurricanes. Locals tell us that the storm surge swept ashore at 22 to 24 feet high and with considerable velocity. The first three to five blocks inland from the shore were essentially wiped clean. Antebellum homes were badly damaged (see Figure 8.4); many were swept away. Jefferson Davis' shoreline home, Beauvoir, was among the most severely damaged. Biloxi was hit extra hard because the storm surge continued around the east end of town and swept in from what is called the "Back Bay."

Biloxi is home to Keesler Air Force Base, the second largest medical center in the Air Force. It provides medical care for approximately 75,000 eligible beneficiaries in the Gulf Coast area. Apart from that, beautiful sandy beaches, warm weather, and casino gambling mean that tourism and retirement living drive the local economy. The beaches did not go away, but the cities had to clean enormous amounts of refuse and debris from the

FIGURE 8.4 Biloxi, Mississippi, March 15, 2007—Repairs continue approximately 18 months after Hurricane Katrina damaged this home along the Gulf Coast. (Photograph by Lucy A. Arendt.)

beaches and the water, and they had to put devastated public utilities and buildings back in place so they could resume services. Efforts were made to ensure that the replacements would be more robust against hurricanes. Biloxi, particularly, took pains to exercise land use planning and controls that would put housing on safer ground. A considerable amount of prime land along the shore was set aside for recreational purposes.

The casino owners rebuilt quickly. Eighteen months after the storm, some were already back in business. Chain hotels and restaurants rebuilt at least some facilities. Several years after Katrina, the shore remained largely devoid of private, permanent housing, filled instead with temporary housing. The need for hotels and restaurants has become as strong as it was before the hurricane. Biloxi and Gulfport are taking the resources they have and building on them. The resources are hard to duplicate elsewhere in the country. Between hurricanes, at least, they provide employment and tax base.

Do Not Do Much Other Than Restore Infrastructure and Housing

Los Angeles adopted a "meet our basic obligations" strategy for business recovery following the Northridge Earthquake. The city and state worked quickly to restore the badly damaged Santa Monica Freeway and restored utilities to the damaged areas. However, the city left to private and not-for-profit groups almost all efforts to help local businesses reestablish themselves. From the city's standpoint, the strategy worked: people are employed and there are businesses in the damaged areas. The problem for individual business owners and for at least some of their customers is that many businesses failed in the aftermath because their circumstances changed so much, only to be replaced by other businesses owned by other investors.

The City of Los Angeles' approach is understandable in its context. Although damage was extensive, it did not cripple the metropolitan area. It did not seriously threaten the regional economy. Nor did it result in a substantial blow to local governments' property tax base. And, even though many individual business owners lost their businesses and their assets, others were willing and able to fill in for them, so residents were able to get what they needed when they needed it, albeit from new sources. Moreover, many governments do not think it is important or appropriate for them to help private organizations recover from disasters. In this view, they simply reflect federal policy.

So, What Works Best?

Everyone knows that a salesperson's life is a lot easier when he or she is selling what everyone wants. Communities with a great location, super amenities, a vibrant economy, low crime rates, great schools, and fine housing at low cost will not have much trouble with economic development. On the other hand, few communities have all that. Worse yet, a good location can change into a not-so-good location as markets shift, as tastes change, and as new products and new technologies replace old ones. For the communities that do not have everything going for them and that also suffer an extreme natural hazard event, the prospects of developing a viable economic base to support a sustainable community can be bleak.

If we, the authors, knew what to do to create strong economies in places without them, we might be busy doing that: working, charging high fees, and setting up franchises in communities around the world. We have, however, learned some things that seem to help. First, it makes lots of sense to evaluate your community as realistically as possible to learn what competitive advantages, if any, it might have for one or another economic base. Sometimes, it will be difficult to come up with more than a dream of what might be "if only." Other times, it might require bold strokes to move in considerably different directions. The key appears to be envisaging what might be both possible and desirable and then working to facilitate the transformation.

Moving in a bold new direction sometimes actually works. Wisconsin, in the late 1880s, was perhaps the nation's primary wheat producer. Disease, however, destroyed the crops. Minnesota and the Dakotas opened as farming areas, and Wisconsin was then left without much of an economic base. One of the University of Wisconsin's regents believed that Wisconsin could convert its farms to dairy and cheese production. The idea was unpopular among farmers: milking was woman's work. However, the university's revitalized Department of Agriculture went to work. It introduced year-round milking, silos and silage, dairy cooperatives, agricultural short courses, and a host of inventions to facilitate producing and marketing milk and creating cheese. By 1910, the agricultural transformation was essentially complete. It is a remarkable story of how government can seed a massive economic transformation (Nesbit 1973).

Note the characteristics of this success story. State residents could see for themselves that what they had been doing (wheat farming) was no longer successful. They could see other locations taking what had been their competitive advantage. The need to identify a successful niche was paramount; else, their families would starve and they would lose their family farms. Next, experts worked hard to provide technological solutions that they trained farmers to use. Hence, the cost to switch was externalized to the University of Wisconsin. Finally, the state not only helped farmers to switch what they produced, it also helped them to identify new markets for their products. Virtually everything that could be done to facilitate the massive change was done.

It seems to make considerable sense to work hard to retain the most desirable elements of the community's economic base following a disaster. Helping an existing industry or business is probably more productive and possibly less expensive than trying to attract a new employer from somewhere else or to create a new economic base.

PITFALLS TO AVOID

Pitfalls exist in every endeavor. It is particularly easy to fall into them when under the pressure of trying to address a spate of new problems and urgent needs. Here, we describe the primary pitfalls we observed while studying postdisaster communities.

Confusing Municipal Recovery with Community Recovery

It is important to distinguish between municipal and community recovery. There is a significant difference between the legal entity of the local government corporation and the community it serves. The legally defined spatial boundaries of a municipality may or may not coincide with the "natural" community. The complexities of American urban settlements and the arbitrariness of municipal boundaries within those settlements result in situations in which municipalities and communities are seldom coterminous. Several communities may exist within one large municipal jurisdiction, or only part of one or more communities may exist within a municipality.

Like any other business enterprise, local governments frequently suffer great losses from extreme natural hazard events. In Princeville, North Carolina, and in Gulfport, Mississippi, city hall was ruined and made uninhabitable by their respective extreme natural hazard events. Homestead's city-owned electric utility was destroyed and, two decades after the hurricane, city hall was so rife with mold that it had to be replaced. Across the country, municipalities suffer significant declines in revenue and revenue-generating capacity as extreme natural hazard events destroy the real property tax base and reduce sales tax revenues.

More often than we can count, local officials said to us, "Don't tell anybody I said this, but this (insert kind of extreme natural hazard event) is the best thing that ever happened here." We were never sure of exactly what they meant, but we think it is something like this: "Nobody died, but we were able to get rid of lots of old housing; we have all new (schools, streets, waste water treatment facility, water supply system, administrative buildings, parks [check all that apply]); and they were paid for by the federal government. The city is essentially debt free. How much better can it get?"

Local officials who say that sometimes have failed to differentiate between recovery of the governmental enterprise and recovery of the community, neighborhoods within it, families, and individuals. Some officials may think that community systems will restore themselves to preevent order if the city simply provides infrastructure and works to rebuild its revenue base; others may think they have no mandate or responsibility for doing more. Moreover, we think that the official probably is using a definition of recovery limited to the replacement of artifacts and excluding the reestablishment of interrelationships among the members of the community and between the community and the local government. The built environment served to support those interrelationships, however old and apparently dysfunctional some of the built environment components may have been. Public housing, for example, often decried as a magnet for crime and other problems, gives lower-income residents a place to call home. When it is replaced by higher-rent apartments and other types of housing, lower-income residents may no longer be able to live in the community. This has happened in New Orleans (Flaherty 2012). Some will say this is a positive outcome, until and if they realize that many lower-income people staff the restaurants, hotels, and other service businesses that cannot afford to pay higher wages and sustain their bottom line. New Orleans has been learning this latter lesson the hard way. For a city that relies on tourism as does New Orleans, not having affordable housing for those who fill service jobs is an obstacle to economic recovery.

Most higher-level local government managers we have talked with generally see municipal and community recovery as two sides of the same coin: the community needs an effective local government and the local government needs a community with a relatively strong economy to provide jobs, a secure future for residents, and a tax base sufficient to meet the revenue needs of the local government. We think most local officials have two implicit goals: recovery of the municipal enterprise and helping the community system to recover. They are committed to the latter goal to the extent they understand what constitutes recovery, to the extent that they have the resources to do so, and to the extent that they believe they have the responsibility and the mandate to do so.

Assuming Everyone Has the Same Recovery Goals

People in different roles often have different perspectives and do not necessarily share the same goals. The city government might want to have a bigger, better downtown retail area, while retailers may want to be close to their customers at or near the city's periphery. City officials may believe it makes good sense to remove housing in a particular area prone to flooding and turn it into a nature preserve, although those who live there may not want to leave. The continuing conflicts in New Orleans following Katrina drive home this point. Rebuilding the Lower Ninth Ward makes little sense from the perspective of creating safe housing in a safe environment. After all, the area flooded and was inaccessible for months after Hurricane Katrina. Now, the area is wiped almost clear of homes: remnants of the neighborhoods that once filled the area are slabs, porches, and parts of fences.

Some people, however, see the rebuilding issue as one of individual property owner rights, as a social issue, or as a racial matter. Nearly 60 percent of the homes in the Lower Ninth Ward were owner-occupied before Katrina, compared to 46 percent for New Orleans overall (Wagner and Edwards 2006). From their perspective, the area would be safer if the Army Corps of Engineers were to build and maintain a levee system to withstand a Category 5 hurricane. After all, they say, other areas of the world (e.g., the Netherlands) that are prone to flooding have much more resilient flood protection, and no one questions individuals' rights to live in these otherwise unsafe areas. Likewise, homes were quickly

FIGURE 8.5   Lower Ninth Ward, New Orleans, Louisiana, March 21, 2014—Two homes that have been rebuilt in the Lower Ninth Ward illustrate different expectations for future flooding. The home in the foreground has been elevated a full story, while the home in the background has been elevated only a few feet. (Photograph by Lucy A. Arendt.)

rebuilt in the Lakeview neighborhood, a predominately white neighborhood, despite flooding that destroyed much of its housing. Many, though not all, of the homes that were rebuilt in both neighborhoods were built to withstand flooding and storm surge (see Figures 8.5 and 8.6).

The conflict over rebuilding the Lower Ninth Ward continues years after Katrina, with no comprehensive solution yet in sight. One factor clearly affecting the rate of rebuilding in both the Lower Ninth Ward and Lakeview neighborhoods is the residents' financial capacity for rebuilding. Although homeownership was relatively high in the Lower Ninth Ward, the value of homes was lower than in the Lakeview neighborhoods, and it is highly probable that the residents of Lakeview occupied higher economic strata, enabling them to expend personal finances in addition to using private insurance and government support to rebuild. One of the authors has taken photos throughout New Orleans since Katrina, and has noted that many homes were rebuilt exactly as they were pre-Katrina in the Lakeview neighborhood, causing no apparent turmoil in the city. Since both the Lower Ninth Ward and the Lakeview neighborhood remain below sea level, one might think that the media scrutiny applied to rebuilding in one (the Lower Ninth) would be matched by the media scrutiny applied to rebuilding in the other (Lakeview). And yet, this does not appear to be the case.

FIGURE 8.6 Lakeview, New Orleans, Louisiana, March 20, 2014—
Two homes that have been rebuilt in the Lakeview neighborhood display
different expectations for future flooding. The home in the foreground
has been elevated a few feet, while the home in the background has been
elevated significantly higher. (Photograph by Lucy A. Arendt.)

Clearly, the Rebuilding Issue Is a Complicated One

Conflict also emerges sometimes when mitigation projects are undertaken
following the disaster. In Grand Forks, North Dakota, an expanded and
enlarged levee system was planned for construction. During the design
process, conflict arose between those who were scheduled to be inside
the flood protection levees and those who were going to be left outside.
To the extent that local residents would pay anything for the mitigation
measure, tax dollars generated from those outside the wall would be
used, of course, to protect those inside the levee. Officials (and those
scheduled to be on the inside) argued that it would be too expensive and
impractical to put everyone inside. Many believed they had a valid point.
Such conflicts can change who is elected to what positions in a community. More than one mayor has been replaced somewhere because
of something said or done during the aftermath of an extreme natural
hazard event.

People from the state or federal government sometimes have objectives that are slightly different from those of local officials with respect
to the disaster. Local officials want to see their community recover.
Individual staff members from other levels of government typically

share that concern but are charged with ensuring that regulations are followed, monies are spent and accounted for appropriately, and projects are completed. Their primary job is to administer those programs efficiently and effectively. We might hope that the goals of all levels of government would dovetail but that kind of congruence is not assured.

At the same time, local officials sometimes seem less concerned with the plight of individuals and of individual businesses than with aggregate measures of population, employment, income, and with ensuring that the physical manifestations of the disaster are no longer apparent. Most individuals who had losses were concerned, at some level, with the well-being of the community, but their focus was usually on themselves, their families, and their friends and neighbors.

The lesson is clear. The criteria for evaluating recovery vary across levels of analysis and perspectives. It is difficult, often impossible, to get everyone to agree to a specific course of action, since it is difficult to create solutions in which everyone gains or at least breaks even. Once again, the Garbage Can Decision Making Model described earlier (Cohen et al. 1972) helps us to understand why getting everyone on the same page and moving forward collectively can be a daunting and sometimes overwhelming task.

Losing Track of the Big Picture

It is particularly difficult to keep an open mind on issues, to identify and explore options, and to make objective decisions when one's community has been devastated, and the struggle for survival and recovery is being waged. Several things work against us when we try.

First, it is often difficult to deal with the fact that many people in the community long to, and expect to, return to what used to be "normal." Most people really dislike ambiguity, much less being torn irrevocably from their accustomed surroundings and routines. Many work diligently to return to the past so they can pick up where they left off. However, unless there were no social, economic, and political consequences from the event, that cannot be done. We all know that communities change every day; if they do not change, they do not survive. Usually, however, the change is sufficiently slow and marginal that people acclimate to it without conscious recognition of their adaptive behaviors. They are able to shop at their favorite stores, drive on their favorite thoroughfares, attend their favorite church, and so on. In times of great change, however, local officials must communicate clearly and convincingly that life will go on, that there will be changes, and that everyone is working hard to ensure that those changes will be for the better.

Second, it is extremely difficult to see the big picture clearly when one is awash in urgent demands. Consequently, local officials need regular reality checks during the aftermath, and it is best to get them from people who do not have a stake in local outcomes. Consultants with integrity—those who are more interested in solving problems than in selling solutions—are useful, particularly when the contract calls for the consultant to tell the truth as best as he or she sees it. One of the most dysfunctional things we saw in communities trying to recover was "group shift" that induced people to believe in something entirely implausible and to engage in and promote highly risky personal investments. Also widespread and problematic was the phenomenon of "group think," wherein people silence their disagreements and present an illusion of unanimity (Janis 1982). Ultimately, conflicts must be raised and addressed. Burying them yields problems that fester and threaten to undermine recovery efforts.

We advocate the use of dispassionate analysis. The most successful communities took the time to think through their plans and proposals, and to subject them to serious scrutiny from multiple perspectives by people committed to sound planning and decision making. The value of an external review cannot be overstated.

Assuming Things Will Work Out as Anticipated: Unanticipated Events and Events beyond Your Control

We are constantly amazed at how many people believe that, once they have set a course of action, things will work out just as they had planned or imagined. We suppose that it is comforting to live with that fantasy, at least until it falls apart. As we have frequently mentioned in this book, the reality is that we do not live in a world of certainty. We live in a world of uncertainty and, often, ignorance. Even our best laid plans are subject to the impacts of unanticipated events and events beyond our control.

It may be inevitable that once humans match up a solution with a problem, they have a tendency to assume that things will work out exactly as they imagined, hoped, or visualized they would. Having made the causal leap that "if I do x, then y will surely happen," they charge ahead vigorously and with determination, oblivious to flaws in their logic and to changing circumstances that make the plan impractical. Moreover, they often become resistant to well-meaning criticism. Humans often create faulty causal models, fail to identify pitfalls, and ignore unknown probability distributions and unanticipated consequences. They are subject to their cognitive biases (Stanovich and West 2008). Often, they fail more because they find a solution to the wrong problem than because they fail to solve the correct problem. Sometimes decisions have to be made quickly but not as often as is generally thought.

No matter how diligently you rake in the autumn, you cannot get every leaf. Likewise, there is no way to control every outcome in the recovery process. One reason it is so difficult is that many things that happen during the aftermath are surprises and have multiple different outcomes, each of which could plausibly occur. Accurately predicting the outcome of a series of sequential events, each of which has a probabilistic outcome, is, at best, unlikely. The fact that things are happening simultaneously makes prediction and therefore control even more difficult.

Because the consequences continue to unfold for months, sometimes years, after the event, it is useful to try to identify what is happening in the community at any given time. What trends appear to be emerging? How likely is each to continue? What apparent anomalies are manifesting themselves? Are they the precursors of trends to which one should be attentive? Are we prepared to deal with new and changing realities?

We think it is possible for state and local government to seed the community with projects and investments that help to swing decisions by others toward the desired path of community recovery. We think, too, that local governments can use pricing to encourage some things and discourage others. For example, if a state government does not want development pressures in a pristine wilderness area, one way to increase the cost of developing the land is to not put roads or freeway interchanges in the area. Similarly, local governments can make it easier to do what is desirable and harder to do what is not desirable. It is a way to use the power of the public purse and the police power to leverage desired paths and outcomes.

Assuming It Will Work Here Because It Worked There

It is tempting to look to other communities to learn what they did and, if it led to good outcomes, to do the same thing in one's community, hoping for the same outcomes. It has become clear to us by looking at communities across the United States that have experienced disasters that context is critical in determining whether a solution in one community will work in another. In short, just because it worked or did not work there does not mean that it will work or not work here.

The lesson is that there is no cookie cutter or instant pudding solution to community recovery. Some things are essential but not necessarily sufficient. It is critical to get the basic utilities, infrastructure, and services up and running. It is critical to help ensure adequate housing and to facilitate private efforts to get needed private services back in operation.

Beyond that, however, recovery efforts should be determined based on the unique context of the community and not on what someone did somewhere else. What will it take to move the community down a path consistent with its values and goals?

Forgetting about Path Dependency

The streets in the old part of more than one city were laid out by deer trails, hardened as they became cow paths, and, finally, institutionalized with pavement. The typewriter keyboard was designed so that the letter arms would not stick on one another as they struck the ribbon to make an impression. Only a few die-hards still use mechanical keyboards, but the arrangement of computer keyboards remains the same. Likewise, what local government does early in the aftermath tends to set a pattern for what follows. As we mentioned earlier, "soft paths" is a phrase sometimes used to describe courses of action that are revocable, courses of action from which retreat is possible without devastating consequences. Soft paths are desirable when the decision maker sees too much uncertainty to commit irrevocably to a specified course of action. The goal when taking the soft path is to maximize flexibility and minimize narrowing of possibilities. The challenge is to relieve the situation while still leaving room for more sensible options to be explored and perhaps implemented as more information is obtained, and until uncertainty is reduced to manageable levels. Once the concrete hardens, it is a little late to change one's mind about where the structure should be sited.

CHAPTER 10

What to Do before the Next Disaster

In a previous chapter, we noted that it is common practice to take steps to either preclude or reduce losses in advance of the most common and frequent potentially damaging events we face. The examples are almost endless: seat belts, crash-absorbing designs in automobiles, building codes, regular dental checkups, health insurance, storm water retention ponds, and so forth. As a result of such precautionary actions, auto deaths per hundred thousand miles driven have declined, buildings are far less likely to fail in small or moderate earthquakes, smallpox is essentially eradicated, people who have frequent dental checkups tend to have more teeth, and places employing good stormwater practices have less minor flooding, other things being equal.

In the same way, it makes sense for residents and local governments to make their communities more robust and more loss resistant before an extreme natural hazard event brings the community to its knees. Community recovery from a devastating natural hazard event is costly, time-consuming, and never guaranteed. No community can be made safe against the rarest and most extreme events, but what can be done is to make the community robust against losses from more frequent smaller and moderate events that can, absent precautions, result in extensive losses, major inconvenience, and the need to devote enormous time and resources to recovery.

This chapter is about how to build a more disaster-resistant and resilient community without breaking the community bank. We know that governmental budgets have little room these days for discretionary expenditures, so building a disaster-resistant community must be done inexpensively and cost-effectively. We also know creating a resistant and resilient community cannot be done all at once and that it is a never-ending job; community decision-making processes must incorporate creating and enhancing disaster resistance and community resiliency as an integral and routine part of resource allocation.

Enhancing resistance and resiliency is not a new activity to be added to local governments' list of things to do. It is simply ramping up activities that are already accepted and undertaken as a routine part of community decision making. When deciding on building a new school, for example, communities routinely make sure the school is located where traffic patterns do not pose a high risk to children, that it is not in a floodplain, that it is not next to a firm working with dangerous chemicals, and so forth. When local government builds a new wastewater treatment facility, most states review the plans to ensure the technology and design will do what is intended: to protect public health and the environment. It is a simple ramp up to review designs to ensure that the facility itself is resistant to predictable natural hazard events. Building disaster resistance and resiliency into a community is simply not a new idea; the new idea is to extend the existing practice to embrace out of the ordinary yet generally predictable events that, without precautions, usually result in emergencies, extensive damage, loss of life, and unnecessary and long-lasting costs.

Even though making a community safer by anticipating the unexpected and preparing for it is nothing new, issues and obstacles inevitably arise before and during decisions about resource allocation. Issues and obstacles should be anticipated by those advocating a more resistant and resilient community.

PREREQUISITES FOR TAKING PRECAUTIONS AGAINST RISKS ASSOCIATED WITH EXTREME NATURAL HAZARD EVENTS

Frequently, we mitigate the likely consequences of those events that we perceive to be likely enough to cause us real harm in the near future. Sometimes we decide on our own to take those precautions. Other times, public policy requires that we do so: seat belts and bicycle helmets are mandatory in some locales, there are penalties for driving under the influence of drugs or alcohol, and we have special speed limits in school zones. We are not particularly likely, however, to take precautions when they are not required or when contemplating events that occur infrequently but that hold the potential for generating far more damage and that, should they occur, require extraordinary efforts from which to recover.

Alesch, Arendt, and Petak (2012) studied hospital organizations faced with State of California requirements to strengthen their older facilities to meet newly adopted standards designed to protect the facilities against earthquake forces. Their work led them to conclude that a set of prerequisite conditions existed that must be met before formal organizations take precautions against known but relatively infrequent extreme events. These prerequisites are congruent with those listed by March and Olsen (1977), but the authors believe they are more complete and augmented with various nuances. The authors believe that the prerequisites are likely to apply to local governments, other formal organizations, or, for that matter, individual households. Here, rather, than list and discuss a laundry list of obstacles for taking precaution against extreme natural hazard events that are very likely to threaten us personally, we have arranged this discussion of obstacles in terms of that set of prerequisites.

Prerequisite 1: Awareness of the Risk and an Appropriate Risk Perception

The first prerequisite for taking action is for responsible decision makers to be aware that the hazardous event may occur and that if it does it may well generate significant adverse consequences for them, their organizations, or their community. This awareness is not a trivial matter. It has not been that many years since we understood that asbestos is a hazardous material, identified the location of the most dangerous fault lines, understood the probability of colliding with large pieces of space debris, and learning about a host of other phenomena that we now know are dangerous realities. Almost every year, physical and social scientists learn of new perils: perils with likely consequences that grow in saliency as we become increasingly interdependent and as the slack between complex social systems is diminished.

Risk awareness is only part of the first prerequisite to action. Risk perception follows from risk awareness. Even if one is aware of the risk, action depends on the decision maker perceiving the risk as being of danger to him or her, the organization, or the community. Analysts have studied how people perceive risks in relation to themselves extensively over the past few decades. People regularly underestimate the likelihood of some hazardous events and overestimate the likelihood and consequences of others. Slovic (2000) and others have made us aware that it is not only the awareness of specific hazards that affects our anticipatory response to them, but it is our judgments, often subjective, of the saliency of the individual hazard to us. That is, our judgment about how likely the event is to happen in a relevant time frame and how likely it is that I (we) will suffer adverse consequences from it.

Slovic (2000) discusses risk perception in this way:

> Whereas technologically sophisticated analysts employ risk assessments to evaluate hazards, the majority of citizens rely on intuitive risk judgments, typically called "risk perceptions." For these people, experience with hazards tends to come from the news media, which rather thoroughly document mishaps and threats occurring throughout the world. (p. 220)

Perceptions of the risks associated with various phenomena and activities vary significantly among people depending on the information they receive, how they process it, and how they interpret it in terms of themselves and their experience. Most certainly, the nature and proximity of hazards creates dramatically different risks and risk perceptions in different places in the world today.

Thus, in order to meet the demands of the first prerequisite, the potential hazard mitigator must know that a hazard exists and perceive the risks associated with the hazard to be relevant to him or her: the risk must be salient to those who would take precautions. Pundits sometimes quip that elected officials have a limit of issue saliency equal to the amount of time left before the next election. Perhaps, but, if a prudent decision maker knows a risk exists, he or she may be likely to ask what the chances are that the event will occur anytime within the reasonably near future. It is a good question. Scientists can sometimes provide estimates of when an extreme natural hazard event will occur and how big it is likely to be. Recent history can suggest how often an event will occur and how ugly it might be. Part of the difficulty in assessing risks for lay people may come from how analysts choose to communicate the risks. Too often, those of us who conduct disaster field research have heard, "They said it was the 500-year flood; I guess we're safe for another 499 years," or some such comparable statement stemming from a major misconception.

Prerequisite 2: Conviction That Something Can Be Done to Protect One's Self against the Likely Consequences of the Event

Locus of control is a well-known personality trait associated with individuals' generalized beliefs about the extent to which they can influence the outcome of events. A set of organizational decision makers predominantly comprising individuals with an internal locus of control is likely to develop a collective sense of potency (Shea and Guzzo 1987). As described by Shea and Guzzo (1987), a collective sense of potency is a key group-level factor that determines "real-world, real-time group effectiveness" (p. 26). A self-reinforcing loop is created as high potency teams seek sometimes negative information to enhance the effectiveness of their decision making, which in turn enhances their decision making, which in turn enhances their collective potency, and so on.

If, on the other hand, one believes that severe earthquakes occur when an omniscient and omnipotent Greater Being decides we should suffer because we have been disobedient or annoying, then one is also likely to believe that it really does not matter what one does, unless it is to proselytize to sinners or to sacrifice a virgin or two. If an individual believes it is God's will that his or her favorite college football team lost its fourth postseason bowl game in a row, then it probably does not matter to this individual what the coach does or does not do; the outcome is out of his hands. Thus, the second prerequisite for implementing measures to protect against extreme natural hazard events is that one has confidence that some action or actions can be taken to alleviate the potential event or the damage it might generate.

Belief about locus of control is relative; one might feel efficacious with respect to some phenomena or some level of natural hazard event, but not others. Most of us understand that Earth is likely to collide with some form of space debris that is sufficiently large to make human life on this planet extinct. Most of us do not believe we can individually do much to keep that from happening, but many of us also think that, in time, with hard work, we, collectively, will be able to reduce the probability that such an event will occur. Thus, part of the internal locus of control has to do with our level of confidence that we can both take action and that the same action will very likely provide the desired level of protection. Prudent policy makers will want to know the extent to which any precautions that might be taken are likely to provide protection against the hazard.

Prerequisite 3: Belief That It Is in Our Best Interest to Act Now

Individuals and organizations frequently have more ways to use resources than they have resources. When given a choice of how to use those resources, most individuals and organizations will try to make what they consider rational choices. Consciously or subconsciously, most people appear to consider the marginal utility of a dollar spent to reduce a set of risks compared with the marginal utility of spending that money on something else on the "wish" or "need" list.

The choice is complicated because we often have to make crude approximations of the marginal costs and payoffs (March and Simon 1958) that will accrue and because not all decision makers have the experience and expertise to accurately weigh and assess the available data. To further complicate the decision, one must make judgments about whether acting now is clearly preferable to acting next month or next year. This necessarily involves trade-offs even for an individual decision maker, but becomes more difficult when the decision involves a number of actors, each with somewhat different perceptions, value sets, and agendas.

Expectancy theory (Porter and Lawler 1968; Vroom 1964) suggests that organizations and their key decision makers are motivated to act when they expect adequate rewards for doing so. In general, the greater the potential rewards, and the stronger the link between performance and rewards, the greater the motivation to act (Vroom 1964). If, however, the means for implementation are beyond the ability of the individual or organization, then action is unlikely. Similarly, if decision makers see a strong link between effort (e.g., implementing a specific hazard mitigation measure) and performance (e.g., increasing a hospital building's resistance to seismic forces), the greater the motivation for them to act is likely to be.

Perhaps the most frequent objection to enhancing community resistance and resiliency is that it will cost money that is needed elsewhere. Every community has a different marginal utility of money and different sets of urgent needs, so the challenge is inevitable. It is easier to sell the need for enhanced resistance in the wake of an extreme natural hazard event that causes serious losses either in the community or in a neighboring community. Flooding in a remote part of China is not likely to get a city council in Mythical, Iowa, excited about the prospect of spending more money on stormwater retention, but when it happens in an adjacent community and citizens are calling their local alderperson late at night, priorities can change. Proximity and perceived similarity tend to affect salience, intention to act, and action.

A dominant argument against taking additional precautions against events is that, if they have a statistical probability of happening to the community, at most, in only 1 percent of the years that pass, it may not happen in our lifetime, why should one spend the money now to reduce the risk? This might be viewed as burying one's head in the sand. At another level, however, it has to do with the present value of a dollar spent now to save, perhaps, $10 at some unknown future time. Even if the discount rate employed in a present value equation is exceptionally low, the value of that dollar spent now may be negligible. In an era and in a society that looks for short-term profits and quick returns on investments, spending money on hazard mitigation may not seem like a good investment.

A somewhat different choice may be made if one asks this question: How much am I willing and able to spend now to protect against some dire consequences in the future? This poses the hazard mitigation question as one of "buying insurance." We each have somewhat different perceptions of risk, our ability to protect ourselves, and the marginal value of a dollar in hand today. In the case of moderate natural hazard events, like periodic flooding, mitigation outlays may be viewed as buying insurance. Just as employers that emphasize worker safety expect to experience lower worker compensation insurance rates, communities that take precautions may reduce property owners' insurance premiums and protect themselves against likely large, unexpected costs in the future. From that perspective, the outlay for precautions taken now may seem less like money down a rat hole. Moreover, creating precautions that protect against multiple perils simultaneously makes sense because the cost of such precautions can be distributed across several potential adverse events.

Prerequisite 4: An Acceptable Solution Must Exist

A problem may be defined as a condition in which one's perceptions of the present or of the likely future is at odds with that which the viewer perceives to be desirable. The disparity between what is desired and what is perceived can cause an individual or an organization to search for alternatives that will help close the disparity between the perceived and desired state of affairs. As previously described, March and Simon (1958) created a simple, robust model of organizational decision making. When faced with a decision, their model suggests, organizations will continue to seek alternatives as long as they believe there is a better solution that can be found for less than the cost of a continued search. Organizations are likely to take action when a critical mass of key decision makers believes the situation will be made better by taking the action now rather than either deferring the action or not taking action at all. Later, March and Olsen (1977) concluded that at least one of the proposed solutions available to decision makers must appear to them to be viable. If a proposed solution is perceived as too expensive, too likely to be ineffective against the threat, or too difficult, either technologically or politically, to implement, then it will not be viewed as a viable solution.

Not only must a proposed hazard mitigation policy make financial sense today, it must also be congruent with the organization's or community's current goals (Vroom 1964), and align with its priorities. Communities will evaluate the costs associated with a given hazard mitigation measure, and assess the likelihood that the costs will increase or decrease in a given period. Likewise, communities will consider the potential contribution or benefit of a given hazard mitigation measure to the community's current versus future goals. Such benefit–cost

ratio analysis will be critical to choosing from an array of hazard mitigation measures. Of course, the specific array of goals and priorities will be
unique to a given community or organization. Consequently, a hazard
mitigation practice that makes sense this year for one organization may
not make sense for another until next year, even later, or never. If an
organization's decision makers do not believe that a given mitigation
measure will significantly increase the organization's ability to achieve
its goals (e.g., serve its community), then the mitigation measure is likely
to be dismissed.

Further, thoughtful decision makers concern themselves with two
other basic questions. First, how safe is safe enough? Second, is there
sufficient evidence that the proposed course of action will be sufficiently
effective to provide the desired level of safety? These two questions lead
inevitably to another fundamental question: How much am I (are we)
willing to spend to protect ourselves from losses that might occur should
the event occur, be strong enough, be close enough, and have a sufficient
duration to do us harm?

These questions have probably been asked since humans first started
assembling teams to attack mammoths for meat. They have never been
easy questions to answer. They involve value judgments and our values
vary considerably from person to person. Moreover, we simply do
not know enough about most hazards and most precautions to make
exceptionally reliable estimates about effectiveness. Nonetheless, decision makers have to arrive at answers to those questions for action to
be taken.

Part of the answers has to do with the reliability of estimates concerning the risks faced. Earthquakes are a good example. We know they
occur. We know where they occur most frequently. We have reliable probability distributions as to the frequency of occurrence of events releasing
various magnitudes of energy. On the other hand, we have considerable
difficulty reliably predicting when and where they will occur in a given
place within a century or so. It is entirely probable that not even all the
dangerous earthquake faults in California have been mapped. In addition, reliable estimates of the effect of an earthquake on a structure can
be made if we constrain the calculation by specifying the nature and magnitude of ground motion, direction of ground motion, estimated performance of the underlying soil and geology, and estimated stresses placed
on various components of the structure. Analysts can say "if this, if that,
and if the other thing, then this will probably occur." Unhappily, this still
leaves quite a bit of residual uncertainty for individual decision makers.
Structural engineers and earth scientists are able to make estimates that
are more reliable almost every year, but, still, the choice of how safe is
safe enough for the individual property owner is largely subjective. One
must know the end goal to ascertain what "safe enough" means.

Unfortunately, not all precautions taken against extreme natural hazard events are risk free; some have inherent risks associated with them. We have noted previously in this book, for example, that there are only two kinds of levees: those that have failed and those that are going to fail. When they do fail, they sometimes generate great adverse consequences. Bridges, too, sometimes fail even when carefully designed. Even buildings built to a building code sometimes fail. Nothing is for sure.

Of course, not all failures of precautionary steps are cataclysmic. When one considers buildings, for example, one can talk about various levels of structural and nonstructural performance following an earthquake. The lowest standard of performance would be collapse prevention. This is sometimes called a "life safety" performance standard: that means that all or most of the occupants at the time of the earthquake would be able to exit the building safely, but the building would most likely face subsequent demolition. The next level of performance would be that there would be damage to structural and nonstructural elements of the building as well as damage to its contents, but occupants could evacuate safely and the building might be reoccupied and used following repair. An even higher level of performance would be that the event generates so little damage to the building and its contents so as to permit immediate reuse. Whether it is actually open for business will, of course, depend on what happens to the building's supporting infrastructure (streets, water, energy) and adjacent buildings.

Other things being equal, the higher up the performance scale, the more costly the precautions required. It is one thing to bolt a building to its foundation; it is quite another to provide the building with base isolation. Even so, structural engineers are quick to say that various buildings or structures are designed to perform up to a given level of stress; if the event exceeds or is substantially different from the forces anticipated and accounted for in the design, the building may not perform at the desired level. What we know for sure is that, if one wants a building or other structure to perform well against events with great destructive potential, it will cost a great deal more than planning safety for a smaller event or lower performance.

Given the uncertainty surrounding the likelihood that an extreme natural hazard event will affect us directly, how can one make an informed decision about how safe is safe enough? The decision comes down to both political and personal choices. In some states, authorized policy makers have decided, at least temporarily, how safe is safe enough for certain kinds of risks and have enacted statutes, codes, and ordinances demanding our compliance. In other cases, the consumer must decide. Am I willing to work in an unreinforced masonry building in Los Angeles? How much am I willing and able to spend now to be reasonably sure that, if this bad thing happens, my family will be adequately protected? How much to spend to buy a unit of safety typically begins with an assessment of one's resources and a judgment about the utility of a dollar spent on protection against a dollar spent, for example, on food, clothing, medicine, or some other thing more "essential" than protection against some unlikely event.

Another concern has to do with incremental improvements in safety. Illustratively, whenever a new feature is added to a building code to enhance hazard resistance, it affects only those buildings that are built subsequent to adoption of the policy; existing buildings are unlikely to have incorporated that safety feature. The exception is when a provision in a building code is made retroactive to existing buildings, such as the case in some areas of sprinkler systems in buildings that have high occupancies. Zealous proponents of enhanced safety are sometimes disconcerted when the enhancements are made marginally in the community; marginal improvements make communities marginally safer, but may not do so fast enough to satisfy some advocates. The problem, of course, is that it is patently unreasonable to tear down an entire city and to rebuild it to meet standards that we think are good enough today, only to be augmented tomorrow when we learn more. We make incremental improvements, as funding is available, and as the public and private "will" permits.

Prerequisite 5: The Individual or Organization Must Have the Capacity to Act

Even if the preceding four prerequisites are met, an individual or organization may still fail to implement hazard mitigation measures.

Agenda Space and Contextual Dynamics

March and Olsen (1977) posit a crowded agenda as a reason action is sometimes not taken on an issue. Other issues and concerns may crowd out time to think about reducing the likely consequences of uncertain events.

Local government agendas are heavily influenced by time-triggered events, such as budget approval deadlines, but they are also affected by event-triggered concerns. Now that events occurring everywhere are communicated broadly in a matter of minutes, contextual dynamics are increasingly important influences on even local government agendas. School shootings in a distant state move concern about student safety toward the top of the agenda in other states. Global climate change and attendant variability in rainfall and temperature push issues like water supply and conservation to the top of the agenda in some places. As political conservatives in state legislatures work to cut costs, taxes, and "governmental interference" by the state, they often mandate that local governments take on those tasks and costs. This forces local governments, often themselves under state-imposed spending limits, to focus their attention on how to do a lot more with a lot less. The community context changes, often rapidly, and those changes greatly affect local government concerns and the ordering of items on the agenda.

"Brush fires" may push aside strategic thinking, and advocates of mitigating natural hazard risks typically struggle to get their concerns at or near the top of the organizational agenda. Moving risk reduction to the top of the local government agenda benefits from having a persistent inside advocate dedicated to reducing exposure and vulnerability to extreme events. March and Olsen's "garbage can" model actually requires a strong and persistent inside advocate to promote consideration of an issue and a solution (1977). Unfortunately, a disaster in another community often creates an opportunity for moving hazard mitigation to the top of the agenda, especially if it appears to locals that the same kind of disaster could very well occur in their community. Again, proximity and similarity affect salience, intended action, and action.

In thinking about a community's decision makers, especially those in local government, it makes sense to consider the leadership of organizations, including members of the top management team. Research on top management teams shows that the issues considered and dealt with depend in part on the functional background (e.g., finance, human resources) and experience of the top managers (Hambrick and Mason 1984). As stated in Alesch, Arendt, and Petak (2012):

> Getting an issue on the top management team's agenda is often a function of power differentials and advocacy (Arendt, Priem, and Ndofor 2005). Issues supported by powerful factions in the organization and championed by powerful advocates are more likely to be addressed (Finkelstein 1992). Unfortunately for those interested in hazard mitigation, members of the top management team are unlikely to have much experience in hazard mitigation. Instead, top managers tend to have functional expertise in finance, marketing, production (i.e., how the organization transforms inputs into outputs), human resources, R&D, and legal issues. (p. 142)

Mitigating hazards, particularly infrequent but dangerous events, does not fit into any of these categories. As a result, the top management team in most organizations—whether a for-profit firm, nonprofit organization, or government agency—is unlikely to have a strong advocate for hazard mitigation. Given the background of most upper-level decision makers, hazard mitigation is not likely to have a white knight at the top level very often.

Resource Availability

For many, if not most, local governments in the first two decades of the 21st century, money for discretionary activities in America is particularly scarce. We frequently hear, "It's important, but we just have too much on our plate right now."

Costs are always a consideration. Typically, though not always, the costs of mitigating against a natural hazard event are a function of the level of protection desired and the damage potential of the hazard against which protection is sought. Illustratively, the costs of creating a building that has a high probability of being safe for immediate reuse in the event of an earthquake measuring 5.0 on the Richter scale would be much less than providing the same level of protection against a much greater earthquake. This, too, affects the how safe is safe enough consideration.

Many other factors contribute to how much it would cost to give reasonable assurance of a given level of safety against a given extreme event. First, it is much less expensive to integrate hazard resistance into a building during the initial design stage than it is once the building is built, the concrete has cured, and retrofitting the building is required to meet that level of safety. We have been told by structural engineers that engineering earthquake safety into a building from the start is likely to add only about 5 to 7 percent to the building costs, whereas retrofitting a building to get the same level of safety could be extraordinarily expensive.

Second, some mitigation is extremely low cost. For example, it makes sense and costs very little to put emergency generators above the expected 100- and 500-year flood depths. Not placing air handling and air conditioning units on an unprotected flat roof in hurricane country is almost a no-brainer and only requires some advance thought in building design. In hurricane zones, it does not cost much more to put 100 mile-per-hour glass in hospital windows than it does to put in weaker panes. Where one might expect terrorist explosions, blast-proof glass can be specified in designs.

Political Culture and Context

It is no secret that some states have more liberal or more conservative political cultures than others do. Political cultures vary among states and even among communities within the same metropolitan areas. Political culture affects the extent to which state or local governments act to reduce the likely consequences of extreme events. The local government's political environment may inhibit or prevent the adoption or implementation of hazard mitigations that would otherwise be extremely helpful in reducing the consequences of natural hazard events. Some states do not even require that all local governments adopt and enforce building codes. Interestingly, a Web site exists for those interested in buying a book titled *No Building Codes: A Guide to States with No Building Codes*. It is described by the purveyors as "a must-have guidebook for the ambitious owner-builder seeking to find the perfect state to build a home without the hassles of adhering to difficult building codes and the inspectors! Don't be shackled down from building your dream home because of these stringent building codes" (Herb 2010, para. 1). Bastions of Tea Party advocates, property rights organizations, or survivalists may reject any or all proposals to spend tax money on hazard mitigation or enhanced resistance to natural hazard events. In such places, regulating development in floodplains may be viewed as taking away one's use of property without compensation.

OTHER CONCERNS: MORAL HAZARD, LEARNED HELPLESSNESS OR DEPENDENCY, AND POLITICAL OPPORTUNISM

Moral Hazard

Moral hazard is the risk that the presence of a contract or a policy will affect the behavior of one or more parties to benefit from the policy by increasing its risk-taking behavior (Kunreuther and Pauly 2006). Used most often in connection with the insurance industry, the term refers to an insured party taking additional risks because of the existence of the policy, and because the insured believes that he or she will not have to bear the consequences of taking the risk. The term is increasingly appropriate in connection with federal and state disaster assistance. Federal government assistance in disaster areas was once viewed as a compassionate act. It was not institutionalized, but considered by Congress on a disaster-by-disaster ad hoc basis. That is no longer the case; disaster assistance is codified in federal statutes and the means by which it is allotted are specified. There is some reason to believe that this policy has contributed to a reduction in self-reliance and on taking responsibility for the consequences of one's actions (or inaction, as the case may be). Platt (1999) asks the question "At what point does compassion lead to 'codependency' whereby potential disaster victims and the federal protectors become locked into a repetitive cycle of loss, compensation, reconstruction and new losses" (p. 11)?

Those who expect others to bear their losses have presumably always been with us, but it appears that public policies have created enhanced incentives for people to expect that others will pay for their bad judgment or bad luck. Following the 1994 Northridge Earthquake, we asked a local businessperson about damage and losses. He replied that his place of business, very near the epicenter of the temblor, was not damaged at all. When asked why, he said that he was required to have the building "engineered" and insured against earthquake damage as a condition of getting a federal small-business loan. When we subsequently asked about his home, he said it was completely destroyed. "Did you have insurance on the house?" we asked. "No," he replied. "I thought the government would cover my losses."

In 2008, heavy rains fell on much of the Midwest, including Wisconsin. Lake Delton is one of Wisconsin's resort and water recreation centers. The community is built around a man-made lake. The dam withstood the flood of water from the rain, but a narrow strip of land, mainly composed of sand, that held the lake from flowing into the Wisconsin River far below it, did not. As the rain fell, the sand comprising the strip of land disappeared into the river, taking three houses with it and badly damaging two others (see Figures 9.1 and 9.2).

FIGURE 9.1   Lake Delton, Wisconsin, June 23, 2008—Rains created flooding and a dam break which caused the lake to drain. (FEMA/ Robert Kaufmann.)

FIGURE 9.2 Lake Delton, Wisconsin, June 23, 2008—Houses fell into the emptied Lake Delton as the side banks collapsed. (FEMA/Robert Kaufmann.)

The Village of Lake Delton had previously opted not to participate in the National Flood Insurance Program so none of the homeowners was able to purchase insurance from the National Flood Insurance Program. Then Governor Doyle, relying on a law that allows the state to take immediate possession of property in emergencies, proceeded to have the State Department of Transportation condemn the uninsured, failed properties that had been built upon the filled-in natural course of the stream that created Lake Delton and the state compensated the five property owners almost $2 million. Why, then, one might ask, should a community participate in the National Flood Insurance Program and why should homeowners whose property is at risk buy insurance? The state's actions simply exacerbated the moral hazard problems associated with natural hazard events (*The New York Times* 2008; WIBA 2008; Wisconsin Dells 2008).

Following the devastating Hurricane Sandy, Congress decided that the National Flood Insurance Program, which through the decades has provided deep subsidies to policyholders, would have to raise its rates to something approximating the actual actuarial costs of providing insurance coverage. Such an action would have the effect of greatly reducing the subsidy to presumably knowledgeable risk takers. The angry response by those who have received the subsidy for decades was not surprising: they were steadfastly opposed to paying the costs associated with their decision to live in an extremely dangerous place. As this is written, Congress is considering action to postpone the insurance rate increases for some time to come. This is an obvious instance of moral hazard (Kunreuther and Pauly 2006): those who are most at risk buy insurance subsidized and underwritten by those who do not take the risk.

Learned helplessness or learned dependency exists when a person perceives that his or her efforts will not have any effect on the desired outcome of a situation and thus becomes dependent on others to bring about the desired effect (Seligman 1975). As defined by Rabow, Berkman, and Kessler (1983), "learned helplessness is an acquired state that develops when an organism (1) fails to perceive contingencies between behavior and outcome, (2) expects frustration and failure because of past experiences, (3) does not receive rewards for expended efforts, and (4) feels hopelessly lost for solutions to environmental demands" (p. 425). Learned helplessness is not the same as moral hazard, but often leads to the same outcomes since those who see themselves as unable to take responsibility often demonstrate the same desires as those who are simply unwilling to take responsibility for their actions or choices or for whatever befalls them. Learned dependency is often associated with the cycle of poverty, which is thought to be perpetuated by both structural social and cultural factors as well as learned individual behaviors transmitted between generations. Social scientists are not entirely agreed on what generates and maintains learned dependency, but generally agree that it does exist among those with certain mental illnesses and among many who live in intergenerational poverty or oppression (Rabow et al. 1983).

Regardless of the reasons for learned dependency, if it is exhibited by a large proportion of the population in a devastated area, recovery is inhibited and the chances that the local population will act to build a more robust and disaster resilient community are slim. Learned helplessness interferes with collective efficacy, one of the building blocks of community recovery. If people do not believe that they can be the agents of their own salvation, they may find themselves waiting in vain for others to assist. On the other hand, learned optimism enables people to perceive that negative events are not directed at them personally and that any setbacks are temporary rather than permanent (Seligman 1998). Optimism that is widely distributed in a community is expected to contribute to a positive sense of collective efficacy (Bandura 1997), in which people have confidence that together they can overcome obstacles and achieve great things.

When people demonstrate collective efficacy, they are more likely to move forward and to be cheered on while doing it. In the United States, in particular, people seem to love stories of those who "pull themselves up by their bootstraps," who survive "against all odds," and who "get to work" in the aftermath of a disaster. In a blog post issued by the White

House, Joplin, Missouri, resident Sue Adams is quoted as saying, "You know what's amazing? People are moving here. People that came to help are coming back and staying ... We're not going to let it beat us. We going to come back and we're going to come back better than ever" (Compton 2012, para. 46). Says Julia Lewis, another Joplin resident, "We didn't wait for people to help us—we jumped right now and got started. It is something everyone in Joplin can be proud of. We can do anything and we can help each other because that is how strong we are" (Compton 2012, para. 51).

Political Opportunism and Ideological Schism

Elected officials invariably make a great show of support for their constituents who are adversely affected by an extreme natural hazard event. Local officials routinely pledge that the community will rebuild bigger and better than ever. Federal officials pledge financial support. Members of Congress typically introduce legislation to provide resources over and above what the Stafford Act would provide the afflicted community. Sometimes, that legislation is enacted and provides a substantial windfall to the affected. Television crews film elected officials wearing blue and gold FEMA (Federal Emergency Management Agency) baseball caps and leaning from the open doors of helicopters to survey the destruction. Disasters are a gold mine of photo opportunities. If all communities were disaster resistant and resilient, most of those opportunities would never occur.

Greed and political opportunism manifest themselves particularly in the instance of proposed legislation concerning the provision of exceptional disaster assistance. Following Hurricane Sandy, for example, members of Congress who had previously proposed and voted for legislation to provide special assistance to their constituencies after their own disasters, over and above Stafford Act provisions, voted against similar aid to those who suffered losses from Sandy (Friedman 2013; Meyer 2013; Pascrell 2013; Ungar 2013). Most of the votes were along partisan lines, reflecting deep-seated Congressional schisms. Others may be explained more by individual representatives being more concerned about how their constituents will vote than about how someone else's constituents will vote.

GOALS AND MEANS FOR MITIGATING THE RISKS ASSOCIATED WITH EXTREME NATURAL HAZARD EVENTS

We perceive four basic goals of mitigation: (1) reducing the occurrence of the extreme event, (2) reducing exposure to it, (3) reducing vulnerability to it, and (4) creating the means for rapid replacement and repair of damage. Though these basic goals are simply stated, advocates for building resistance and resiliency have many tools and approaches at hand to accomplish them.

Even the most ivory-towered, vine-covered professor or safety advocate knows that we cannot make an entire community resistant to the full array of likely extreme natural hazard events all at once. Even when prudent mitigators can build resistance into structures at low cost during design, all the money spent still adds up, making it important to make informed choices about risk reduction priorities. The most obvious means for mitigating the risks associated with hazardous events are not always the most cost-effective. Various approaches to building resistance and resiliency are listed here.

Reducing the Likelihood of the Damaging Event

Not much can be done to prevent earthquakes. Nor do we yet know how to preclude space debris from striking Earth. We can, however, reduce the frequency, size, and duration of events such as wildfires in suburban areas and river flooding. Fires at the nexus of suburban development and wild areas can be controlled by removing dry brush fuel and by leaving open space between buildings and fire prone areas. Dams and levees are preferred by many to control flooding and river flow, but other means exist. Increasingly, people are coming to the realization that it makes more sense to adapt to rivers than it does to try to control natural events. Plantings, marshes, swamps, and retention facilities in strategic locations slow or reduce runoff. Parks and open spaces in and around cities help ensure that rivers, when flooding, do less damage.

Some impoverished countries have actually created situations in which extreme natural hazard events are largely the consequence of human action. Haitians, for example, too poor to buy other fuel, have denuded hillsides of trees and vegetation for use as charcoal fuel. Estimates suggest that more than 98 percent of the country has been stripped of its trees for use as fuel (Masters 2008). As a consequence, rain brings mudslides, destruction of homes, deaths, and more poverty (Knox 2012).

Reducing Community Exposure to the Potentially Damaging Event

Even though not much can be done to reduce the occurrence of natural hazard events, communities can and should reduce their exposure to those events where possible. It is foolish to permit construction on property subject to landslides, avalanches, river flooding, storm surge, lava and pyroclastic flows, and other events that are essentially inevitable. The challenge, of course, is that the most dangerous locations are often the most desirable in terms of scenery and access to amenities. People love to live near water; it is peaceful, scenic, and beautiful—until it is pouring into your house, submerging everything to the rafters.

Sometimes, facilities have to be built in areas subject to the effects of extreme natural hazard events; we do not build harbors or marinas inland, away from the water. Beach umbrellas are sold and rented at the beach. Downhill skiing takes place on the sides of mountains where avalanches may sometimes occur. Being in a place that is exposed to certain natural hazard events is sometimes downright foolish, but sometimes it is simply the right or most appropriate thing to do. When it is the right thing to do, it makes sense to reduce the vulnerability of the asset.

Local communities can prevent construction in vulnerable locations through the police power (zoning, eminent domain, etc.), but also through the power of the purse. Land purchases or gifts from private organizations and individuals can take land that should not be built upon permanently from the inventory of places to build. That land can be put to good use both as a hazard reduction tool and as wildlife habitat and or recreational areas.

FEMA has a program that helps to provide "buyout" funds for communities in which certain properties are repeatedly flooded. Importantly, "FEMA does not buy houses directly from the property owners. Acquisition or Buyout projects, while 75 percent funded by FEMA, are administered by the State and local communities. The State and local communities work together to identify areas where buyouts make the most sense" (FEMA 2012b, para. 3). Essentially, the local government can use federal funds to help it to buy the property and remove it from use. Such buyouts are intended to save future allocations of funding that would be needed in the event of another disaster, for example, river flooding. Tax increment funding programs can be employed to acquire property within an area (subject to state and local provisions) and to improve it to better serve the community. This could be done by replacing vulnerable structures with structures that are better sited and less vulnerable to natural hazards. Increased revenue from the site repays bond issues.

Reducing the Vulnerability of That Which Is Exposed

It is not rocket science: if a structure or activity must take place in a dangerous location, then it is important that the structure be made less vulnerable to the most likely events. Either that or the structures should be such that, when destroyed, not much of value is lost. A beachside cabana or shack selling fried clams lost to a hurricane is not a great loss, but the destruction of a city's wastewater treatment facility to the same event is. Two factors are evident in this example. First, the total replacement cost of any structure should be considered before siting it in a given location. How many months or years of average revenue might be needed to rebuild the structure? Second, how important is the structure to how many people and the overall community? Cabanas make a day at the beach more pleasant, but they are not necessary to a community's safe functioning.

Trade-offs are part of life. Unfortunately, those who want others to bear the costs of their risk-taking are inclined not to make trade-offs between exposure and reduced vulnerability. In situations where risk takers are unwilling to take adequate responsibility for the consequences that are likely to accrue to innocent parties, local government is obliged to ensure that the offending structure is either built somewhere else or that its vulnerability to the hazard is sufficiently reduced to meet standards. Communities cannot assume that individuals serving their self-interest will yield positive consequences for the community.

Harden in Place

Sometimes it makes good sense to simply harden a structure or facility against potential hazardous events. Many historic sites and facilities are built along rivers or harbors where they are subject to storms and flooding. It may well make sense to increase the resistance of those existing structures rather than to move or replace them. In Los Angeles, historic buildings and sites, including Olvera Street at the center of the original village, have been retrofitted to resist earthquake forces. Harbor facilities can hardly be moved inland, but along the Gulf Coast, they had better be able to withstand predictable storm surges and hurricane winds. Hardening in place does not always require serious engineering. It may be enough to store fuel and locate emergency generators above flood level.

Employ "Soft Mitigation" Tactics

What is the worst that could happen? Decision makers need to imagine the worst-case—yet likely—scenario for their organization or community, conduct a hazard vulnerability analysis, and then take action. In Wisconsin, for example, a major earthquake is not a likely occurrence. An EF3 tornado, on the other hand, is definitely possible. Even more probable, given the high number of rivers and lakes in the state, is major flooding. Most communities in the state would do well to anticipate such an event.

Insuring against probable losses from likely events is necessary for local governments, organizations, and individuals. In our experience, self-insurance is essentially no insurance. Insuring with a reliable, financially sound insurance firm is the best way to ensure that money will be available to help individuals, businesses, and local governments recover quickly with relatively little pain and anguish. Be careful, however, to ensure that the company from which the insurance is purchased is financially viable following a regional disaster. Make certain, too, that the policies purchased provide the desired coverage.

Store valuable records so that they are safe from almost any possible extreme natural hazard event. No community wants official property, criminal, and other legal documents to be destroyed because the records were in the basement that flooded. Store hard and electronic files in multiple locations to preclude decades of painful, expensive litigation. Backup electronic files often and regularly, and store them where they can be quickly retrieved, perhaps off-site, "in the cloud," or in another physical locale.

Conduct emergency training exercises often because people change jobs and locations. It is important for people to know how to secure their job posts, how to exit, where the first aid kits and spare parts are, and all of the other things that would otherwise be a mystery when the lights go out and strange noises appear from nowhere. Ensure that the right people are involved in the training. In our experience, this means everyone, at least everyone who works in a given organization (Arendt and Hess 2006). No one can predict who will be working when the hazardous event happens; formal leaders may not be on premises or reachable. As recommended by Arendt and Hess (2006, p. 55):

> It is not enough for people to read and hear about what they should do in the event of an emergency. Actual practice or enactive mastery is the gold standard for learning to do something well and feeling confident about one's ability to perform effectively that same something in the future (Bandura, 1997). To that end, hospital staff members should have the opportunity to *physically* practice what will happen in an emergency, over the course of more than one day, in order to simulate the real conditions of a disaster or extreme event.

Work with others in the community. If, for example, the community's economy is vulnerable (for any of many possible reasons), do not wait for a disaster to work with local employers. If you do, it will be too late. Local officials should talk with major local employers or groups of smaller employers to learn what it is that the community can do to help ensure that the employer will remain viable and profitable and, perhaps most of all, in the community. Some employers are likely to say they want lower taxes, special deals, or whatever, but, once past that, discussions can take place about helping to ensure adequate employees, space for expansion, transportation access, and other matters about which the local government can provide assistance, thus building a more economically resilient community.

THINGS TO DO NOW, BEFORE THE NEXT DISASTER

Here is a list of things to begin right now, long, we hope, before an extreme natural hazard event threatens a disaster in your community.

Develop and Maintain a Risk Inventory and Risk Assessment

Every community needs a continuing inventory of the problems it faces and those that are on or just over the horizon. Being blindsided is never good politics or policy. Despite this assertion, it seems that at least some people prefer denial to acknowledgement of risk. We are reminded of the Broadway production *The Wiz*, in which the title character sings a song imploring her subjects, "Don't bring me no bad news." Frankly, government leaders ought to implore residents, businesses, and other officials to bring them bad news early, while there is still time to do something about it. That is the purpose of the risk inventory and assessment: identifying likely sources of difficulty so something can be done now to keep it from happening or to reduce its consequences.

It is unlikely that one person or one agency can create the inventory of risks faced and conduct a thorough risk assessment, primarily because the risks will appear in a variety of activities and functional areas, including public works, human resources, finance, recreation, and so forth, and not be within the purview of any single department. In such cases, city planners, usually trained to look at the community as a system, will be helpful.

Developing the inventory and assessing risks is not a one-time activity. As one potential risk is alleviated, it is entirely likely that one or more will appear to take its place. This requires that the inventory and the risk assessments be a continuing activity and that action priorities be established and assigned. Those responsible for the action must be held accountable. Often, it is possible that some or much of the work required will be conducted by community groups and associations outside government.

What about criteria? What should be high on the list? John Platt (1969) wrote an article titled "What We Must Do." Platt's priorities were arranged by a relatively simple set of criteria. He looked at how many people would be affected adversely if the event should occur, how serious the consequences would be for them, and how soon it was likely to occur if nothing were done to stop it. The more people, the more serious the impact, and the sooner it was likely to happen determined essentially how high a priority was placed on addressing the risk. That seems sensible. It also makes sense to address risks that comprise low-hanging fruit. If it is easy and inexpensive to reduce the risk, do it now.

Make Some Plans

Making a recovery plan before a disaster actually occurs may sound like a fool's errand. While every extreme natural hazard event generates unique consequences and problems, some of those consequences are almost universal among natural hazard events. The plan should address the most likely of the issues that are likely to emerge. Having a protocol for who will be responsible for what, will save time and minimize conflict during and following the emergency. A close friend who flew transport planes in the Vietnam War says, "Having a check list is very handy, particularly when bullet holes begin to appear in the cockpit." Thus, having a response plan with assigned responsibilities is important before the event occurs. Moreover, it is critical that the protocol be continually updated and that those with assigned roles know their range of responsibility and that of others. Incumbents change often, so regular training is essential.

The community plan should incorporate strategies for addressing problems that are very likely to emerge, based on the most likely natural hazard events that will affect the community. If it looks as though evacuation is likely to be needed, for example, the plan had better specify how the evacuation process will be handled. During Katrina, a number of nursing and health care facilities each contracted to ensure that sufficient ambulances would be available to evacuate patients needing an ambulance (Arendt and Hess 2006). Unfortunately, most of them contracted with the same firm: a firm that did not have access to enough ambulances when everyone needed some at the same time. Do not let something like that happen to your community. Question assumptions about how an evacuation might happen. Hospitals in New Orleans were surprised by their inability to use land-based evacuation. At least one had to create a makeshift helicopter landing to evacuate not only its patients, but patients from a nearby hospital as well (Arendt and Hess 2006). In a city prone to flooding, land-based evacuation does not seem practical. Figure 9.3 illustrates the futility of imagining otherwise.

An important part of the plan is action steps to be taken before the extreme natural hazard event occurs to put the precautions in place that are called for by the inventory of risks and the risk assessments. If the community economy is vulnerable to an extreme event, then take action to help those parties that are critical to the economy do what is important for them to become robust, resistant, and resilient. One thing we hope readers of this book understand at this point is that it will not be enough to think only of clearing debris and restoring power and water. The community's full array of functions is needed to ensure a resilient community. If some of those functions are operating at suboptimal levels

FIGURE 9.3 New Orleans, Louisiana, Tuesday, August 30, 2005—
Cars on the streets of New Orleans are flooded to the top of the wheel
wells. (FEMA/Marty Bahamonde.)

before an extreme natural hazard event, odds are extremely good that
the community will struggle mightily in the aftermath.

Develop a Shared Vision

It is commonplace that local governments will be encouraged, following
an extreme event, to involve the community in developing a vision for
the community's future. That is not something that can be done in an
afternoon with coffee and cookies supplied by a generous contributor.
What is desirable has to be congruent with what is possible. Working out
the vision should certainly involve members of the community, but, following the disaster, many community members will be busy trying to get
their lives together again. It is better to have a vision in place before the
disaster and to have been working toward achieving the vision before
the event. If the event results in part or all of the preevent vision being
unrealizable, then modify that aspect of the plan and the strategy for getting from here to there, but do not put off making important basic decisions concerning what is possible and desirable until the community is in
turmoil. Use the existing plan to help quell the turmoil. Individuals under
stress may not make the decisions they would make in calmer times.

Get Necessary State Government Policies in Place

The Business Civic Leadership Council (BCLC) in Washington, DC, was created by the U.S. Chamber of Commerce in consideration of chamber members that give considerable support to communities that experience disasters. In brief, these members wanted assurances that the money they gave would have a lasting positive impact. In 2008, the authors of this book were commissioned by the BCLC to devise a list of the most important things state governments should do to facilitate community disaster recovery (Business Civic Leadership Council 2009). During the course of that study and studies that had been previously conducted in communities that had experienced disasters, it became clear that several critical policies should be adopted by state governments before the next disaster. The primary reason was that the adoption of such policies would greatly reduce conflict, negotiations, and other transaction costs during the postevent turmoil and struggle for recovery.

Each of the policies recommended in that report, if adopted, would facilitate both hazard mitigation and community recovery from disasters. State governments are unlikely to think about and act on these policies without prompting and support from local governments and local communities. Therefore, it makes sense for local governments to learn from those who have suffered disasters and to seek the adoption of these policies before the next disaster.

Assisting with Local Government Financial Plights

Several of the recommended policies have to do with establishing financial arrangements for local governments before the disaster occurs. In Chapter 5, we discuss financial problems that local governments experience in the aftermath of extreme natural hazard events. State-level policies should be put into place to help local governments address those problems. Iowa, in the wake of major flooding, recently enacted legislation that provides for postdisaster funding both for schools that lose enrollment and for those that get unexpectedly large numbers of students due to the extreme natural hazard event. This is intended as an equitable plan for the short run and, if needed, the longer run. Every state should have such a policy. Few do.

A second set of state-level policies affecting local government finance has to do with tax revenue. Ad valorem property taxes (see Chapter 5) typically plummet following devastating extreme events. So, too, do centrally collected and locally shared taxes. The State of Florida was induced to enact a law that provided jurisdictions badly damaged by Hurricane Andrew with the net increase in sales tax revenues experienced in nearby localities not damaged by the hurricane (Florida Legislature 1993, p. 11). As described in Chapter 5, the agreement was for 3 years, not nearly sufficient time for Homestead and Florida City to recover to the extent that the level of their preevent sales tax revenues was reached.

Without adequate revenue, local jurisdictions have little chance of maintaining adequate levels of service to residents, much less rebuilding their community. Every state should develop policies for providing financial assistance to local governments to make up the difference between insurance proceeds and tax revenue that would have been generated for a period sufficiently long to permit community recovery. How long will this be? Well, this of course depends on the damage wrought and the full array of resources available to assist the community in restoring all of its functions. In at least some cases, the community may need help for up to 10 years.

States can also provide revolving loan funds to help communities undertake recovery activities, just as they do for municipalities building certain kinds of new facilities. Many of the revolving loan funds provide for subsidized interest rates and provide a boon to devastated communities at low cost to the state.

Insurance

Individuals can buy flood insurance from the National Flood Insurance Program through their private broker if the municipality within which they live agrees to adopt policies and practices stipulated by the flood insurance program. These policies and practices are designed to reduce the risks associated with flooding. Not every municipality subject to flooding participates in the program. Thus, many homeowners subject to flooding do not have access to insurance. State governments should work to ensure that all communities within the state that are potentially subject to flooding participate in the national flood insurance program. States and local governments should also work to educate their constituencies about the limits of homeowner's insurance and the need for specialized insurance (for flooding, earthquake, etc.).

The federal government leaves regulation of property and casualty insurance firms to the states. Not all states perform their regulatory obligations equally well, but it is important to recovery that property owners and local governments have appropriate property and casualty insurance policies at appropriate rates available from viable insurers. Insurance payments for losses are a valuable resource for stimulating and facilitating disaster recovery. In Florida following Hurricane Andrew, 11 property and casualty insurance firms failed, leaving policyholders stranded.

Permits and Licensing

After every disaster, communities are swamped with applications from residents and contractors to undertake various repair or replacement activities. Some want to become licensed plumbing, roofing, electrical, or building contractors in the damaged community. Others want building and specialty code permits and inspections so they can open badly needed restaurants and day care centers. State governments should expedite permitting and licensing businesses that are needed in the early aftermath and should consider statewide licensing of contractors and specialty trades workers, just as many states license barbers and beauticians.

Infrastructure Inspections

States are responsible for inspecting most bridges, dams, and highways. A failed dam in an urban area is likely to generate severe adverse consequences, yet state governments as a whole are notoriously lax in inspecting and certifying bridges, dams, and levees. Given the extraordinary potential for extreme consequences from failed dams and bridges, state governments must be pressured to adopt and enforce appropriate policies and practices.

In addition to these suggested policies, we offer a few, final paragraphs that emphasize—one more time—the essential need for both mitigation and disaster preparedness at the community level. From everything we have observed personally and learned from others, communities have the best shot at recovering when they engage in serious recovery planning before disaster strikes.

Local governments need to engage in what may be called "fact checking" and "ground-truthing." If our community is hit by a tornado, earthquake, flood, hurricane, and so forth, what is likely to happen? For example, how will we go about identifying sources of assistance? Who on staff has experience with the kind(s) of disasters most likely to strike our community? What is the obligation of local versus state versus federal government in terms of resources and timing of resource distribution?

What many local governments will discover, if they do their fact checking in earnest, is that they will likely be eligible for far less support than they think makes sense, that the support will take longer to arrive than hoped, and that the support will require documentation to a degree that local officials have never experienced. People might think of this fact checking as a tabletop exercise, not of response in the traditional sense of search and rescue and all of the activities that occur in the immediate aftermath of a disaster, but in terms of what happens next. And next.

One item that must be driven home is that the Stafford Act defines federal assistance for public assistance and individual assistance as being supplemental to state and local efforts and insurance. "Supplemental" necessarily means that there is an expectation that some significant portion of the full costs of the disaster will be borne by individuals and their insurance companies, along with local and state governments and their insurance policies. Federal assistance is not intended to cover all of the costs associated with a disaster. Sometimes, to the chagrin and extreme disappointment of those affected, no federal assistance is provided.

As a good colleague reminded us, disasters need not be catastrophic in order to present a fiscal disaster for most communities. Returning to the Stafford Act, when considering the public assistance aspect, the state and each affected county must both meet per capita loss thresholds. These thresholds are around $1.30 per capita for the state and about $3.30 for the county (McCarthy 2010). If the state does not meet its threshold, it is not eligible for public assistance, and the counties are not eligible even if one or more counties have met the county threshold. If the state meets its threshold, only those counties that meet the county threshold are eligible. States can help their county and local government officials by sharing these loss thresholds—and the likely range of actual costs—so that these officials can begin to understand exactly what will need to happen in order to receive federal assistance. It would also be helpful for local government officials to be made aware of situations in which counties did not meet the per capita loss thresholds and were therefore not included in the disaster declarations. Finally, explaining that even when all criteria are met, the maximum payout will be no more than 75 percent of the loss should help decision makers to internalize that investments in mitigation will prove wise in the wake of disaster.

As baffling as the criteria for public assistance may be, the criteria for individual assistance are even less clear and potentially more difficult to meet. The Code of Federal Regulations states that there are no set thresholds for recommending individual assistance. Factors to be considered are concentration of damages, trauma, special populations, voluntary agency assistance, insurance, average amount of assistance by state, and economic declarations. Recent federal legislative efforts have focused on trying to quantify the factors and balance fiscal outlays so that both smaller and larger communities are treated equitably (Davis 2014).

States are ranked as small, medium, and large, and there is guidance suggesting what a state should be able to handle based on its size. The authors' home state, Wisconsin, is considered a medium-sized state. As such, it is expected to handle an event in which an estimated 582 homes would suffer major damage or be destroyed. This number may not seem particularly high to someone imagining a large urban center, but for many smaller localities, this number is enormous. Even when a state does qualify for individual assistance, the limit is approximately $31,000 per household. Again, these numbers are not shared in an attempt to garner greater federal support for individuals and their communities, but rather to inform local government officials about the fiscal realities to be faced after an extreme natural hazard event. In brief, the fiscal realities are ugly. Better to spend money mitigating and preparing, rather than waiting for a check after a disaster that may never come.

As we draw to a close, it is the authors' sincere wish that communities, including especially local governments and community leaders, will take the initiative to consider the myriad impacts that an extreme natural hazard event might have on their community, and take the steps needed to facilitate community recovery. Following the tradition of the late Edward R. Murrow, we sign off by saying, "Good night and good luck."

References

Acevedo, Melissa, and Joachim I. Krueger. 2004. "Two egocentric sources of the decision to vote: The voter's illusion and the belief in personal relevance," *Political Psychology*, 25(1): 115–134.

Aldrich, Daniel P. 2012. *Building resilience: Social capital in post-disaster recovery*. Chicago, IL: The University of Chicago Press.

Alesch, Daniel J., Lucy A. Arendt, and James N. Holly. 2009. *Managing for long-term community recovery in the aftermath of disaster*. Fairfax, VA: Public Entity Risk Institute.

Alesch, Daniel J., Lucy A. Arendt, and William J. Petak. 2012. *Natural hazard mitigation policy: Implementation, organizational choice, and contextual dynamics*. New York: Springer.

Alesch, Daniel J., and William Siembieda. 2012. "The role of the built environment in the recovery of cities and communities from extreme events," *International Journal of Mass Emergencies and Disasters*, 30(2): 197–211.

Alexander, David. 2005. "An interpretation of disaster in terms of changes in culture, society and international relations." In Ronald W. Perry and Enrico L. Quarantelli (Eds.), *What is a disaster? New answers to old questions*. Xlibris Corp.

Arendt, Lucy A., and Daniel B. Hess. 2006. "Hospital decision making in the wake of Katrina: The case of New Orleans." Research supported by the Earthquake Engineering Research Centers Program of the NSF under award to the Multidisciplinary Center for Earthquake Engineering Research (MCEER) (via EEC-9701471 grant). Technical Report MCEER-06-SP01 (http://mceer.buffalo.edu/publications/Katrina/06-SP01.asp).

Arendt, Lucy A., Richard L. Priem, and Hermann A. Ndofor. 2005. "A CEO-Adviser model of strategic decision making," *Journal of Management*, 31: 680–699.

Ashby, William Ross. 1958. "Requisite variety and its implications for the control of complex systems," *Cybernetica*, 1(2): 83–99.

Bandura, Albert. 1997. *Self-efficacy: The exercise of control*. New York: W. H. Freeman/Times Books/Henry Holt & Co.

Barry, John M. 1998. *Rising tide: The Great Mississippi Flood of 1927 and how it changed America*. New York: Simon & Schuster.

Bashan, Amir, Yehiel Berezin, Sergey V. Buldyrev, and Shlomo Havlin. 2013. "The extreme vulnerability of interdependent spatially embedded networks," *Nature Physics*, 9: 667–672.

Batty, Michael. 2007. *Cities and complexity: Understanding cities with cellular automata, agent-based models, and fractals*. Cambridge, MA: The MIT Press.

Becker, Christine. 2009. "Disaster recovery: A local government responsibility," *Public Manager Magazine*, 91(2), March: 6–12.

Benjamin, Ernest, Adel M. Bassily-Marcus, Elizabeth Babu, Lester Silver, and Michael L. Martin. 2011. "Principles and practice of disaster relief: Lessons from Haiti," *The Mount Sinai Journal of Medicine*, 78(3): 306–318.

Bentley, Callan. 2011. "The Mineral, VA earthquake of August 23, 2011—UPDATED," *American Geophysical Union Blogosphere*. Last modified August 23, 2011. http://blogs.agu.org/mountainbeltway/2011/08/23/the-mineral-va-earthquake-of-august-23-2011/.

Bentley, Ian, and Georgia Butina. 1990. "Urban design." In S. Gleave (Ed.), *Architects Journal*, 192(17): 61–71.

Bertalanffy, Ludwig von. 1968. *General system theory: Foundations, development, applications*. New York: G. Braziller.

Bogert, Nick. 2013. "Battered city of Gary, Ind., considers shrinking 40 percent to save itself." Last modified June 19, 2013. http://inplainsight.nbcnews.com/_news/2013/06/19/18956862-battered-city-of-gary-ind-considers-shrinking-40-percent-to-save-itself.

Bolin, Robert. 1993. *Household and community recovery after earthquakes*. Boulder, CO: University of Colorado, Institute of Behavioral Science, Program on Environment and Behavior, Monograph No. 56.

Brooks, Mary Jo. 2013. "In tornado aftermath, what residents of Moore can learn from Joplin," *PBS Newshour*. Last modified May 22, 2013. http://www.pbs.org/newshour/rundown/2013/05/what-moore-okla-can-learn-from-joplin.html.

Brown, Frank Dexter. 2001. "The destruction of Princeville, the nation's oldest black-governed community." Last modified April 9, 2001. www.seeingblack.com/x040901/princeville.shtml.

Bruine de Bruin, Wändi, Andrew M. Parker, and Baruch Fischhoff. 2007. "Individual differences in adult decision-making competence," *Journal of Personality and Social Psychology*, 92(5): 938–956.

Buchanan, David A. 2011. "Reflections: Good practice, not rocket science—Understanding failures to change after extreme events," *Journal of Change Management*, 11(3): 273–288.

Buldyrev, Sergey, Roni Parshani, Gerald Paul, H. Eugene Stanley, and Shlomo Havlin. 2010. "Catastrophic cascade of failures in interdependent networks," *Nature*, 464: 1025–1028.

Burdeau, Cain. 2012. "Last Katrina FEMA trailer leaves New Orleans." Last modified February 15, 2012. http://cnsnews.com/news/article/last-katrina-fema-trailer-leaves-new-orleans.

Burgelman, Robert A., and Andrew S. Grove. 2007. "Let chaos reign, then rein in chaos—repeatedly: Managing strategic dynamics for corporate longevity," *Strategic Management Journal,* 28(10): 965–979.

Business Civic Leadership Council (BCLC). 2009. "State governments and community disasters: A critical role." Washington, DC: Business Civic Leadership Council.

Carr, Lowell Juilliard. 1932. "Disaster and the sequence-pattern concept of social change," *American Journal of Sociology,* 38(2): 207–218.

Center for Disaster Philanthropy. 2014. "The disaster life cycle." *Learning Center, Issue Insights.* Accessed March 12, 2014. http://disasterphilanthropy.org/learning-center/issue-insights/the-disaster-life-cycle/.

City of Biloxi, Mississippi. 2008. Comprehensive Annual Financial Report, City of Biloxi, Biloxi, Mississippi, Fiscal Year Ended September 30, 2006. Accessed December 13, 2008. http://www.biloxi.ms.us/PDF/CAFR06.pdf

City of St. Peter, Minnesota. 1995. Comprehensive plan. City of St. Peter, Minnesota.

City of St. Peter, Minnesota. 2004. Comprehensive plan. City of St. Peter, Minnesota.

CNN Reports. 2005. *CNN Reports: Katrina—State of emergency.* Kansas City: Andrews McMeel Publishing.

Coates, Sam, and Dan Eggen. 2005. "A city of despair and lawlessness," *The Washington Post.* Last updated September 2, 2005. http://www.washingtonpost.com/wp-dyn/content/article/2005/09/01/AR2005090100533.html.

Coffman, Keith. 2013. "Colorado evacuations continue as flood crest moves downstream." Accessed September 17, 2013. http://www.reuters.com/article/2013/09/17/us-usa-colorado-flooding-idUSBRE98B0KM20130917.

Cohen, Michael D., James G. March, and Johan P. Olsen. 1972. "A garbage can model of organizational choice," *Administrative Science Quarterly,* 17(1): 1–25.

Comerio, Mary C. 1997. "Housing issues after disasters," *Journal of Contingencies and Crisis Management,* 5(3): 166–178.

Comerio, Mary C. 1998. *Disaster hits home: New policy for urban housing recovery.* Los Angeles, CA: University of California Press.

Comfort, Louise K. 1994. "Self-organization in complex systems," *Journal of Public Administration Research and Theory: J-PART,* 4(3): 393–410.

Compton, Matt. 2012. "Joplin: One year later." *The White House blog.* http://www.whitehouse.gov/joplin.

Cox, Robin S., and Karen-Marie Elah Perry. 2011. "Like a fish out of water: Reconsidering disaster recovery and the role of place and social capital in community disaster resilience," *American Journal of Community Psychology*, 48: 395–411.

Cutter, Susan, Bryan J. Boruff, and W. Lynn Shirley. 2003. "Social vulnerability to environmental hazards," *Social Science Quarterly*, 84(2): 242-261.

Davis, Rodney. 2014. "Reps. Davis, Shimkus, Schock, Kinzinger, Bustos, Enyart introduce bipartisan legislation to bring fairness to FEMA disaster declaration process." Press release. Last updated January 23, 2014. http://rodneydavis.house.gov/media-center/press-releases/reps-davis-shimkus-schock-kinzinger-bustos-enyart-introduce-bipartisan.

Dynes, Russell R. 1989. *"Conceptualizing disaster in ways productive for social science research."* Working paper #80. University of Delaware, Disaster Research Center.

Eggler, Bruce. 2009. *"Census population estimate for New Orleans for 2008 too low, Mayor Ray Nagin says.* Last modified October 2, 2009. http://www.nola.com/politics/index.ssf/2009/10/census_population_estimate_for.html.

Federal Emergency Management Agency (FEMA). 2011a. "National disaster recovery framework: Strengthening disaster recovery for the nation." Last modified September 2011. http://www.fema.gov/media-library-data/20130726-1820-25045-5325/508_ndrf.pdf.

Federal Emergency Management Agency (FEMA). 2011b. "National disaster recovery framework: Community planning and capacity building recovery support function." Last modified September 2011. http://www.fema.gov/pdf/recoveryframework/community_planning_capacity_building_rsf.pdf.

Federal Emergency Management Agency (FEMA). 2012a. "Presidential disaster declaration." Last modified June 22, 2012. http://www.fema.gov/public-assistance-local-state-tribal-and-non-profit/presidential-disaster-declaration.

Federal Emergency Management Agency (FEMA). 2012b. "Hazard mitigation assistance—property acquisition (buyouts)." Last modified December 27, 2012. http://www.fema.gov/application-development-process/hazard-mitigation-assistance-property-acquisition-buyouts.

Federal Emergency Management Agency (FEMA). 2013a. "Disaster case management program guidance." Last modified March 1, 2013. http://www.fema.gov/media-library/assets/documents/31253.

Federal Emergency Management Agency (FEMA). 2013b. "Community disaster loan program." Last modified October 25, 2013. http://www.fema.gov/community-disaster-loan-program.

Finkelstein, Sydney. 1992. "Power in top management teams: Dimensions, measurement, and validation." *Academy of Management Journal*, 35: 505–538.

Finney, Caitlin, Erene Stergiopoulos, Jennifer Hensel, Sarah Bonato, and Carolyn S. Dewa. 2013. "Organizational stressors associated with job stress and burnout in correctional officers: A systematic review," *BMC Public Health*, 13(1): 1–13.

Flaherty, Jordan. 2012. Post-Katrina reforms in New Orleans continue to disenfranchise African-Americans, poor. Last modified August 29, 2012. http://truth-out.org/news/item/11192-reform-and-its-discontents.

Florida Legislature. 1993. "Hurricane Andrew and sales tax." *1993 Summary of general legislation.* Page 11. http://www.law.fsu.edu/library/collection/FlSumGenLeg/FlSumGenLeg1993.pdf.

Forrester, Jay Wright. 1969. *Urban dynamics.* Cambridge, MA: MIT Press.

Free Press Staff. 2014. "Where does Detroit's bankruptcy go from here? Here's a road map to how it may play out," *Detroit Free Press*. Last modified January 1, 2014. http://www.freep.com/article/20140101/NEWS01/301010014/Detroit-bankruptcy-end-of-year.

Freilich, M. 1963. "Toward an operational definition of community," *Rural Sociology*, 28 (June): 117–127.

Friedman, Dan. 2013. "Colorado Republicans in Congress vote for disaster assistance for their own state despite fighting to deny aid after Hurricane Sandy," *New York Daily News*. Last modified October 1, 2013. http://www.nydailynews.com/news/politics/colorado-republicans-vote-disaster-assistance-denial-article-1.1473395.

Furedi, Frank. 2007. "The changing meaning of disaster," *Area,* 39(4): 482–489.

Fussell, Elizabeth. 2007. "Constructing New Orleans, constructing race: A population history of New Orleans," *Journal of American History*, 94 (Dec. 2007): 846–855.

Garner, Marcus K. 2014. "In Atlanta snow storm, it's social media to the rescue," *Atlanta Journal-Constitution*. Last updated January 29, 2014. http://www.ajc.com/news/news/in-snow-storm-its-social-media-to-the-rescue/nc6Kc/.

Gersick, Connie J. G. 1991. "Revolutionary change theories: A multilevel exploration of the punctuated equilibrium paradigm," *Academy of Management Review,* 16(1): 10–36.

Gillette, Becky. 2006. "Business interruption insurance can save the day—or not," *Mississippi Business Journal*. Last updated July 17, 2006. http://msbusiness.com/blog/2006/07/17/business-interruption-insurance-can-save-the-day-8212-or-not/.

Global Terrorism Database. 2013. Accessed November 28, 2013. http://www.start.umd.edu/gtd/.

Grafanaki, Soti, and John McLeod. 2002. "Experiential congruence: Qualitative analysis of client and counsellor narrative accounts of significant events in time-limited person-centred therapy," *Counselling and Psychotherapy Research*, 2(1): 20–32.

Gratz, Roberta Brandes. 2010. *The battle for Gotham: New York in the shadow of Robert Moses and Jane Jacobs*. New York: Nation Books.

Greater New Orleans Community Data Center (GNOCDC). 2013. "Lower Ninth Ward Statistical Area." GNOCDC analysis of data from U.S. Census 2000 Summary File 1 (SF1) and U.S. Census 2010 Summary File 1 (SF1). Last accessed November 1, 2013. http://gnocdc.org/NeighborhoodData/8/LowerNinthWard/index.html.

Haas, J. Eugene, Robert W. Kates, and Martyn J. Bowden (Eds.). 1977. *Reconstruction following disaster*. Cambridge, MA: The MIT Press.

Hambrick, Donald C., and Phyllis A Mason. 1984. "Upper echelons: The organization as a reflection of its top managers," *Academy of Management Review*, 9(2): 193–206.

Hamman, Robin (1997). "Virtual communities," *Cybersociology Magazine*, 20 November. Accessed November 27, 2013. http://www.cybersociology.com/issue_2_virtual_communities/

Hauser, Christine, and Thomas J. Lueck. 2005. "Mandatory evacuation ordered for New Orleans as storm nears," *The New York Times*. Last modified August 28, 2005. http://www.nytimes.com/2005/08/28/national/29katrinacnd.html?_r=0.

Henderson, Donald A. September-October, 1980. "Smallpox eradication," *Public Health Reports (1974-)*, 95(5): 422–426.

Herb, Terry. 2010. *No building codes: A guide to states with no building codes*. E-book available at http://nobuildingcodes.com/.

Hess, Daniel B., and Lucy A. Arendt. 2006. "Critical care in crisis: Decision making in New Orleans' hospitals," In Natural Hazards Center (Ed.), *Learning from catastrophe: Quick response research in the wake of Hurricane Katrina*, pp. 177-213. Boulder, CO.

Hillery, George A. 1955. "Definitions of community: Areas of agreement," *Rural Sociology*, 20:111–124.

Houston, J. Brian, Betty Pfefferbaum, and Cathy Ellen Rosenholtz. 2012. "Disaster news: Framing and frame changing in coverage of major U.S. natural disasters, 2000–2010," *Journalism & Mass Communication Quarterly*, 89(4): 606–623.

Huffman, Alan. 2005. "The unkindest storm: Hurricane Katrina shattered many of the Gulf Coast's historic districts." Last modified September 16, 2005. http://www.preservationnation.org/magazine/story-of-the-week/2005/the-unkindest-storm.html#.UpojANJDu8A.

Huler, Scott. 2004. *Defining the wind: The Beaufort scale, and how a 19th-Century admiral turned science into poetry.* New York: Crown.

Hunter, Larry W., and Sherry M. B. Thatcher. 2007. "Feeling the heat: Effects of stress, commitment, and job experience on job performance," *Academy of Management Journal,* 50(4): 953–968.

Iacovelli, Debi. 1999. "The Saffir/Simpson Hurricane scale: An interview with Dr. Robert Simpson," *Mariners Weather Log,* 43(1): 10–12.

Iwan, William D. 2006. "Preface to the Special Issue on the Great Sumatra Earthquakes and Indian Ocean Tsunamis of 26 December 2004 and 28 March," *Earthquake Spectra,* 22(3): xi–xii.

Janis, Irving L. 1982. *Groupthink: Psychological studies of policy decisions and fiascoes.* Boston: Houghton Mifflin.

Joint Legislative Audit Bureau. 2004. "Best practices report: Local government user fees," Madison, Wisconsin. Last modified April 2004. http://legis.wisconsin.gov/LAB/reports/04-0UserFeesFull.pdf.

Juliusson, E. Ásgeir, Niklas Karlsson, and Tommy Gärling. 2005. "Weighing the past and the future in decision making," *European Journal of Cognitive Psychology,* 17(4): 561–575.

Kammerbauer, Mark. 2008. "Evacuation and return—crisis mobility in New Orleans following Hurricane Katrina," *Environment, Forced Migration & Social Vulnerability International Conference,* October 9–11, Bonn, Germany.

Kast, Fremont E., and James E. Rosenzweig. 1972. "General systems theory: Applications for organization and management," *Academy of Management Journal,* 15(4): 447–465.

Katz, Daniel, and Robert L. Kahn. 1978. *The social psychology of organizations.* New York: Wiley.

Kiel, L. Douglas. 1995. "Chaos theory and disaster response management: Lessons for managing periods of extreme instability." In Gus A. Koehler (Ed.), *What disaster response management can learn from chaos theory,* Conference proceedings (CRB-96-005), pp. 186–210. Sacramento, CA: California Research Bureau, May 18–19.

Kieper, Margie. 2006. "Hurricane Katrina storm surge, part 5: St. Bernard Parish, LA." *Weather Underground 16 Part Series.* Last accessed December 2013. http://www.wunderground.com/education/Katrinas_surge_part05.asp.

Klein, Kenny. 2013. "Has New Orleans recovered?" *The Huffington Post.* Last modified December 4, 2013. http://www.huffingtonpost.com/kenny-klein/has-new-orleans-recovered_b_4374931.html.

Knox, Richard. 2012. "Before Sandy hit U.S., storm was a killer in Haiti." *NPR.* Last modified October 31, 2012. http://www.npr.org/blogs/health/2012/10/31/164045691/before-sandy-hit-u-s-storm-was-a-killer-in-haiti.

Koehler, Gus A. 1995. "What disaster response management can learn from chaos theory." In Gus A. Koehler (Ed.), *What disaster response management can learn from chaos theory*, Conference proceedings (CRB-96-005), pp. 2–41. Sacramento, CA: California Research Bureau, May 18–19.

Kroll-Smith, J. Stephen, and Stephen R. Couch. 1991. "What is a disaster? An ecological-symbolic approach to resolving the definitional debate," *International Journal of Mass Emergencies and Disasters*, 9(3): 355–366.

Krugman, Paul R. 1996. *The self-organizing economy*. Cambridge, MA: Blackwell Publishers.

Kunreuther, Howard, and Mark V. Pauly. 2006. "Insurance decision-making and market behavior," *Foundations and Trends in Microeconomics*, 1(2): 63–127.

Kushma, Jane. 2007. "Role abandonment in disaster: Should we leave this myth behind? *Natural Hazards Observer*, 31(5): 4–5.

Levine, Joyce N., Ann-Margaret Esnard, and Alka Sapat. 2007. "Population displacement and housing dilemmas due to catastrophic hurricanes," *Journal of Planning Literature*, 22(1): 3–15.

Lewin, Kurt. 1951. "Problems of research in social psychology." In D. Cartwright (Ed.), *Field theory in social science: Selected theoretical papers*, pp. 155–169. New York: Harper & Row.

Lite, Jordan. 2008. "50-state ills: Workers, ex-N.Y.ers from across the nation report WTC ailments." Last modified April 30, 2007. http://www.nydailynews.com/news/50-state-ills-article-1.213120.

Litke, Jim. 2005. "New Orleans' thin blue line stretched to breaking point." *Officer.com*. Last modified September 5, 2005. http://web.archive.org/web/20080626165548/http://www.officer.com/article/article.jsp?siteSection=15&id=25779.

Louisiana Justice Institute. n.d. "No way to treat our people: FEMA trailer residents 30 months after Katrina." Last accessed December 1, 2013. http://www.louisianajusticeinstitute.org/files/all/docs/LJI_FEMA_Trailer_Report_Publication.pdf.

Macon County Chamber of Commerce. 2012. "Montezuma." Last accessed November 30, 2013. http://www.maconcountyga.org/Histmtz.html.

March, James G., and Herbert A. Simon. 1958. *Organizations*. New York: Wiley.

March, James G., and Johan P. Olsen. 1977. *Ambiguity and choice in organizations*. Oslo: Universitetforlaget.

Martel, Brett. 2006. "Storms payback from God, Nagin says," *The Washington Post*. Last modified January 17, 2006. http://www.washingtonpost.com/wp-dyn/content/article/2006/01/16/AR2006011600925.html.

Massey, Joseph Eric, and John P. Larsen. 2006. "Crisis management in real time: How to successfully plan for and respond to a crisis," *Journal of Promotion Management,* 12(3/4): 63–97.

Masters, Jeffrey. 2008. "Hurricanes and Haiti: A tragic history," *Weather Underground, Inc.* http://www.wunderground.com/hurricane/haiti.asp.

McCarthy, Brendan. 2009. "Despite drop in crime, New Orleans' murder rate continues to lead nation," *The Times-Picayune.* Last modified October 5, 2009. http://www.nola.com/news/index.ssf/2009/06/despite_drop_in_crime_new_orle.html.

McCarthy, Francis X. 2010. FEMA's disaster declaration process: A primer. *Congressional Research Service,* RL34146. Last modified March 18, 2010. http://assets.opencrs.com/rpts/RL34146_20100318.pdf.

McCarthy, Kevin, D. J. Peterson, Narayan Sastry, and Michael Pollard. 2006. "The repopulation of New Orleans after Hurricane Katrina," Technical Report. Santa Monica, CA: RAND Gulf States Policy Institute.

McGrath, Joseph E. 1976. "Stress and behavior in organizations." In Marvin D. Dunnette (Ed.), *Handbook of industrial organizational psychology*, pp. 1351–1395. Chicago: Rand McNally Co., Inc.

Meyer, Theodoric. 2013. "Why 58 representatives who voted for Hurricane Katrina aid voted against aid for Sandy," *Propublica.* Last modified January 18, 2013. http://www.propublica.org/article/the-58-representatives-who-voted-for-katrina-aid-and-against-sandy-aid.

Mileti, Dennis. 2006 *Holistic disaster recovery: Ideas for building local sustainability after a natural disaster.* Fairfax, VA: Public Entity Risk Institute.

Miller, Russell. 1983. *Planet Earth: Continents in collision.* Alexandria, VA: Time-Life Books.

Mitchell, James K. 2004. "Re-conceiving recovery." Keynote address to the Recovery Symposium, Napier, New Zealand, July 12–13.

Morgan, Gareth. 1986. *Images of organization.* Newbury Park, CA: Sage Publications.

Morris, Frank. 2011. "For Joplin's children, tornado's effects persist," *NPR.* Last modified September 15, 2011. http://www.npr.org/2011/09/15/140476898/for-joplins-children-tornados-effects-persist.

Morrison, David, Clark R. Chapman, Duncan Steel, and Richard P. Binzel. 2004. "Impacts and the public: Communicating the nature of the impact hazard." In M. J. S. Belton, T. H. Morgan, N. H. Samarasinha, and D. K. Yeomans (Eds.)., *Mitigation of hazardous comets and asteroids.* Cambridge: Cambridge University Press.

Mumford, Lewis. 1938. *The culture of cities.* New York: Harcourt, Brace and Company.

Mumford, Lewis. 1961. *The city in history*. New York: Harcourt, Brace and World.

National Public Radio. 2008. "Transcript: Former New York Mayor Rudy Giuliani," *Special series: The Republican convention*. Accessed November 27, 2013. http://www.npr.org/templates/story/story.php?storyId=94254610.

National Research Council. 2012. *Disaster resilience: A national imperative*. Washington, DC: The National Academies Press.

National Weather Service. 2005. "Urgent weather message for New Orleans, Louisiana." Archived from the original on January 20, 2008. Last accessed November 30, 2013. http://web.archive.org/web/20080120002429/http://www.srh.noaa.gov/data/warn_archive/LIX/NPW/0828_155101.txt.

Nesbit, Robert C. 1973. *Wisconsin: A history*. Madison, Wisconsin: The University of Wisconsin Press.

Nigg, Joanne M. 1995. "Disaster recovery as a social process," Preliminary paper #219. Newark Delaware: Disaster Research Center, University of Delaware.

Norris, Fran H., Susan P. Stevens, Betty Pfefferbaum, Karen F. Wyche, and Rose L. Pfefferbaum. 2008. "Community resilience as a metaphor, theory, set of capacities, and strategy for disaster readiness," *American Journal of Community Psychology*, 41: 127–150.

Nossiter, Adam. 2007. "Whites take a majority on New Orleans' Council," *New York Times,* November 20. Accessed December 5, 2008. http://www.nytimes.com/2007/11/20/us/nationalspecial/20orleans.html?_r=1&ref=us&oref=slogin.

Olinger, David and Bruce Finley. 2013. "Colorado flood: Dams break in Larimer and Adams counties; overflowing in Boulder." Accessed September 13, 2013. http://www.denverpost.com/environment/ci_24080336/.

Oliver-Smith, Anthony, and Susanna M. Hoffman (Eds.). 1999. *The angry earth: Disaster in anthropological perspective*. London: Routledge.

Olsen, Lise. 2005. "City had evacuation plan but strayed from strategy," *Houston Chronicle*. Last modified September 8, 2005. http://www.chron.com/news/hurricanes/article/New-Orleans-strayed-from-evacuation-plan-1491205.php.

Pascrell, Bill. 2013. "Colorado Congressmen sponsor legislation to use portion of Sandy aid they voted against to assist their constituents," Office of U.S. Representative Bill Pascrel, Jr., 8th Congressional District of New Jersey. News release on September 30, 2013.

Paton, Douglas. 2006. "Disaster resistance: Integrating individual, community, institutional, and environmental perspectives." In D. Paton and D. Johnston (Eds.), *Disaster resistance: An integrated approach,* pp. 308–318. Springfield, Illinois: Charles C. Thompson.

Payne, Ed. 2014. "Winter storm part deux: This time, we're ready, says Georgia." CNN. Last updated February 10, 2014. http://www.cnn.com/2014/02/10/us/winter-weather/

Peisah, C., E. Latif, K. Wilhelm, and B. Williams. 2009. "Secrets to psychological success: Why older doctors might have lower psychological distress and burnout than younger doctors," *Aging & Mental Health,* 13(2): 300–307.

Perrow, Charles. 1984, rev. ed. 1999. *Normal accidents: Living with high-risk technologies.* Princeton, NJ: Princeton University Press.

Perry, Ronald W. 2005. "Disasters, definitions and theory construction." In Ronald W. Perry and Enrico L. Quarantelli (Eds.), *What is a disaster? New answers to old questions.* Xlibris Corp.

Perry, Ronald W., and Enrico L. Quarantelli (Eds.). 2005. *What is a disaster? New answers to old questions.* Xlibris Corp.

Platt, John. 1969. "What we must do," *Science* (New Series), 166(3909): 1115–1121.

Platt, Rutherford H. 1999. *Disasters and democracy: The politics of extreme natural hazard events.* Washington, DC: Island Press.

Plyer, Allison. 2008. "March 2008 New Orleans population growth slow in first quarter 2008." *Greater New Orleans Community Data Center.* Last modified April 24, 2008. http://www.gnocdc.org/media/GNOCDCApr24-08.pdf.

Porter, Lyman W., and Edward E. Lawler. 1968. *Managerial attitudes and performance.* Homewood, IL: Dorsey Press.

Quarantelli, Enrico L. 2001. "Disaster planning emergency management and civil protection: The historical development of organized efforts to plan for and to respond to disasters." Unpublished manuscript held at Disaster Research Center University of Delaware, Newark, DE.

Rabow, Jerome, Sherry L. Berkman, and Ronald Kessler. 1983. "The culture of poverty and learned helplessness: A social psychological perspective," *Sociological Inquiry,* 53(4): 419–434.

Rappaport, Ed. 1993. "Preliminary Report: Hurricane Andrew, 16–28 August, 1992." Miami, FL: National Centers for Environmental Prediction, National Hurricane Center, National Oceanic and Atmospheric Administration, December 10. http://www.nhc.noaa.gov/1992andrew.html

Renschler, Chris S., Amy E. Frazier, Lucy A. Arendt, Giancarlo P. Cimellaro, Andre M. Reinhorn, and Michel Bruneau. 2010. "Developing the 'PEOPLES' resilience framework for defining and measuring disaster resilience at the community scale," *Proceedings of the 9th U.S. National and 10th Canadian Conference on Earthquake Engineering,* July 25–29, Toronto, Ontario, Canada.

Research Institute on Christianity in South Africa (RICSA). 2010. *Definitions for RICSA's Poverty Project*. Last accessed May 1, 2010. http://web.uct.ac.za/depts/ricsa/projects/publicli/poverty/pov_def. htm.

Rodriguez, Havidán, and Russell Dynes. 2006. "Finding and framing Katrina: The social construction of disaster," *Social Science Research Council*. Posted June 11, 2006. http://forums.ssrc. org/understandingkatrina/finding-and-framing-katrina-the-social-construction-of-disaster/.

Roese, Neal J., and Kathleen D. Vohs. 2012. "Hindsight bias," *Perspectives on Psychological Science,* (7): 411–426.

Rubin, Claire B. with Martin D. Saperstein, and Daniel G. Barbee. 1985. *Community recovery from a major natural disaster*. Boulder, CO: University of Colorado, Institute of Behavioral Science, Program on Environment and Behavior, Monograph No. 41.

Schaufeli, Wilmar B., Michael P. Leiter, and Christina Maslach. 2009. "Burnout: 35 years of research and practice," *Career Development International*, 14(3): 204–220.

Schiller, Daniela, Marie-H. Monfils, Candace M. Raio, David C. Johnson, Joseph E. LeDoux, and Elizabeth A. Phelps. 2010. "Preventing the return of fear in humans using reconsolidation update mechanisms," *Nature*, 463: 49–53.

Seligman, Martin E. P. 1975. *Helplessness: On depression, development, and death*. San Francisco, CA: W.H. Freeman.

Seligman, Martin E. P. 1998. *Learned optimism*. New York: Pocket Books.

Shea, Gregory P., and Richard A. Guzzo. 1987. "Group effectiveness: What really matters?" *Sloan Management Review*, 28(3): 25–31.

Simon, Herbert A. 2000. "Bounded rationality in social science: Today and tomorrow," *Mind & Society*, 1(1): 25–39.

Sioutas, Michalis, Wade Szilagyi, and Alexander Keul. 2013. "Waterspout outbreaks over areas of Europe and North America: Environments and predictability," *Atmospheric Research*, 123: 167–179.

Slovic, Paul. 2000. *The perception of risk*. Sterling, Virginia: Earthscan.

Small Business Administration. 2012. "Frequently asked questions about small business." Last modified September 2012. http://www.sba. gov/sites/default/files/FAQ_Sept_2012.pdf.

Smith, Stanley K. 1994. "Population projections: What do we really know?" Monograph No. 1, *Bureau of Economic and Business Research*, University of Florida, May.

Smith, Stanley K., and Christopher McCarty. 1996. "Demographic effects of natural disasters: A case study of Hurricane Andrew," *Demography*, 33(2): 265–275.

Solomon, Ed. 1997. *Men in Black*. DVD. Directed by Barry Sonnenfeld. Culver City, CA: Columbia Pictures Corporation.

Spence, William, Stuart A. Sipkin, and George L. Choy. 1989. "Measuring the size of an earthquake," *Earthquakes & Volcanoes*, 21(1): 58–63.

Stanovich, Keith E., and Richard F. West. 2008. "On the relative independence of thinking biases and cognitive ability," *Journal of Personality and Social Psychology*, 94(4): 672–695.

Steinberg, Laura J., Nicholas Santella, and Corrine B. Zoli. 2011. "Baton Rouge Post-Katrina: The role of critical infrastructure modeling in promoting resilience," *Homeland Security Affairs*, 7, art. 7: 1–34. Last accessed November 29, 2013. www.hsaj.org.

Stover, Carl W. 1989. "Evaluating the intensity of United States earthquakes," *Earthquakes & Volcanoes*, 21(1): 45–53.

Texas Tech University. 2006. "A recommendation for an Enhanced Fujita-Scale (EF-Scale)." Lubbock, Texas: Texas Tech University, Wind Science and Engineering Center.

The New York Times. 2008. "Storm causes dam to collapse in Wisconsin." Last modified June 10, 2008. http://www.nytimes.com/2008/06/10/world/americas/10iht-storms.5.13618154.html?_r=0.

Tierney, Kathleen, Christine Bevc, and Erica Kuligowski. 2006. "Metaphors matter: Disaster myths, media frames, and their consequences in Hurricane Katrina," *The Annals of the American Academy of Political and Social Science*, 604 (March): 57–81.

Tierney, Kathleen. 2005. Personal conversation.

Tushman, Michael L. 1977. "Special boundary roles in the innovation process," *Administrative Science Quarterly,* 22(4): 587–605.

Ungar, Rick. 2013. "GOP Congressmen who begged for federal aid in disasters striking home district vote against Sandy aid," *Forbes.* Last modified January 4, 2013. http://www.forbes.com/sites/rickungar/2013/01/04/gop-congressmen-who-begged-for-federal-aid-in-disasters-striking-home-districts-vote-against-sandy-aid/.

U.S. Army Corps of Engineers. 2006. "Performance evaluation of the New Orleans and Southeast Louisiana hurricane protection system." June 1, 2006. http://www.nytimes.com/packages/pdf/national/20060601_ARMYCORPS_SUMM.pdf.

U.S. Geological Survey (USGS). 2013a. *The Modified Mercalli Intensity Scale.* Last modified January 9, 2013. http://earthquake.usgs.gov/learn/topics/mercalli.php.

U.S. Geological Survey (USGS). 2013b. "100% chance of an earthquake." Last modified January 9, 2013. http://earthquake.usgs.gov/learn/topics/100_chance.php.

U.S. National Archives and Records Administration. 2010. Code of federal regulations. Title 13. Disaster loan program.

Veiga, Christina. 2012. "After Hurricane Andrew, Homestead's ball park remains a symbol of what might have been," *Miami Herald*. Last modified August 23, 2012. http://www.miamiherald.com/2012/08/23/2965486/after-hurricane-andrew-homesteads.html.

Verhoef, Erik T., and Peter Nijkamp. 2004. "Spatial externalities and the urban economy." In Roberta Capello and Peter Nijkamp (Eds.), *Urban dynamics and growth: Advances in urban economics*, 88–120. New York: Elsevier.

Vroom, Victor. 1964. *Work and motivation*. New York: Wiley.

Wagner, Peter, and Susan Edwards. 2006. "The economy in numbers: New Orleans by the numbers," *Dollars & Sense*, Issue 264. http://www.dollarsandsense.org/archives/2006/0306wagneredwards.html.

Whoriskey, Peter. 2007. "New Orleans repeats mistakes as it rebuilds," *Washington Post*. Last modified January 4, 2007. http://www.washingtonpost.com/wp-dyn/content/article/2007/01/03/AR2007010301593.html.

WIBA: Madison's News/Talk Station. 2008. "Flood emergency." http://www.wiba.com/pages/flooding.html.

Wilson, Jacque, and Matt Smith. 2014. "Two inches of chaos: What Atlanta's leaders were doing while the snow fell." CNN. Last modified February 1, 2014. http://www.cnn.com/interactive/2014/02/us/georgia-snow-timeline/.

Winchester, Simon. 2002. *The map that changed the world: William Smith and the birth of modern geology*. New York: Harper Collins.

Wisconsin Dells. 2008. "Lake Delton, Wisconsin." Last modified July 22, 2008. http://www.wisconsin-dells-wi.com/lake-delton-wisconsin.htm.

Wisner, Ben, Piers Blaikie, Terry Cannon, and Ian Davis. 2004. *At risk: Natural hazards, people's vulnerability and disasters*, 2nd ed. London: Routledge.

Withington, John. 2010. *Disaster! A history of earthquakes, floods, plagues, and other catastrophes*. New York: Skyhorse Publishing.

WLOX-TV (Biloxi, Gulfport, Pascagoula). December 6, 2008. http://www.wlox.com/.

Wolshon, Brian. 2006. "Evacuation planning and engineering for Hurricane Katrina," *The Bridge: Linking Engineering and Society*, 36(1): 27–34.

Wright, James D., Peter H. Rossi, Sonia R. Wright, and Eleanor Weber-Burdin. 1979. *After the clean-up: Long-range effects of natural disasters*. Beverly Hills, CA: Sage Publications.

Yates, F. Eugene (Ed.). 1987. *Self-organizing systems: The emergence of order*. New York: Plenum Press.

Index